LAVIL

LAVIL

LIFE, LOVE, AND DEATH IN PORT-AU-PRINCE

EDITED BY

PETER ORNER AND EVAN LYON

FOREWORD BY

EDWIDGE DANTICAT

VOICE OF WITNESS

VERSO

London • New York

For Adrienne and Family
In Memory of Loutchama

VOICE OF WITNESS
First published by Verso 2017
© Verso and Voice of Witness 2017

The moral rights of the authors have been asserted

1 3 5 7 9 10 8 6 4 2

Verso
UK: 6 Meard Street, London W1F 0EG
US: 20 Jay Street, Suite 1010, Brooklyn, NY 11201
versobooks.com

Verso is the imprint of New Left Books

ISBN-13: 978-1-78478-682-3
ISBN-13: 978-1-78478-684-7 (US EBK)
ISBN-13: 978-1-78478-683-0 (UK EBK)

British Library Cataloguing in Publication Data
A catalogue record for this book is available from the British Library

Library of Congress Catalog-in-Publication Data

Names: Orner, Peter, editor. | Lyon, Evan, editor. | Voice of Witness
(Organization), sponsoring body.
Title: Lavil : life, love, and death in Port-au-Prince / edited by Peter
Orner and Evan Lyon ; Voice of Witness.
Other titles: Life, love, and death in Port-au-Prince
Description: New York : Verso Books, [2017] | Series: Voice of witness
Identifiers: LCCN 2016046169 | ISBN 9781784786823 (alk. paper)
Subjects: LCSH: Port-au-Prince (Haiti)—Biography. | Port-au-Prince
(Haiti)—Social conditions—21st century. | Port-au-Prince
(Haiti)—Economic conditions—21st century. | Haiti Earthquake, Haiti,
2010—Personal narratives. | Interviews—Port-au-Prince (Haiti) |
Haiti—Social conditions—21st century. | Haiti—Biography.
Classification: LCC F1929.P8 L38 2017 | DDC 972.94/52—dc23
LC record available at https://lccn.loc.gov/2016046169

Typeset in Garamond by MJ&N Gavan, Truro, Cornwall
Printed in the US by Maple Press

CONTENTS

APPENDICES

FOREWORD

by Edwidge Danticat

It is the morning of the feast of Corpus Christi, fête Dieu, in Port-au-Prince. The sun rises early and fast, along with a chorus of voices singing hymns. Altar boys in flowing white robes and girls in long, spotless communion dresses weave rosary beads through their gloved fingers, or adjust crowns of white flowers on their heads. The parents walk at their children's side, their beaming faces glowing in the hot sun. "He must be present in my life every day," they sing. *Fòk li prezan chak jou nan vi mwen.*

Corpus Christi processions are meant to commemorate Christ's body, in pain, but Haitians have plenty of their own pain. The procession circles a makeshift displacement camp where mothers are bathing their children in buckets of cloudy water in front of the layers of frayed faded tarp they call home. Before entering the crowd with her grandmother, my six-year-old U.S.-born daughter, who is returning to Port-au-Prince for the first time since the January 12, 2010 earthquake, repeats something she's told us many times since we landed in the city. "I thought everything was broken."

Built for 200,000 people yet home to more than 2 million, Port-au-Prince is a city that constantly reminds you of the obvious, as though you were a six-year-old. No, everything is not broken. And no, not all the people are dead. Every person in that procession, and every person living in the city, bears that communal testimony, and Port-au-Prince is a testimonial city. It is a city that everything—fires, hurricanes, earthquakes, political upheaval—has conspired to destroy, yet still it carries on, in part due to the resoluteness of its people, a few of whose stories you will read about here.

The republic of Port-au-Prince, as it is often called, is a city of survivors. Even those who would like to see the country decentralized or have the capital moved elsewhere talk about creating another Port-au-Prince, a different one for sure, but an improved version of the old one. Still, Port-au-Prince is also a heartbreaking city. It is a city where a restaurant that charges over twenty American dollars for a steak might stand inches from some place where others are starving. It is a city where the dead can lie in a morgue for weeks as the family clamors for money to pay for the burial.

It is also a city where paintings line avenue walls, where street graffiti curses or praises politicians, depending on who has paid for them. It is a city of so much traffic that it has become a city of back roads, short cuts that rattle your body through hills, and knolls that at first don't seem passable. It's a city of motto taxis, which are better fitted for such roads. It is also a city of cell phones, where conversations often end abruptly because someone's prepaid cards have run out of minutes. It is a city, as one of Haiti's most famous novelists, Gary Victor, has written, where people who might run toward bullets will flee the rain, because the rain can reconfigure roads in an instant and can take more lives in a few minutes than a gun. It is also a city of commerce, a city of entrepreneurs, a city of markets where the vendors are as numerous as the products being sold, a city where I once saw a woman walking through the streets with a cluster of grapes, like many people have in their refrigerators, that she was selling by five or ten. Must I even say that it is a city of dreamers?

It is a city of music, from the vendors who sing the values of their wares, to the konpa blasting from the colorfully painted tap tap camions and lotto stands, to the lyrical laments rising from open-air

Protestant revivals to the drums throbbing from the Vodou temples. It is a city of street pharmacists whose giant cones of pills look like mosaic art. It is a city of canal-clogging used clothes—pèpè—foam food boxes, and un-recyclable plastic. It is a city of smoke and haze, of trash being burnt, of dust-covered trees.

It is now also a city of tremors, tremors that are sometimes felt based on your level of experience with previous tremors, where you might be sitting with someone and that person feels the earth shake and you don't feel a thing. It is a city where sometimes you both feel the tremors and panic equally, especially when others have dashed outside or leaped out of windows in fear. Traumas are sometimes as visible as amputated limbs in Port-au-Prince and sometimes they linger deep beneath the surface, like phantom limbs. Port-au-Prince is a city of seen and unseen scars.

This book too is filled with narratives of seen and unseen scars. It is a book about choosing to live and not to die in Port-au-Prince, to fight, to survive, to thrive. You will read here about residents of Port-au-Prince who though they share a city, a nationality, live very different realities, based on their level of access, their age and schooling, their neighborhoods, and the amount of time they've spent in that city. There are testimonials from street merchants, teachers, doctors, professors, activists, young people, old people. There are also testimonials from people like me, people who were born in or used to live in Port-au-Prince, but who now make their home elsewhere.

The gatherers of these stories are wise to (aside from the act of translation) allow the voices here to speak for themselves, to tell their own stories. There are many post-earthquake stories here, but the January 12, 2010 earthquake is not Port-au-Prince's only story, nor is it the only story of many of the people you will hear from here. There are also plenty of testimonials involving political instability, lack of access to health care and educational opportunities, and incidents of violence that preceded the earthquake. Particularly heartbreaking are the testimonials of sexual violence told by women who, even when they make every effort to prosecute their attackers, end up threatened, persecuted, and not receiving justice.

One might expect these testimonials and others to contain nothing but self-pity and heartbreak, but like Port-au-Prince, many of the people who tell their stories here have an unconquerable will that lifts them beyond their daily pain. Embracing hope, even as they fight for basic rights and necessities, these men and women exemplify determination and fortitude not only as survivors, but as narrators of their own stories. These testimonials are not about people who elsewhere might be considered downtrodden; they are about people who are indeed present in their own lives and are searching for ways to make this much-tried-and-tested city, and their country in general, not only a better and more humane place for themselves, but also for their neighbors, as well as for future generations.

INTRODUCTION

PART I: THE VOICES
by Peter Orner

The narratives collected here are edited from interviews and conversations conducted in Port-au-Prince at various times over a four-year period between August 2012 and February 2016. This is a book about a city of 2.6 million (when the metro and adjacent areas are accounted for) that experienced the most devastating man-made disaster in recent history. We say man-made because a vast number of the more than 200,000 casualities caused by the 7.0 magnitude earthquake that struck Haiti on January 12, 2010 occurred as a direct result of widespread substandard building.[1] Untold thousands were crushed by the rubble created by collapsing structures. But we wish to make clear from the outset that this book does not revolve exclusively around the earthquake, although the catastrophe plays a profound, life-altering role in many of the following stories. It could not be otherwise. No one in Haiti, or in Haiti's far-flung diaspora, was unaffected by the ruin the earthquake left behind.

Lavil is a book about life—and death—in a vibrant and complex political, economic, and cultural capital. Port-au-Prince, like Haiti

---

[1] For more on urban planning and the earthquake's impact on Port-au-Prince, see Appendix IV, page 327.

itself, is often described as poor. Yet poverty, although pervasive, has never been, and never will be, *the* story of Port-au-Prince. To say a person is poor tells us very little about who someone is, wherever that person happens to live. The minute you begin to listen to someone, anyone, they become something far more than the adjectives we use as a shorthand to describe them.

But Haiti has always been subject to drastic oversimplification by outsiders searching for an easy explanation for its real and perceived failures as a nation-state. Haiti is frequently described in the U.S. media as a unique sort of basket case. Why does this image persist? It may be because many discussions of Haiti begin with the fact—the glorious fact—that it is the only nation on earth born out of a successful slave revolt. In 1804, after defeating France on the battlefield, Haiti became an independent nation. However, often, too often, this fact is immediately followed by a recitation of the fact that Haiti is now "the poorest country in the western hemisphere." It as if to suggest that the latter fact must necessarily, and almost naturally, mitigate the power of the former.

This is not the place to delve deeply into intricate Haitian history, but it is important to remind readers that Haiti's revolution came in the wake of two other far more internationally famous revolutions. But neither France (which had just lost a war) nor the Americans were prepared to recognize, much less support, a revolution carried out by people considered to be racially inferior. These nations, for the most part, couldn't even quite believe that it had happened in the first place. An army of blacks defeats Napoleon? In the words of the late anthropologist and University of Chicago professor Michel-Rolph Trouillot, "The Haitian Revolution thus entered history with the peculiar characteristic of being unthinkable even as it happened."[2]

If Haiti's liberation were supported, what would that mean for the future of American slaves?[3] What would it mean for lucrative colonies

---

[2] Michel-Rolph Trouillot, *Silencing the Past* (Boston: Beacon Press, 1995).

[3] Haiti wasn't recognized as an independent country by the United States until

throughout the world? The Haitian revolution wasn't merely ignored, it was actively undermined—and worse—from the beginning.[4]

The need to oversimplify Haiti and its problems resurfaced in earnest after the earthquake. On January 14, 2010, two days after the initial devastation, while people were still alive under rubble, David Brooks in the *New York Times* argued that culture was responsible for, among other things, corruption and the lack of state-of-the-art building codes.

We're all supposed to politely respect each other's cultures. But some cultures are more progress-resistant than others, and a horrible tragedy was just exacerbated by one of them.[5]

Brooks also cites the progress-resistant influence of Vodou and the notion that "child-rearing practices often involve neglect in the early years and harsh retribution when kids hit nine or ten" as apparent evidence of the average Haitian's personal responsibility for the disaster.

Mr. Brooks, I'd like to introduce you to Adrienne Phatal, mother of three. Her story might well alter some of your thoughts on what you refer to sweepingly as Haitian "child-rearing practices." Or Jean Pierre Marseille. Jean is a father of six. He adopted one of his daughters after she was orphaned in the recent cholera epidemic, but, as he says, "She's my daughter. I gave her a birth certificate. I consider her one of my own." Or Marielene Lene, a mother of six who also takes care of a relative as if he were her own, and who does her best

---

fifty-eight years later, in 1862, the second year of the Civil War. For more on the timeline of Haiti's history, see Appendix I, page 293.

[4] In 1825, France essentially indebted Haiti for generations by "charging" it 150 million gold francs for Haiti's own independence. The amount was eventually negotiated down to 90 million francs, but that still represents nearly US$21 billion in today's dollars. In the first of many interventions, in 1915, the United States, under Woodrow Wilson, invaded Haiti ostensibly to "protect U.S. interests." For more on the history of Haiti, see Appendix I, page 293.

[5] *New York Times*, January 14, 2010.

to send them all to school while earning the equivalent of US$2.50 a day.[6] Or Johnny Destanville, father of a toddler born four years after the earthquake. "I had all these beautiful dreams of going to university but those dreams were shattered," he told us. "I'm hopeful for my son. As a teacher, I will be able to help my son and I have faith that God will help me provide for him." I could go on and on. The struggle of parents, of single mothers, of fathers, to survive economically—and otherwise—is a dominant theme of this book, because the majority of the people we talked to, and the majority of the people in Port-au-Prince, have very little money, and no savings. This doesn't make them one monolithic entity by any means, but the challenge of finding enough food, enough work, and enough cash to support one's family and send the children to school is the daily business of most residents of Port-au-Prince, as it is in so many cities across the world. A grand, noble history and intractable poverty do not make Port-au-Prince unique. But we would suggest that the majority population of the city, and the country as a whole, has been plagued, largely, and since the very beginning, by an unprecedented combination of brutal and self-serving governments and brutal and self-serving foreign intervention. Human rights—and these include the right to food, the right to shelter, the right to health, the right to "security of person" (all promises of the Universal Declaration of Human Rights)—of most Haitian citizens have been indiscriminately trampled upon since before and after the country was founded.

In some respects this *is* also a book about how a city functions in the complete absence of accountable government. We found that in spite of the lack of many basic services that citizens of many countries take for granted, Port-au-Prince functions (often astonishingly well under the circumstances) through an intricate network of social, family, and economic networks. Sometimes these networks result in

---

[6] Tuition is required for most schools in Haiti. Parents spend on average the equivalent of US$130 per child per year on tuition and other school costs.

tragic situations, such as those described by Juslene Marie Innocent, who was sent to live with relatives in Port-au-Prince with the promise of educational opportunities as a *restavek*, but was instead forced to work under difficult and violently abusive conditions.[7] Other narratives, like that of Denis Clermont, give a sense of how family love and support can help one through a time when the world itself became unrecognizable.

Of unfortunately special note is the fact that the global problem of sexual assault is so much a part of the lives of women from all sections of Port-au-Prince. Of this plague, Juslene told us that because so many women "are out every day looking for work, shopping for food for the children in the markets, we're constant targets of abuse by men."

Over the four years we spent working on this book, we spoke, formally and informally, with more than a hundred current and former residents of Port-au-Prince and its immediate environs. We were welcomed into many homes. We talked with people on the street, in tents, cafés, supermarkets, offices, taxis, tap taps, cemeteries, hospitals, parks, schools. Across Port-au-Prince, we spoke with teachers, merchants, gravediggers, activists, doctors, reporters, artists, mothers, fathers, lawyers, housekeepers, merchants, masons, bricklayers, firefighters. We also spoke with individuals currently living outside their city and country, people who make up the large Haitian diaspora in the United States.

We wish we had the space to include them all, as everyone who took the time to speak with us provided yet another insight into life in Port-au-Prince. A number of these interviews were conducted on multiple occasions over the course of many hours. Others are much shorter and the result of a brief encounter, often on the street, amid the noise of the traffic and commerce.

---

[7] In Haiti, children who are used as unpaid domestic servants are known as *restaveks*. For more information, see the Glossary, page 309.

We see our role as collectors of stories, as listeners, and we've tried here to include stories, and parts of stories, that, one way or another, had an impact on us. Although some of our narrators, such as Lamothe Lormier, Eve Emanuela, Gina, Lians,[8] provide important context, and we provide a few appendices and footnotes for critical context, our approach has been decidedly non-academic. We haven't set out to teach through the stories included here. Our choice to avoid making this a book that tries to teach lessons about Port-au-Prince or Haiti is best explained by something novelist Lyonel Trouillot[9] said while chain-smoking through an interview on his front lawn:

> I believe once you get into the business of telling stories, if the reader is smart, he should ask the question, "Why does he tell me this story and not another one?" There is a vision of the world somewhere in that decision. But it doesn't have to be like one plus one equals two. It doesn't have to be as if you're giving a lesson or a message.

Therefore: No message, no lesson, no comprehensive answers, no quick fixes. But we hope to help debunk oversimplified notions of life in Haiti, and in Port-au-Prince in particular, by providing a curious reader with a multiplicity of voices from the city. While there have been a great number of books written about Haiti, especially in recent years, few of them focus exclusively on Port-au-Prince, and even fewer that forefront the voices of residents of the city themselves. Subjects covered in these narratives run the gamut from health

---

[8] Some of the narrators requested we not use their full names.

[9] Lyonel Trouillot is author of *Street of Lost Footsteps* (among many other works of fiction and nonfiction), a harrowing and lyrical novel detailing one long night of violence and love in Port-au-Prince. He is also Michel-Rolph Trouillot's brother and a member of what Edwidge Danticat calls one of Haiti's most fertile literary families, one that also includes a sister, the novelist Evelyn Trouillot (*Infamous Rosalie*), and noted Kreyol scholar and children's book author Jocelyne Trouillot. I like to imagine what dinner-table conversations were like in their house growing up.

care (including mental health) to education, history to literature, economics to the environment, the earthquake to the problematic international response, political upheaval to the ongoing epidemic of violence against women. Some reach back in time; others exist entirely in the present moment. Many of the stories are intimately personal in nature. A good number of these narrators—mothers and fathers, daughters and sons—are as all people everywhere, preoccupied above all with family and love.

After the earthquake President Obama said, "To the people of Haiti, we say clearly, and with conviction: you will not be forsaken, you will not be forgotten." I don't doubt the sincerity of this statement at the time the president said it. There were millions of people who also genuinely believed it. I do wonder how it is possible for us—and the president was speaking for all Americans—to have such short memories. Consider this book a small attempt to make good on President Obama's promise.

Coeditor Evan Lyon brought with him to this project decades of experience in Haiti as a physician, music teacher, and writer, and he also brought fluency in Kreyol and bottomless affection for Haiti. Senior associate editor Laura Lampton Scott provided heroic coordination and essential editorial guidance. Martine Fleurius, Marvens Joseph, Gasline Laguere, Katie Kane, Doug Ford, Sarah Broderick, and Yukio Tominaga devoted countless hours to the project as editors, interviewers, or translators. Students in the Graduate M.F.A. program at San Francisco State University made pivotal contributions. The attorneys and staff at the *Bureau des Avocats Internationaux/* Institute for Justice and Democracy in Port-au-Prince, including Mario Joseph, Eve Emanuela, Brian Concannon, and Nicole Philips welcomed us and supported the project from the beginning. Daniel Tillias of SAKALA (Community Center for Peace and Alternatives in Cité Soleil) and Jessica Hsu of Haiti Communitere provided their time and expertise.

And this book would simply not exist without the dedication and commitment of Jean Pierre Marseille—journalist, husband, father, and longtime resident of Port-au-Prince. Not only did Jean Pierre himself conduct many of the interviews and translations you are about to read, he also generously provided us with commentary on life in his city, as well as his own remarkable life story. Born in the Bahamas to Haitian parents, raised in Haiti and the U.S. before being deported back to Haiti, Jean Pierre's insights and unvarnished observations appear throughout the text. There are as many views of Port-au-Prince as there are residents of this great and battered city on the coast of the Gulf of Gonâve. That said, if any one person could possibly embody the spirit of Port-au-Prince—its sleepless, kinetic energy, its sense of optimism in the face of cruel economic realities—it might well be Jean Pierre Marseille. As Jean Pierre himself put it:

> They're hustling. Everywhere. In every neighborhood you go, you will find people selling. Yes, everybody's selling something. That's the life in Port-au-Prince. Everybody's making commerce. You don't make much, but you make something for tomorrow.

PART II: LAVIL/THE CITY
by Evan Lyon

It is often said, "Haiti is a rural nation." This is true to my experience of Haiti. I have spent the majority of my time in Haiti living and working in the mountainous Plateau. The incredibly poor roads, where they exist, and innumerable tracks and trails everywhere else, conspire to make the region feel vast, though the nation is slightly smaller than the U.S. state of Maryland. Much of Haiti remains inaccessible to motorized transport of any kind. For our patients who live five to six hours on foot or by animal from the nearest hospital, the rural reality of present-day Haiti can be a matter of life or death, much like it has been for centuries. Aside from poor roadways, other critical infrastructure such as safe drinking water, quality housing and schools, and electricity have never reached these places. Haiti is a small nation, but measured by travel and hardship, it becomes much larger.

For several years, my work as a physician and community health worker centered in the medium-sized city of Hinche, the governmental seat of the département du Centre, the Centre Department.[10] From the Port-au-Prince airport, the seventy-mile trip to Hinche usually took five to six hours in a four-wheel drive truck. When the mud was deep it took longer. If the rivers rose, it didn't happen at all. I'll never forget taking a single-prop airplane to Hinche several years after I first made the trip by road. By air, the trip took thirty minutes, and as we landed on the dirt airsptrip on the edge of Hinche, I nearly cried with frustration at all the hours previously lost to travel by road.

The majority of Haitians still live mostly rural lives. Much of Haitian culture—family, food, memory, and religion—remains rooted in rural life. There's a beautiful expression in Kreyol, *kote ou se moun?*, that's often translated as "where are you from?" But a more literal translation is more revealing—"where are you a person?" Most Haitians who have immigrated to either Port-au-Prince or outside the country retain this distinction. I live in Port-au-Prince, but I'm a person in Verrettes or Saint-Marc or Les Cayes.

Recognizing this truth that many residents of Haiti are persons elsewhere, we have still decided to title this collection of narratives *Lavil. The City*. The capital city, Port-au-Prince, is most often simply called Lavil, familiar and imposing in the same breath. The City has grown exponentially in recent decades, the result of millions of pulls and pushes, many reflected in the stories that follow. This expansion isn't unique to Port-au-Prince or Haiti. Urbanization is an important

---

[10] The Centre Department is one of Haiti's ten *départements*, the country's largest administrative division. For more on Haiti's administrative divisions, see the Glossary, page 309.

force worldwide; the UN reports that a majority of the world's population now lives in urban areas. The proportion of city dwellers worldwide is expected to rise to 66 percent by 2050. In Haiti at the time of the earthquake, nearly one in three Haitians were living in and around Port-au-Prince.

Though so much of Haiti's culture seems drawn from its rural nature, the Haitian capital dominates the nation in a way few principal cities do—demographically, economically, politically, and, importantly, in terms of outsiders' impressions of the country. This is certainly true since the dark years of the Duvalier family dictatorship, despite the reality that their brutally efficient Tonton Makout were mostly a rural paramilitary.[11] The political turmoil following Baby Doc's ouster in 1986 centered around the City and Jean-Bertrand Aristide (himself a person in Port Salud on the southern coast) was a parish priest among the urban poor in Port-au-Prince.[12] Haitians displaced from homes around the country by natural disaster or deprivation often make their way to Port-au-Prince. Haitian deportees from the U.S. are relocated to Port-au-Prince. And the massive gears of the international aid establishment via NGOs and the UN runs first through Port-au-Prince. To understand something of life in Haiti, one needs to grapple with Port-au-Prince.

Prior to the earthquake on January 12, 2010, Port-au-Prince had become swollen from decades of growth far beyond the capacity of its infrastructure. Rapid, poor-quality building was certainly a leading contributor of death and injury once the tremors started. Since the disaster, problems with urban planning have been rightly recognized, with significant attention paid to the crumbled buildings and general

---

[11] The *Makout* were a feared paramilitary group under the Duvalier regimes during the second half of the twentieth century. For more on the Makout, see the Glossary, page 309. For more on the Duvaliers, see Appendix I, page 293.

[12] Jean-Bertrand Aristide was elected president of Haiti in 1990 and removed by coup in 1991. He returned to the presidency in 1994–95 and then was again elected in 2000. For more on Aristide, see Appendix I, page 293.

lack of infrastructure.[13] But the people who built these buildings—often with little more than hope—have stories. And many stories of those who were working, eating, learning, loving, raising children, scratching out a living, or simply finding a corner of shade at the time of the earthquake are now gone forever. We hope this book will work against this terrible loss.

My personal introduction to Haiti began in Port-au-Prince where I first visited as a volunteer music teacher in the summer of 1996. I arrived at the invitation of an American musician and friend with long-standing ties to Haiti, but I didn't speak a word of Haitian Kreyol and was unprepared for most of what I found. I'm sure I slept poorly that first night in the stillness and heat and in anticipation of what the following months would bring. My first morning in Port-au-Prince, I was told there was to be a big funeral at the Episcopal Cathedral adjacent to Ecole Sainte Trinité, and no one was available to play the organ. I came to Haiti to teach a piano but I wasn't very comfortable with the organ. I didn't mention that when I was asked to fill in. I managed, at the three-tiered keyboard of the massive pipe organ—the only one in Haiti.

Fifteen years later, this beautiful cathedral, the organ, and the surrounding school were all destroyed by the earthquake.

I lived in Port-au-Prince for a year and a half during my first visit, then spent the next thirteen years back and forth to Haiti working to provide health care and address poverty with a nonprofit organization called Partners In Health and its Haitian partner Zanmi Lasante.

On January 12, 2010 at 4:53 p.m. I was in clinic caring for people living with H.I.V. in Montgomery, Alabama—applying skills I had learned in Haiti to aid another community. During that first night, like everyone connected to Haiti, I did not sleep. It was nearly

---

[13] For more on urban planning and the earthquake's impact on Port-au-Prince, see Appendix IV, page 327.

impossible to gather news from loved ones in Haiti, or much information at all. Like many who cared about Haiti, I felt I had no choice but to return and help. Four days later I was on a plane to Port-au-Prince. The scene so soon after the disaster was indescribable.

During those first days after the earthquake, many remarked how peaceful the streets of Port-au-Prince seemed, even as open spaces were being claimed as camps for the displaced. The darkness and silence of the capital was broken only by the candles or cooking fires and the hushed sounds of crying, conversations, and prayer. Dozens of Zanmi Lasante doctors and nurses, as well as a few foreign volunteers, circulated throughout Port-au-Prince until 2 and 3 a.m., moving supplies, transporting the injured, and organizing to provide assistance wherever a foothold could be found.

In stark contrast to our experience in the capital, media outlets around the world began reporting on increasing insecurity and the threat to foreign aid workers in Port-au-Prince. We witnessed hundreds of calm and organized aid shipments and read in the press about unruly crowds and near riots. One breathless article reported that the doors of the national penitentiary had been thrown open, allowing 4,000 dangerous prisoners to run amok in the streets. In reality, prisoners had escaped, but since 80 percent of those incarcerated in Haiti are in pretrial detention, most of those in jail had only been accused of a crime. Nonetheless, a compelling and alarming narrative was set in motion, paralleling centuries of how the outside world has skewed its view of Haiti, often to serve self-interested beliefs. We hope the voices in this book, the stories shared with us, will help to counter this enduring unwillingness and inability to see Haiti clearly.

And we hope that readers will come to better understand the city at the center of Haitian life. Perhaps the most important reason we decided to call this book Lavil is because, through our conversations with narrators, Port-au-Prince emerged as a character in nearly every story, including the majority that could not be included.

EXECUTIVE EDITOR'S NOTE

by Mimi Lok

The narratives in this book are the result of extensive oral history interviews conducted over a four-year period with over a hundred men and women. Most interviews were conducted in Port-au-Prince and the surrounding suburbs, though a few interviews took place with Haitian citizens living outside of Haiti, either temporarily or permanently. These recorded interviews were conducted by Peter Orner, Evan Lyon, Jean Pierre Marseille, and a large team of interviewers and translators.

With every Voice of Witness narrative, we aim for a novelistic level of detail in order to portray narrators as individuals in all their complexity, rather than as case studies. We do not set out to create comprehensive histories of human rights. Rather, our goal is to compile a collection of voices that offers accessible, thought-provoking, and ultimately humanizing perspectives on what can often seem like impenetrable topics.

The stories themselves remain faithful to the speakers' words (we seek final narrator approval before publishing their narratives), and have been edited for clarity, coherence, and length. In a few cases, some names and details have been changed to protect the identities of our narrators and the identities of family and acquaintances. The narratives themselves have been carefully fact-checked, and are supported by various appendices and a glossary included in the back of the book that provide context and some explanation of the history of the region.

We thank all the men and women who generously and patiently shared their experiences with us, including those whom we were unable to include in this book. We also thank all the frontline human rights defenders working to promote and protect the rights and dignity of all men and women throughout Haiti. Without the cooperation of these human rights advocates, this book would not be possible.

Finally, we thank our community of educators and students who inspire our education program. With each Voice of Witness book, we create a Common Core-aligned curriculum that connects high school students and educators with the stories and issues presented in the book. Our education program also provides curriculum support, training, and site visits to educators in schools and invested communities. Visit the Voice of Witness website for free lesson plans, additional interview material, and to find out how you can be part of our work: voiceofwitness.org.

Mimi Lok
Executive Director and Executive Editor
Voice of Witness

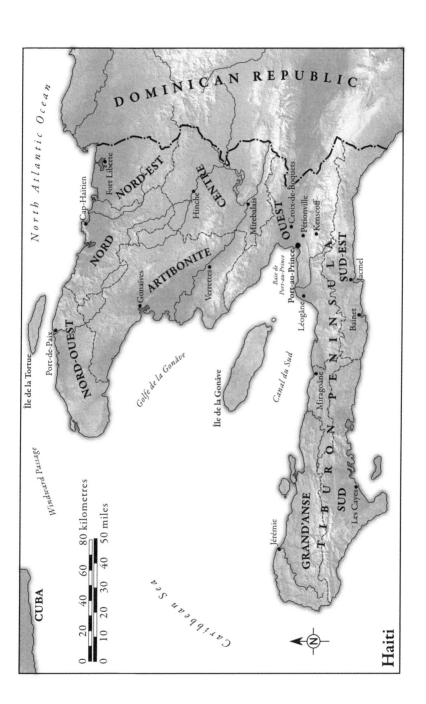

Haiti

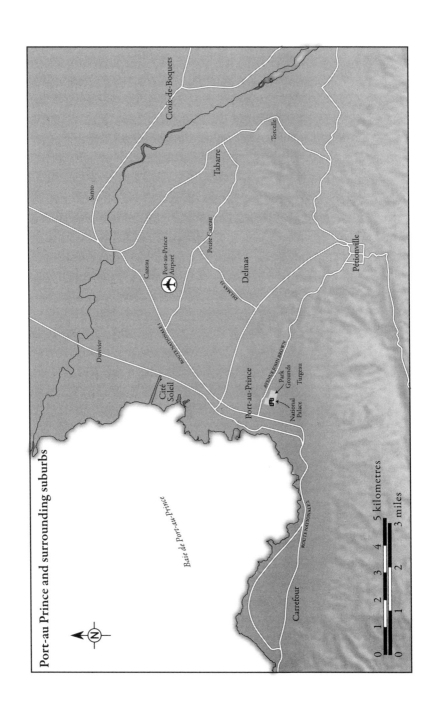

Port-au-Prince and surrounding suburbs

A more complex symbol, which has given me greater possibilities of expressing the tension between geometric rationality and the entanglements of human lives, is that of the city.

—*Italo Calvino*

One of the questions I was frequently asked when I was interviewed about *Twilight* was, "Did you find any one voice that could speak for the entire city?" I think there is an expectation that in this diverse city, and in this diverse nation, a unifying voice would bring increased understanding and put us on the road to solutions. This expectation surprises me.

—*Anna Deavere Smith*

People bring their illusions with them when they come to Port-au-Prince.

—*Dany Laferrière*

After the earthquake, I finally felt equal to everyone else.

—*Bazile Bermante*

I have medicine for roaches and I have traps for rats. And I have things to wipe down your traps for rats. I have poison for roaches. I have spray for mosquitoes. I have poison for cats. And I buy anything that has secondhand batteries. I'll buy mattresses. I'll buy any old sofa you have. You have any old secondhand jewelry that you don't want? Broken chairs? Anything that you have in your house that you want to throw away? I'll buy it. I'll buy it for regular money. Cash money. Secondhand refrigerators? Old inverter batteries, car batteries you're not using any more? I will buy them all with cash money. Have anything? What do you have?

—*Roving Merchant on Lalue (John Brown Avenue)*

MARIELENE LENE

39, fish merchant

Marielene makes a living selling dried salted fish that she carries in a wooden crate. She cuts pieces off of the fish with a knife for customers, depending on how much they want and how much they can afford. For twenty years, she sold wood for cooking and construction until it became illegal.[1] A busy mother of four, she originally came to Port-au-Prince to seek medical care for her son but remained in the city because of the lack of opportunity back home. Her husband remains on the farm andeyo *(literally "outside," meaning outside of Port-au-Prince), though occasionally he visits Marielene and the children in the city. Though she is small, she speaks forcefully in a deep voice.*

We spoke with Marielene in downtown Port-au-Prince in a vacant lot across the street from where Haiti's White House used to be before the earthquake on January 12, 2010.

I am under the sun every day. Yes, dried fish is my business. *Aranso*, it is called. You buy a case from a wholesaler and then sell it. If someone wants it for 20 Haitian dollars, you sell. If they want it for 10 Haitian dollars, you sell. For 5 Haitian dollars, even if it's just 1 goud, you sell.[2] You sell, you sell, you sell. It's a business that goes up and down.

---

[1] In 1923, forests covered as much as 60 percent of Haiti. By 2010, forest cover had dwindled to less than 4 percent.

[2] Generally the Haitian dollar refers to approximately 4.5 gouds. Therefore, 20 Haitian dollars equals 90 gouds or approximately US$2.50.

You have to be in the street every day. If you stay in your house, you won't be able to get ahead. I walk through the street singing, *Aranso! Aran Sel!* Normally if you do your business right, you can make 50 Haitian dollars a day. Sometimes as much as 60. But there are other times it's 30 Haitian dollars. And this is my only business right now. This is the only thing that's helping me. I pay the children's school. I have six children of my own. I have another child of my little brother who is in my hands, and I pay for his school. If I have even 100 Haitian dollars I try to stretch it to send my children to school. I buy a few things on credit. I have a few clients I can work with like this. I buy a bag, a pair of shoes on credit. My children need shoes for school. All on this little case of dried fish. Six kids …

I'm from the first section of Belle Fontaine, in the commune of Croix-des-Bouquets.[3] I lived with my parents near Belle Fontaine's springs. I have four brothers and one sister. We used to work the earth, cultivating. We planted corn and beans, and we traded animals. We had so little. Sometimes we worked and didn't make any profit at all. For a long time my parents didn't have the means to send me to school. I didn't attend until I was ten years old. I made it to the second grade. That was when I started to care for myself.

My older sister's name is Jezula Lene. She is the one who taught me the pinewood business. Our parents couldn't do much for us, so we had to fend for ourselves. That's life *andeyo*.[4] We would walk a lot to buy wood from people near a forest called Mars Rouge. We would buy it, cut it in smaller pieces, and repack it. Then we would again walk long hours past a place called Ti-Source. The journey to Ti-Source is very long—we'd go up mountains, we'd cross rivers.

---

[3] Belle Fontaine is a village in the mountains southeast of Port-au-Prince. It is part of the commune of Croix-des-Bouquets, which is part of the larger arrondissement of Croix-des-Bouquets, part of which overlaps with the Port-au-Prince metropolitan area. For more on Haiti's administrative divisions, see the Glossary, page 309.

[4] Haitians refer to anywhere in the country outside of Port-au-Prince as *andeyo*, "outside."

Sometimes we camped in the woods, sometimes we walked through the night. At Ti-Source, there would be stationed trucks. We knew all of the drivers. We'd pay about 60 gouds to ride on top of the trucks and arrive in Lavil around 5 a.m. I'd make about 500 gouds per day. Back then, with that money, I could stock my pantry. Now, with 500 gouds, you can't even feed your family for one day.[5]

We sold a little salt also. Sugar too. We stayed in the business for probably twenty years. But then we couldn't work there anymore. People didn't want us cutting down the trees. It was part of some project or another to protect the trees. One night we heard that the state wanted to arrest us for selling wood. So we decided to work all night. This was in the late 1980s when Henri Namphy was president.[6] We worked the whole night and cut down as many trees as we could. When we got to the little spring, even in the night, there were trucks. Truck drivers would come meet us and take our wood to the city. All this so the state wouldn't confiscate the wood we were trying to sell. One time, we were caught, and they took all the wood my sister had. My sister was crying because she didn't know what she was going to do.

ME AND MY HUSBAND, WE COME FROM THE SAME COUNTRY

Me and my husband, we come from the same country. We're from the same section even. We were married in Notre Dame Church in Belle Fontaine. I knew my husband from when we were both small children. He actually started talking to me when I was thirteen years old. But I always told him, "I'm still a child. I've got nothing in life yet." I asked him to give it a break and he did. He waited. We got

---

[5] At the time of the interview, 500 gouds equals approximately US$12.50.

[6] Henri Namphy was a general and interim president of Haiti following the ouster of Baby Doc Duvalier in 1986. For more on Haitian history, see Appendix I, page 293.

married at age twenty-one. My husband is one year older than me. My parents approved of the marriage. It was a big wedding, lots of people, a beautiful day. It was in the church on Sunday, September 28. You know Sundays are the days God has chosen for everyone. You aren't at work. You don't do anything. Everyone came together that day. My mother and father and all my family were there.

When I was married, I was already five months pregnant. After the marriage, we had very little. The little bit that we could find, we resigned ourselves to it. There were many days we passed without eating. You have no choice but to sit with this truth. After the marriage, people came to us and when they had a little to share they shared it. We did the same with our neighbors. That time was a time of hunger. When you could find a little something, you ate it, and when you couldn't find anything you spent the day hungry. It was only here in the city that we could buy a little rice to take back to the provinces.

What made me come to Port-au-Prince was my third child. After he was born, he became sick. He would swell up, shrink, swell up, shrink. I had a sister-in-law who lived in Croix-des-Bouquets.[7] She told me about a hospital there. Early in the morning, at 3 a.m., I left home and just me and this little baby walked to the hospital. The Sisters there took care of the child. They gave him medicine. They gave us both a little soap to wash up. They also gave me a little wheat flour and a little corn flour for us to cook. I saw my child begin to get a little better. They told me if I took him back to the provinces, he would not stay better. So I didn't go back. My family gave us a little place to stay. When I finally did visit back in the provinces, life was not good at all. We still had so little money. The children couldn't go to school. So I decided to stay in Croix-des-Bouquets. I started working every day in the street, running in front of trucks, selling this fish.

---

[7] Here Marielene is referring to the town of Croix-des-Bouquets, which is a suburb of Port-au-Prince but is also within the larger commune of Croix-des-Bouquets.

I used to rent the house with the little money I made. Now, I own the house I live in. A friend of mine saw my plight with all the children. She asked her daughter to let me build a room on a piece of leftover land she had. The daughter agreed, and I started building. I used money I had saved to build it. It took me a year to finish the room. In this life, people will help you once, but the next day you've got to figure out how to survive. My sister lives by me. We are in the same situation. She sells the salted fish with me too.

The children love their father. Unfortunately, he doesn't have anything. My husband still works the earth in the provinces. Right now we've planted a few beans, a little corn. Sometimes too much rain makes us lose it all. And sometimes when the rain doesn't fall, the beans are spoiled, and the corn lost too. But he still does this work. He's also very good at taking care of animals. He comes to the city now and then and spends a little time with me and the children, but he always goes back *andeyo*, to the country. Sometimes three months go by and I don't see him. When he's here he messes around with other women in the street. He often has a woman on the side. I really don't let this bother me. There are even times when he gives our little 50 gouds to another woman and I have nothing for the children. But I stay.[8] *Paske se marye nou marye*—when you're married, you're married. You could go and leave one man, thinking another is better, and turn around and it's worse.

I SAW THE HOUSE BEGIN TO SHAKE

That Tuesday, January 12, I had gone out to buy my fish. Just as I was arriving back at home in time to feed my children, I saw the house begin to shake. While the house was shaking, my children ran outside

---

[8] At the time of the interview, 50 gouds equals approximately US$1.25.

yelling "Jesu, Jesu, Jesu." I held onto them. The house crashed down. I had a lot of things broken, but I didn't lose anyone. I saw people who died, people who were crushed. And there were many people sitting on empty ground just like this. Nobody had homes anymore. We all held our children and we sat.

EDNER BRICE

61, tailor, mattress reupholsterer

Edner Brice, a self-taught tailor. He takes to the streets to buy broken mattresses and house utensils from other street vendors and then carries them with a wheelbarrow to his shop at the back of a tin-roofed house he rents in Rue des Miracles. There, he fixes the wares or uses his sewing machine to upholster the mattresses. In his spare time, of which he has little, he likes to play dominoes and cards or watch soccer or a good movie. In 2015, we spoke to Edner, a father of eight, as he was haggling with vendors, expertly maneuvering through the streets of Grand Rue, Rue Saint-Martin, Rue des Césars, Rue du Centre, and back to his shop in Rue des Miracles. As he hawked, we passed buildings destroyed by rain and locals stealing the iron supports. Just prior to the interview, there was an altercation where a young man was shot. Edner remained unfazed.

> Edner: *M'achte kabann an fe, fe a repase, matla box, blende!*
> A woman in Grand Rue: *I have an iron to sell.*
> Edner: *How much?*
> Woman: *50 gouds.*
> Edner: *5 gouds, because I will have to repair it.*
> Woman: *You could offer 6 gouds.*
> Edner: *I only have 5 gouds. Can I give you the rest on my way back? Do you trust me?*
> Woman: *Sure.*

I'm Edner Brice. I am from Pestel. I left there when I was ten years old. Now I'm sixty-one years old. I've been living in the city for fifty-one years now. God has been showing me how to survive. My father was a farmer, and my mother used to sell at the public market. On Saturdays, my father would slaughter a pig or a cow, and they would sell the meat at the market. When I was at my parents' house, I completed the first grade, but when I was ten years old I moved to Port-au-Prince to be with a cousin, and then I didn't go to school. I try to read and write. But life is tough. I have a lot of responsibilities. I have two brothers and two sisters. We sort of are in similar situations. I have other family members, but we are not close and we don't talk.

> Edner: *How much is this box spring?*
> Man on Rue Saint-Martin: *It's 1,700 gouds.*
> Edner: *Man, that's too much!*
> Man: *Give me 1,300 gouds.*
> Edner: *I won't sell it back if I pay that much for it. I have to make a living. I'm willing to buy three.*
> Man: *Okay. You can give me 1,000 gouds for this one and 400 each for the other three.*
> Edner: *Still too much money. I have to repair them. I can give you 400 for all four.*
> Man: *I can't. Offer 500 and it's a deal.*
> Edner: *Okay. I only have 400 now, but I can bring you the rest on my way back.*
> Man: *No problem.*

I was born in 1953 and Duvalier was elected in '57. So the first president I knew was François Duvalier. We didn't have freedom of speech. It was in 1985 when Makouts killed three students at Gonaïves.[1]

---

[1] Gonaïves is a city of more than 300,000 about 90 miles north of Port-au-Prince.

I was thinking that the regime really cannot be trusted if they are starting to kill students. Aristide was part of the people.[2] It was hard for him. The bourgeoisie will never let someone from the people rule them. They would do all they can to put him down. I was able to land a job cleaning the streets because of them. It was okay. I could buy a big *mamit* of rice for some of it and have a lot more left.

My first woman left me. I didn't have enough money to take care of her. When we became involved, I'd already started my business. She was doing housekeeping. She became pregnant. I rented a house for us. Houses weren't so expensive back then. I rented one for a year for 60 gouds. We stayed together for eight years. I didn't have a good job. I couldn't provide for her the way she wanted. We had one child, a girl. She's thirty-nine years old now. We see each other often. I have three grandchildren. They all come by every month or two.

A few years later I got married. My wife and I have had seven children together: Loudie, Ecson, Magdaline, Mackendy, Frantz, Fedner, Marie Sonie. We wouldn't have had so many kids if we didn't have a good life. It's thirty-two years this year. There is no need to go looking for anyone else. We will be together until God calls us to him.

Edner: *How much are those boxes?*
Dealer on Rue des Césars: *300 gouds.*
Edner: *Is that the final price? I have to resell it. Can I offer 30 gouds?*
Dealer: *No. No deal. How about 100?*
Edner: *You won't find a better deal. You know that. You are a businessman like me. You know that I also have to make a living. You'll have to sell it to me at 30 gouds, so that I can sell it back at 35.*

---

[2] Jean-Bertrand Aristide was elected president of Haiti in 1990 and removed by coup in 1991. He returned to the presidency in 1994–95 and then was again elected in 2000. For more on Aristide, see Appendix I, page 293.

Dealer: *No. Sorry.*

Edner: *Okay.*

One of my children became sick and died at seventeen years old. He was sick for seventeen days. He died on our way to the hospital. We still went to the hospital, but when we arrived, the doctor said that he was already dead. It was a curse.[3] Someone who came to see him said that he had three zombies on him. One doesn't need to have known enemies for that to happen. Sometimes a Haitian doesn't like good things to happen to his brother. Even though I don't go to church anymore, I am a church person. I say, like Job, God gave, and God took away; may His name be glorified.

I SAW EVERYTHING FALLING

When the earthquake happened, I was inside, and I felt the earth shake. I saw everything falling. We ran out to an open field. We heard people crying, and saw many people dead. We spent many months sleeping on that field. I had some money saved; that's what I used to feed my family because I couldn't work. I couldn't find work anywhere. People only bought water and food.

I sent my children to an orphanage at Ganthier 4.[4] We didn't have any place for them to sleep. At first the orphanage took good care of them. The only thing was the water. It was making them sick. And also, the kids weren't going to school. So I picked them up.

---

[3] In Haiti, many people believe in supernatural illness or "sent sickness." Even many Haitians who aren't adherents of Vodou share some of these beliefs. Supernatural illness can take the form of a physical object that can harm an individual, but a physical object is not required. Suspicion of a supernatural illness usually stems from jealousy or other interpersonal conflicts, which are then mediated by a Vodou practitioner who sends the sickness to its victim. For more on Haitian Vodou, see the Glossary, page 309.

[4] Ganthier 4 is a neighborhood in the arrondissement of Croix-des-Bouquets, southeast of Port-au-Prince.

They cried so much when they saw me. I wanted my children to go to school. So I sent them back. They spent several months wearing regular clothes to school because their uniforms were lost during the earthquake.

We survived. Neighbor shared with neighbor. It stayed like that until I could work again. Then, everything was fine again. Well, it's hard to walk back with all the things I buy. And there is always a chance that thieves will take my money. Thieves come out as early as 6 a.m. One time I had 500 Haitian dollars stolen. The next day, I had to take out a loan. I have to pay it back with 25 percent interest.

Excuse me, sorry to interupt, but do you know why there's an ambulance?
There was an altercation. Two guys were shooting each other. One stole something. The thief's dead. And the other is on the way to the hospital.

Do you think violence has decreased?
No, I don't.

Please, go on. What are your ambitions?
I want to make more money, but this country doesn't have opportunities. Imagine that someone only makes 3 gouds in a day. Who can live on that? But between the wife and me, we make it work. She sells food. Any food she finds. She goes to warehouses and buys whatever is there. Then she goes to the street and hawks.

> Vendor on Rue du Centre: *I have a mattress box.*
> Edner: *How much is it?*
> Vendor: *100 gouds.*
> Edner: *I give you 40 gouds.*
> Vendor: *No. 80 gouds.*
> Edner: *That is too much. I have to make a living too.*
> Vendor: *Okay. Give me 70 and it's yours.*

Edner: *I will give you 60.*
Vendor: 65.
Edner: *Come on! What is 5 gouds to you? It is a lot to me. I have to resell it and pay someone to carry it.*
Vendor: *Okay. Deal.*
Edner: *Thank you!*

Some of my children are in public school. We don't pay much, but we pay something. I pay 100 gouds for each of them for entrance fee. Then you have to pay for ID badges. Exam sheets, uniforms, shoes, books, et cetera This year has been tough.

If I came into money I would look for another place to stay because I can't stay here if there is unrest. I wouldn't want to move and go live with the masses again. I am hoping to one day live in a quiet neighborhood again.

Edner: *M'achte kabann an fe, fe a repase, matla box, blende!*

FRANTZ SANTIL

40, various work

After immigrating to the United States as a child, Frantz lived in the U.S. for over twenty years. Due to a fight with another man, Frantz was imprisoned and then deported to Haiti. At twenty-seven years old, he returned to a country he could barely recall. We interviewed Frantz on three occasions from 2013 to 2015. The first time, Frantz was seemingly at death's door. He often lost his voice as he struggled to finish sentences and took slow, drawn-out breaths. The second time we spoke, he had made a remarkable physical recovery. In our last conversation, though he had been deported thirteen years prior, he still struggled to reconcile his American and Haitian lives.

2013

Imagine: Not being able to see your family. Not being able to work, to earn a living. Walking on strange streets. Looking around, people looking at you strangely. Everything is strange. How many years can you be strange?

I was born in Haiti on May 16, 1975. My childhood in Haiti wasn't torturous or anything like that. It was just a regular poor peoples' life. Country life. Animals and things. Chickens. But we ate food regularly. The house was in the countryside. A two-room house.

About ten people there. My earliest memories are all blended faces, just mixed up. Relatives. Kind faces. Caring faces.

I don't know how old I was when my mom left for the States. She and my dad probably went together, but they separated once they got to the States. I've gone over it a million times in my mind. My mom ended up getting married to another guy. My dad went and lived with another woman in New York City. He died there when I was about fifteen.

So when someone gets a chance to go to the States, the first thing they do is send for their kid. My mom went to the States and she sent for me. Before that, her dad, my granddad, got to the States and sent for his daughter. It's just a domino effect like that until everybody gets out of here. But not everybody wants to stay in the States, and not everybody goes. They say it's too cold.

When I first came to the States, a man chaperoned me and took me around. And then I lived with my mom and some family in a house, growing up, going to school in Florida. I graduated from Miami North Senior High School.

I liked to travel when I was in the States. I went to art galleries, touched paintings that were worth $300,000 or $400,000. I educated myself. I liked Indiana Jones. I liked to discover things. I liked archaeology.

From four and a half years old until I was twenty-seven, I was living in the States.

THE WAY I GOT DEPORTED
STARTED WITH MICHELLE

The way I got deported started with Michelle. I met Michelle at a movie in Fort Lauderdale—*Jurassic Park*. She spilled my popcorn on the ground, and we bumped heads when we both tried to pick it up at the same time. It was the making of a good story. It turned out to be a tragedy.

We exchanged phone numbers. She lived in Colorado. I got kicked out of my aunt's house in Ft. Lauderdale for running up a $2,000 long-distance bill to Colorado. I got sent to my grandmother's place, and I ran up another bill for like $4,000 there. My parents found out what was going on, that I wanted to be serious with Michelle. So they said, "If you guys want to be serious, be serious."

I decided to go to Colorado instead of running up phone bills. It was December. Her dad, Steve, he's a good guy, a psychotherapist. He picked me up at the Greyhound bus station. I didn't know what I was doing in Colorado. It's freezing. I lived at her dad's place for a while, went jogging with him at the Broadmoor resort. Nice place. Then I got my own apartment with a roommate.

Then I got into trouble. Street fight. Parking lot of the apartment. Police got called. My roommate and I got into a fight with a military guy. This guy, he was just around, socially. The fight was over a girl named Nancy. She was spreading rumors, "Oh, Frantz is my boyfriend now." Not true. I suppose this guy thought he was her boyfriend. And just being macho, being a tough guy, he hit me first. That's the truth. I told the judge that—"He hit me first." And he told the truth, too. But the truth did not set us free. Because it's also true that I hit him in the face with an ashtray. And he bled, severely, from the head and the nose.

I had a lawyer, a state public defender. I was almost able to get mutual combat, which just means fighting. But the judge was very strict. Two black guys. Conservative Colorado. We didn't go to trial. At the pretrial conference, the district attorney was like, "Judge, this is a waste of time. Just send these guys to jail and get this over with."

I pleaded *nolo contendere*.[1] Plea bargain. Assault. Not even assault —conspiracy to commit assault. The public defender told me, "Take six years. You'll do three."

---

[1] Latin for "no contest." In a criminal proceeding, a defendant may enter a plea of *nolo contendere*, in which he does not accept or deny responsibility for the charges but agrees to accept punishment.

So I went to jail. Sentenced six years. The other guy told the truth and was charged, but after about twenty days in jail, he got out. You know, a military guy, he had a lawyer and stuff like that. I ended up doing eight years. Immigration hold. It would have been six years, but I was detained for two years by Immigration.

My parents, both of them, were naturalized citizens before 1982. There's a law that says if both your parents are naturalized citizens of the United States before you are eighteen, then you are the beneficiary of their naturalization because you are a minor. So I fought for a while. It worked for a while.

Then the Immigration Department sent a letter that said, "OK, Frantz, make a decision. Do you want to go to Haiti? Or you're going to stay locked up." I said, "Well, send me to Haiti."

YOU HAVE NOTHING

To get deported, you have to go to Oakdale, Louisiana.[2] You leave from Oakdale at 9 o'clock in the morning. You're put in cuffs. Miami is the last stop in the States. From Miami, you come to Haiti.

You have nothing. No street clothes. Just a prison jumpsuit, a couple letters in your pocket, and your legal box of documents. And you lose your legal box on the way because you're in handcuffs, and it's the marshal guy that's carrying it for you. After a while, he gets tired and drops it off someplace.

The marshal guy walks with you. You don't have any handcuffs on your legs. The marshal said to me, "Frantz, you're a pretty cool guy. Why'd you end up in jail?" I said, "You're a pretty cool guy. Why'd you end up a marshal?" We had a couple laughs.

I was put on a plane, then Haiti. The marshal stayed on the plane. Haitian police were at the bottom of the stairs, put me in some

---

[2] Oakdale, Louisiana, is the site of a major federal migrant detention center and court.

zip-lock type of handcuffs. While the Haitian police were putting the handcuffs on me and other guys who'd been deported, I saw a lot of pots and pans in the middle of the road. I'm seeing things boiling, but not like regular food. I'm looking at this thing, it's all like black and purplish looking, and so I ask somebody, "What is that?"

And they told me, "Well, that's blood. Once they kill the goat or they kill the pig, they collect all the blood and cook it, and then they cut it into pieces like a cake and sell it."

I thought, *Wow, that's not good.* It smelled awful. I don't think that people are supposed to eat blood, you know what I mean? I see people eating it, so to them it's okay. But to me, it's unbelievable.

They tell you to get on this bus. The twenty-six of us were transported to another jail. My legal box never shows up. It stayed at the airport, I guess. All those memories. All those years of letters. I had money from the jail in the States, about $300. In jail, I got a degree in working with children, handicapped children. It all got lost in my legal box. Everything was lost.

To get out of jail in Haiti, it takes patience. And money. My mom came to the jail in Haiti, something that she didn't do in the States. She pulled strings. She had friends in high places.

When I walked out of jail, I thought I saw freedom, a new life. I walked right into the open air, the free space, and talked to people. "Hey, what kind of country is this? Where's the movie theaters?" *"Movie theaters? You must be rich."* "Rich, no, I'm poor. Just like you." *"To go to the movies, you have to be rich."* "Where's the McDonald's?" *"There's no McDonald's in Haiti, buddy."*

There's no manual. There's no instructions. At night, it's dark. There's no electricity. You have to find your way around. I didn't speak much Kreyol. Luckily for me, I caught on quick. But unluckily for other deportees, sometimes they don't. Some recidivize, some can't handle it. Some die in a few days. They do armed robberies. Obviously, desperate times call for desperate measures.

You get poorer by not working. You lose weight by walking so much. Your family, after a while, tells you, "Hey, I don't have no more money." Like right now, I need money to eat, and I can't because my family is saying that they don't have any money right now. "Wait till next week, will ya?" And I can't. Can I wait a week to eat?

Twenty years later, you're still a deportee. On the block, you're not called your name. You're not called "sir," "mister." Still called "deportee." When you first come back, it's okay because you know that's what you are. But when you work toward being a better person, you would think that other people would work toward changing their mentality. But they don't.

IN THE HOSPITAL, YOU PAY FOR EVERYTHING

Now, I'm sick. Even though the blood results are not in my hand, I feel like maybe I've contracted H.I.V. because I hear there's a lot of it around. I finally got a friend to help get me into the hospital. In the hospital, you pay for everything. I don't get food and medication because I can't buy anything. The operation I need, they might do it for free because my condition is getting critical.

I have to fight my way through it. I don't want to die here like this—weak, naked, hungry. It's the worst way to die: weak. I want to be strong again. So I just rest and take medication. If I wasn't strong, I probably wouldn't make it this far, right? If I make it out, I'm going to help out other deportees because it's hard living in the States for twenty-something years and coming to end your life like this.

This was not the plan I had for my life. It was a sorry life, a sad life because it was unsuccessful. Being deported. I guess you just come out here to die. Deported to death.

2015

I remember that you guys gave me a ride to the hospital. My hemorrhoids became so infected that the inflammation and the swelling was causing me not to be able to go to the bathroom. I had a fever and I was losing my appetite. So it was a really scary thing. An intestinal tract infection. So the doctor suggested an operation.

I needed to get some help, so I called Loune from the Partners In Health organization that I used to work with. I worked there with handicapped children for about a year or so. I taught the kids how to speak English, how to use spoons and to feed themselves. So it was a really good experience. Loune is the chief of staff over there. Her boss is Paul Farmer. Paul tried to show me some techniques to resolve the problem. But when those techniques didn't work out, Loune said, "Let me take you to a doctor who can either do an operation or give you some treatment."

But when we got there, the doctor told me it is going to cost me 35,000 gouds. Do you know how much that is in U.S. dollars? That's about 1,000 U.S. dollars.[3] I don't have 1,000 *Haitian* dollars. Loune said don't worry about the money, because she was going to pay the bill for me. It was really good to think of myself as someone who deserved that kind of help.

Getting that sick was like a spiritual awakening. You know when you have some type of near-death experience? And you're fighting to hold onto life? You have these moments where you're praying, "Oh please God. Get me out of this and I'm going to be such an angel and I'm going to become a preacher," and this and that. I had moments like that. I was thinking about all these years of not seeing my friends, my family. They don't even know where I am, dying in that situation. I was like a dog, dying by the wayside and nobody caring or knowing about me. Mostly I was thinking about my family.

After that treatment, it really got better. The doctor recommended that I stay away from certain kinds of foods and spices. And I did. I quit smoking for the most part. That's helped a lot. So here I am

---

[3] At the time of the interview, 35,000 gouds equals approximately US$875. A Haitian dollar generally equals 4.5 gouds, so 1,000 Haitian dollars equals US$112.

today, completely hemorrhoid free. No more intestinal tract infection, but I still occasionally take medication to make sure it doesn't reoccur.

Honestly, I think I feel so much better because I was able to get support from people who knew me as a good person. I think that was a good thing psychologically because I had a lot of anxiety, depression, and stress that was really dominating me. But I think what made me feel really better was not only the medication, but knowing that I had support from these people who appreciated my work and appreciated me as a person.

PORT-AU-PRINCE. IT'S CRAZY.

Port-au-Prince. Whoa, I don't know. It's crazy. What do I hear? What do I see? What do I smell? You smell so many different things: the trash, food vendors on the street, the smell of burning meat and frying chicken and things like that. A lot of noise, a lot of clamor. For example, you hear people always selling things, walking around with things to sell. Some guy is walking around with a refrigerator on his head like, "I got a refrigerator to sell." It's just so much to take in, so much to hear, so much to see. I try to keep myself in an isolated area where I am not so much bothered by the environment out here.

Out of all the cities I have been to in my life, from Florida to Colorado to Ohio, Mississippi, Washington, this is the most unique city. It is hard to imagine how someone is able to survive these cruel and unusual conditions. And I really do mean unusual. Trying to find something to eat is kind of like having to hunt for food. You have hunger pains. It's always hot and sticky. Having to get from one place to another is always a hassle, takes hours. Some place that should take a couple of minutes to get to, but because of the traffic, it'll take hours. It's uncomfortable. That is the gist of it. But you have no choice. I have to walk everywhere I go, so you just have to deal with it.

Describing it would take hours—how people live out here. There's nothing interesting to do. It's very bland, very boring, very depressing. There's no fun, nothing to enjoy. No Six Flags. No miniature golf. It's just dirt and heat and bad water and that's about all there is. I don't have fun. You really have no time for fun. Poor people really don't relax. They just hang around and have a few laughs by the roadside or in the neighborhood. The richer people go to the beach or whatever. But I don't. I really can't afford to, you know.

We try to make the best of the situation that we can.

As you can see, I sleep on the floor since I don't have a bed. Here in this neighborhood, there's a lot of vegetation and there's the ocean right behind you. So when it rains a lot here, you get a lot of these insects, and one of those insects was a centipede. Last week, it was really raining. One of them crawled into the house and lay where I make my bed area. In the middle of the night, I felt something bite me on my thigh. I jumped up and lit my phone, thinking, *Oh my god.* But I paid it no mind because I was thinking, *What harm can this thing do?*

The next day, it gets all infected and swollen and painful. I went to a Haitian doctor, and he said, "Well, you gotta just take some painkillers and some antibiotics." So I go to another hospital, but I couldn't afford the amount of money that they were asking to open it and clean it, so I just left it alone. I'm dealing with it the best that I can. The pain really drains me. It takes a lot of energy when I have to go somewhere. It's really difficult for me to sit, so I have to spend most of my time standing, you know? It's really uncomfortable, but out here, you have to be strong to survive, so I'm just trying to deal with it. Hopefully it's not something that's going to end up killing me.

I'VE LIVED IN MANY NEIGHBORHOODS

I've lived in many neighborhoods. Here in Delmas is pretty laid back, middle class.[4] I've lived in upper-middle-class neighborhoods,

---

[4] Delmas is a large residential and commercial suburb in the northeast of Port-au-Prince, adjacent to the city's airport. Individual neighborhoods in Delmas are

which is a little more stressful, a little more expensive. And I've lived in the ghetto neighborhoods, like Cité Soleil, which was much more enjoyable.[5] You get a feeling of excitement and adventure there, but it turns into danger once there are things going on like the coup d'état of President Aristide.[6]

At the time that I was living in Cité Soleil, Aristide had returned and guys with guns were on the streets trying to take over the government and put Aristide back in power.[7] It got out of hand. It was 2005 to 2008. There was a political uprising and all kind of difficulties. The movement was like an armed street gang, supporters of a political movement that's called Lavalas.[8] They were maintaining the movement through violence and pressure and threatening government agents, and it was really cool to meet some of those characters. They went down in history as the big-time fugitives of Haiti, the wanted men. I used to sit and talk to the guys like this. It was always interesting to listen. And as it turns out, these characters now only live in my imagination, because they're all dead.

The things that I was seeing, they hurt me, to see people being burnt alive or women being shot to death because they were spying or something like that. I've seen a lot of cruel things. Seeing an innocent person being killed because they are a relative to a gangster or something like that, that was always difficult. But you had to adjust

---

referred to by number, since the suburb is organized around numbered streets that radiate out from a central road (for instance, Delmas 45, Delmas 18, et cetera).

[5] Cité Soleil is a large, densely populated unplanned neighborhood of more than 400,000 in northwest Port-au-Prince.

[6] Jean-Bertrand Aristide was elected president of Haiti in 1990 and removed by coup in 1991. He returned to the presidency in 1994–95 and then was again elected in 2000. For more on Aristide, see Appendix I, page 293.

[7] Frantz is describing a paramilitary formed in support of former president Jean-Bertrand Aristide's political party, Fanmi Lavalas. For more information on Aristide, see Appendix I, page 293.

[8] Aristide's leftist political party. For more information, see the Glossary, page 309.

because these were times of war. It was a like civil war, you know what I mean?

In Delmas, it's pretty quiet. But I've been hearing gunshots and a lot of ambulances and things like that during the night. In the morning when I get up, I hear guys in circles having political discussions about who is going to be the next president, how the country is going to become so much better.

Here's a story. This probably started around the election time at the beginning of August. I had a friend—well, a friend or an enemy, I don't know what it was—but he lived near the house that I rent. A young guy, younger than myself. One day he asked me to go help this guy's political campaign by posting his photographs on the walls and spray-painting his name on buildings and stuff like that, and he was going to pay us. I'm telling the dude I don't get involved in things like that. I am not into politics. And he says he's not into politics either—he's just out to get a bit of money. So I'm like, *Well, I'll think about it.*

I didn't give him a quick response, so he went and got somebody else. They went out and were hanging the guy's photographs on walls and spray-painting and stuff like that. And one morning I wake up to his aunts, his cousins, his father screaming, "Rudy's been shot to death." According to what the witnesses were saying, some guys came by with ski masks and heavy guns, what we would consider to be a drive-by shooting. I've been able to find out that another candidate had given a group of guys guns and paid them to stop guys from posting photos of other candidates. The result of that is that this guy ends up getting killed. And it's funny—if I had gone with him, maybe I might have been a victim myself, you know?

No one has been identified. There've been no suspects arrested or anything like that. His brothers and his father, I've noticed since he's been dead, everybody just stays drunk. Really, really drunk. He was an essential part of their household. So they just try to stay drunk to avoid the reality.

I WAKE UP TO THE SOUNDS OF MY CHICKENS EVERY MORNING

My original home is in Port-au-Paix. In Port-au-Paix, I don't feel as tired as I do when I am in Port-au-Prince. It's much more peaceful. I have my own place. I don't have to rent. I have access to water right near my place, the local river, and I can bathe. It's not a dirty river like some places here in Port-au-Prince. This place is much cleaner—flowing water over the rocks. It's cool, refreshing water. It's like going to the beach, and it's in my backyard.

I wake up to the sound of my chickens every morning about 5 o'clock, 6 o'clock in the morning and I go feed them. I take it seriously because chickens are a good source of meat, especially when you don't have funds to purchase food. You can just get a chicken and clean it and it becomes a meal. It's a good resource.

I go to the woods to have that feeling of being connected to nature and learning how to survive in the outdoors. It's much less stressful than in the city, where you don't get shade from the trees, you don't get running water. I don't have to commute to any place, because everywhere you need to go is in walking distance. So I'm trying to build my life out there and I think that once I am able to, I am going to attempt to stay there more often than in Port-au-Prince.

I was born here in the city, because in the countryside, it's difficult to get a birth certificate. So the parents have to come to the city to have the child in order for them to get the birth certificate and get it registered. So I was born in the city, but my family is from the countryside. And since I've been back in Haiti, I've been able to find family members and meet the ones that I forgot and the younger generation that I never knew. It has been interesting to share my experiences in the States. They think it is really cool. They are always asking me about my tattoos. It is amazing how the older generations, like the grand uncles and grand aunts, remember me. They are like, "You've been gone for like twenty-something years, but you're back!"

I was able to pay for my land in monthly installments. I did most of the work myself, gathering friends and relatives, young boys who were willing to help get the blocks put up, get the doors made, and stuff like that. To get a house built out there, maybe cook some food and offer people some incentive to help you out. I'm thinking that the wisest thing for me to do is create a stable living environment in the countryside where I can afford to stay. The reason I come to Port-au-Prince is because I feel that it is easier to find employment here than it is in the countryside—although it has been awhile since I've been able to find work here either.

You don't find enough income in those areas in the countryside. There's not much to do. No electricity, no Internet. It's very difficult. You live in the forest, just live off the land. You eat coconuts. You make a little farm and grow sugar cane and sweet potatoes. I don't know how to farm. I can raise chickens because all you have to do is feed them and put them in the cage at night so wild animals don't eat them or they don't get lost in the woods.

It's difficult for me because I haven't done that all my life, so I come to the capital city where it's easier to find work that has to do with computers and management and stuff like that. Somehow I manage to earn enough while I'm here so I can survive out there for a while until my funds are depleted and I have to come back here. But I do plan on making a farm, and hopefully in the next year or two I'll be able to harvest and have food. I'm starting really small because I don't have any money to start any other way.

I DO ODD JOBS

One thing you learn real quick in Haiti is that only the strong survive. I've had so many friends die here. Just the other day, my friend committed suicide. He just couldn't take it. The pressure that is most difficult here is not being able to eat three meals a day like we're used to in the States. If you're unemployed, you don't have money, and if you don't have money, you can't buy produce.

Generally on a Sunday, you have to give it your best shot to try to get something to eat because you spent all week not eating well. So I save everything that I can throughout the week to make a real special meal on Sundays. It's called ramen noodle. It's one of my favorite things. It's the cheapest and quickest thing I can make. I used to eat it when I was a kid in the United States. You just boil some water, put it in there, and you're ready to go.

I walk because I don't have a vehicle that transports me wherever I need to go. I do odd jobs. I run errands and help people, someone who needs to fill out an application that's in English or something like that.

I try to think of ways to create employment not only for myself but for people here in Haiti. My newest idea came from my experience in Port-au-Prince, watching manual laborers on the streets of Delmas breaking their necks to get day work from those guys in the upscale areas, whether it be for a day or two or just handyman jobs, gardener's jobs, or to wash the boss's clothes. Some people make it and some people don't. The ones that do make it, it doesn't last very long and they're usually cheated out of their money. There's never anything official that says, "This is how much you're going to get paid," or, "You're on a regular schedule." It's all chaos, it's not organized. It leaves people worse off than having no work at all.

I imagined a way to organize a little bit so it can be less of a hassle to them and also gives me some type of employment, like an agency that provides services in the upper-class neighborhoods where they're building hotels and they're repairing things. They always need people but they can't find the people, because some of the people here don't know where to go to get the jobs. Some are not computer literate, so they don't know there are job offers on the Internet.

I've made myself available to teach Haitian people how to use the household appliances that are in those new buildings. For example, the Marriott hotel. It's brand new. It's very nice. And it's got washing machines, but all the buttons are in English. So what I've decided to do is teach people how to use a washing machine so they can be qualified for these janitor and housekeeping jobs. So that's what I'm working on now, what I hope will improve the quality of life for all Haitians.

I MISS MY LIFE

Since I've been here, I'm a stranger in a strange land. I don't think I have what you would consider to be friends. You greet people because it's polite and you have to do certain courteous things for the elderly or children or whatever. But as far as having friends or considering someone to be your best friend? No, I don't have anything like that. I feel like I'm dying. I mean, I'm usually very weak. I don't know if it's stress or depression, but I just don't feel as strong as I used to when I was in the States.

On a scale from one to ten, I think my chance of getting back to the United States is one. But I grew up watching things like *Rocky*—movies that are about something seemingly impossible, but somehow by the end of the movie, there's a victory, someone has overcome an obstacle. So maybe it is an obstacle to get out of Haiti, but I think one day I will be able to, because I really miss my little sisters, my real friends. I miss my life, you know? I would like to go, just to reminisce and spend some time with old friends and pass by the grandparents. They're in the States and I'd like to see them. My first-born child, she's like almost eighteen now. She's got a boyfriend and everything. And I haven't been there. From jail to Haiti it's been almost twenty years. But I still feel as if America is a good place. But I don't know. Maybe I'm wrong.

I think it is unfair to take a guy out of the situation where he spent his whole life. I was twenty-seven years old. I lived in the U.S.

my whole life from the time I was four and a half. I had just gotten engaged to the daughter of a prominent doctor. Everything was ahead of me.

So I had a lot of opportunities to be somebody, and because of a fight with a guy ... And to be treated like just a regular refugee and have your permanent resident papers taken away and be sent back to Haiti, I think that was unfair. I think it was cruel and unusual, to tell you the truth. I'm American, brother. I mean, I don't feel Haitian in my system at all. I mean, the blood in my veins runs red, white, and blue. I am forty this year. I feel like I'm sixty, but I'm forty. I feel like I have a lot of years left, God willing, to live out my dream. And I have no other dream but the American dream.

You have to really get to know Haiti to love Haiti. There are places in Haiti that are really nice, places I enjoy like the countryside, living in the mountains. Whether the United States is better than Haiti depends on how you define "better." Better that you can eat? That you can go to a store? That you can find a job? Instead of having to be unemployed for all your life here? I mean, okay, economically, sure it's better. But what about when you get to the heart of things like your family members that knew you when you were young and your loved ones that you'd never seen before?

I like the fact that I really know that I'm Haitian and I feel it and I see it. I see people that look like me and have the same nose as me, the same ears as me. I feel good about it, to see those people. But feeling Haitian in like a social way? No. Culturally, I don't feel it. I still feel like an American. You know, I like things like baseball and apple pie. Burger King and Olive Garden. I know it's a long shot, but I hope one day to make it back home because Haiti is not my home. No one loves me here. So I hope to click my heels one day three times and say, "There's no place like home" and be back in America.

JUSLENE MARIE INNOCENT

37, laundress and housekeeper

Juslene Marie Innocent, like many girls in rural Haiti, was sent to Port-au-Prince as a restavek at a young age and placed in the home of an aunt.[1] In that house she was sexually abused and raped by her uncle. Eventually, Juslene got a job in the home of people who cared for her. Later, she met the man who became her husband.

Juslene lost most of her family on January 12, 2010. During the earthquake, she lost consciousness and woke to find her husband and her three children crushed under rubble. At the time she was rescued, Juslene was unaware she was pregnant. Six months later, she gave birth to a son.

I met this gentleman years ago and we started dating. His name was Lidye.

About two months into the relationship, I became pregnant. I told Lidye. He said he would rent an apartment for us so we could stay together with the baby. I was still so ashamed that I had to leave my job. I didn't want to tell the kind family I was working for that I was pregnant. They had two daughters. I didn't want to be a bad

---

[1] In Haiti, children who are used as unpaid domestic servants are known as *restaveks*. For more information, see the Glossary, page 309.

example for them. So I left and moved in with Lidye. Lidye was a mason. It wasn't easy for him to find jobs, but he did his best to put food on the table. I went back to work as a housekeeper to help out with the bills. I was twenty-five years old when my first child, Mildred, was born.

After a few years, we got married. We didn't have much money, but we invited both families to the event. My husband had nothing but praises to say about me. He was so proud of me. My aunt that I lived with as a child didn't come to the wedding. She sent her children. Even though my aunt mistreated me, I forgive her. My mother didn't come to my wedding, either. And after the wedding she sent me a letter to apologize for sending me away all those years before. One of my siblings wrote the letter, since my mother doesn't know how to read or write. She called me "my dear." I was so touched, I cried as I read the letter. My mother was finally acknowledging me. She's my mother. She carried me for nine months. I owe her my life. Now I go back to Jérémie to see her when she's sick.[2]

I was with Lidye for seven years. We had four children. Our youngest was still in my belly when the earthquake hit. He's in school now. When he started talking, the first word he said was "father." At about one year old, he asked me for his dad. I told him that my brother was his dad. As he grew up, he figured out that I had lied, and I told him that his father had died during the 2010 earthquake. He cried and wouldn't eat. The neighbors found a way to comfort him by telling him that all the men in the neighborhood were his dads.

Even though he never knew his father, he misses him. I haven't told him about the three siblings he lost in the earthquake. He's too young for it all.

---

[2] Jérémie is the capital of the Grand'Anse Department at the western tip of the Tiburon Peninsula.

I ended up here in Ti Place Cazeau.[3] I have a new daughter, Néhémie. She is eight months old. She says "mommy" and "daddy." The father is a married man. He lied to me about being married.

I think about my husband a lot. Every day. I'm sure we'd be better off if he'd lived. Right now, I do laundry for people. I set the price and the customers give me a barrel of water, soap, and Clorox. I wash from morning until late in the afternoon. Sometimes the skin comes off my hands. Still, the money isn't enough. Many times when the children are hungry, I say to myself, if Lidye was alive, my children wouldn't be hungry. He always worked hard. Anyway, I am not going to question why my husband had to die. God is all knowing.

My son and I are close. He always receives "Very Good" as a grade in school and shares with me what he's learned—the songs and poems. I always show my joy and kiss him to congratulate him. He is a very attentive and a sweet child. He gives me strength to keep fighting for him. I think he is a gift from God.

My children will not suffer the same fate as I. Never. Even if I have to beg in the street. I know what it feels like to suffer as a child. I would never inflict such pain on anyone. Sometimes I am impatient with God, but when I remember what He pulled me through, I regain strength.

The other day, we were going to church. As we were walking, he saw the pastor's car, and he said to me, "Mom, one day I will have a car like this one." I asked him how. My son replied that he will be working one day. Then he will buy his car and drive me and Néhémie around in it. That put a smile on my face. My son has dreams.

---

[3] Ti-Place Cazeau is a suburb on the eastern edge of Port-au-Prince.

I wrote two articles about the earthquake, but not literature, because I was there. That night I walked for three hours. I walked all the way from Delmas 48 to Pétionville because we were sponsoring some writers from abroad who were studying fiction there. I went to make sure they were alive. What I saw in the streets, what I felt myself, and what I saw in the people's faces—I don't have it in me to write a text that would be as powerful. And if literature doesn't add something, why try? Every time people ask me, "Are you going to write a novel about it?" I say, No! And listen, I'm telling you, the worst catastrophe was not the earthquake. It was—it is still going on—it is what the Haitian government and the so-called international community did after. The lies and the social injustice are worse today than before the earthquake. The distance between the rich and the poor. The so-called help, international help, has not in any way helped to restructure this society.

—*Lyonel Trouillot, novelist*

JOHNNY DESTANVILLE
AND
DENIS CLERMONT

Johnny—34, school teacher, construction worker

Denis—24, student

When we first met Johnny and Denis, half brothers ten years apart in age, they were living in a tent camp called Pax Villa, named for the crematorium grounds where the camp was situated.[1] After the earthquake, people retreated to the safety of the crematorium's front lawn, and the camp grew from there. The brothers longed to return to their former lives—Johnny as a teacher and Denis as a student. For four years, they lived in a tent at the Pax Villa camp. The tent was lined with their most valued possessions: Denis's stacks and stacks of books. Over time, the atmosphere at the camp became tense. The owner of the crematorium no longer wanted people camping on his land, and there was competition for limited resources, especially water.

In 2014, the brothers were able to leave the camp, find an apartment, and place Denis back in school. We spoke with the brothers on numerous occasions from 2012 to 2016, both at Pax Villa as well as in their new home in Cité Castro.[2] In 2014, we learned that Johnny had become a father.

---

[1] Pax Villa Camp was located in Delmas 33.

[2] Cité Castro is a neighborhood in Port-au-Prince.

PAX VILLA CAMP, 2013

DENIS

I'm Denis Clairmont. I'm twenty. I grew up in Okai.[3] It's to the south in the countryside where you find a lot of trees, a lot of little birds, and a big running river. And you will find the countrymen doing a countryman's work, farming and things like that. I didn't really know our parents because I was really young at the time we left. The only thing that I remember was seeing that they did a lot of farming to raise food.

I live with Mr. Johnny and my sister Jeanette at Pax Villa camp. Mr. Johnny Destanville is my brother. He's a good brother. We have the same mother but we don't have the same father. Johnny used to come to visit us when I was little. He was living in Port-au-Prince. One day Johnny came, brought a soccer ball, and said, "Let's go play soccer." I was around five or six years old. I remember that he scored against me while I was playing goalkeeper. I was very happy.

JOHNNY

I'm in certain ways responsible for my brother Denis and my sister Jeanette, as much as I can be. When I cannot be, it's up to them.

At the time of the earthquake Denis and I were living together in the ghetto, Cité Castro. There were some guys in the neighborhood that would go off sometimes. But it's not really that bad an area compared to other places. Our house was totally destroyed in the earthquake. It fell completely to the ground.

We came to Pax Villa on January 13, the day after. Before the earthquake, I was a teacher. I taught at a regular private school, ages

---

[3] Okai is another name for Les Cayes, a city of 70,000 on the southwest edge of the Tiburon Peninsula. It is one of Haiti's major seaports.

ten to thirteen. I made 450 gouds a month, which was about $60 US. Some people got paid less, like 300 gouds. I was one of the highest-paid teachers. But the truth is, I became a teacher because there were no other jobs. Teaching, if you can read and know somebody that knows somebody, is one of the easiest jobs to get in Haiti. I knew someone who knew a school director. I spoke to the director and he had me take a test. I passed and qualified to teach in the school.

The test was in French: math, science, social science. This island used to be a French colony. The Spanish fought the French and divided the island in two. In the East, in the Dominican Republic, they speak Spanish. In the West, in Haiti, we speak French and Kreyol.[4] In school, we're more likely to speak French, but we also teach in Kreyol. Money-wise, speaking French is more valuable than Kreyol. It's a class thing. If you go to school, you speak French.

I miss teaching. I miss the kids. There's a special way that they make you feel, when you're working with kids. I love to see a child reach another level. It makes me happy to see the change.

I came to Port-au-Prince when I was young, so young I can't remember my age at the time. My mother couldn't give me an education in the countryside. I know it was hard for her. In order to have a better life for us—even for her—she sent me to the city.

I grew up at my aunt's house in Port-au-Prince. My mother didn't come to see me regularly. She was a farmer and a saleswoman. She was a woman on her own. She was very busy and was surrounded by her extended family. Everybody, at that time, was living in the same *lakou*.[5] The food she would grow, she'd sell. I saw her once in a blue moon. But she worked hard to provide for the family. My mother passed away around January 12, around the time of the earthquake, but it wasn't the earthquake that killed her.

---

[4] For more on the history of the island, see Appendix I, page 293.

[5] A *lakou* is a piece of land that has small houses owned by people from the same family.

Denis is the youngest. Denis and I have been close since we were children. I used to visit him in the countryside. We used to play soccer together and have good times. I remember that time he asked me for a soccer ball. It was easier for me to find money then so I bought a ball, but I couldn't fit it in my bag because it was too big. I brought it to him in a small net. When Denis saw me, he ran to me. I remember that the first thing he took was the ball. [He laughs.] I told him, "You should have taken my bag." He helped me with my bag. He was very happy about the soccer ball. I was moved by how he reacted. If I had more gifts, I would have brought them. I think that the soccer ball is what triggered this love I have for him. I realized that he really loved me. He walked with me in the countryside and showed me around. He told me about the trees and all the different fruits. He also showed me the gardens. Our relationship was very special. He was also obedient. It's nice when a kid listens to you. Even now, he always listens and helps me. He is an adult now, and I listen to him when he gives me advice.

DENIS

During the summer, when Johnny came to visit me, my mother told him that I wasn't going to be able to continue school because she couldn't afford it. And he said he would take me to Port-au-Prince so I could go to school. My brother chose to pay for my school with the little money he was making from teaching.

The night before I left to live with Johnny, I felt wonderful, and I will always remember it. In Haiti, when you're living in the country-side and you go to Port-au-Prince, it's like moving to New York City, the place that everybody wants to move to. I had a lot of emotions. I also felt sad because I was leaving my mother.

On the bus to Port-au-Prince, I felt impatient when we were stuck in traffic. In the countryside, I never saw that many cars in the streets. I wanted to see what the city looked like. I wanted to get to the capital as quickly as possible. The bus was moving and stopping constantly. I was accompanied by another neighbor who was also going to Port-au-Prince. I didn't really have a conversation with her because I was so shy. And the only thing that was on my mind was to arrive in Port-au-Prince and see Johnny. If there wasn't traffic, we would have spent only about three and a half hours on the road. We got on the bus at 9 a.m., and we arrived in Port-au-Prince around 4 p.m.

When I got off the bus, I was looking everywhere. I saw so many people and so many cars in the street. I heard the vendors yelling about their products outside. I was looking for Johnny but I was also curious about the things I was seeing. There were lights and many other things that I wasn't used to seeing. Where I lived, we didn't have all those lights. In our village there was no electricity.

The woman who accompanied me found Johnny first and told me, "There he is." When I first saw Johnny, my heart opened. I hugged him. I didn't jump on him. Johnny greeted the woman and then we got in another car and left.

I remember that Johnny used to take me to a place near the airport. We watched the planes fly. It was something that I hadn't seen before. I felt different, that I was living another life.

JOHNNY

Yes, it started when I brought the ball for Denis. I became very close to him and felt that he had to be by my side. I wanted him to be a part of the life decisions that I was making. When he came to Port-au-Prince, he was my responsibility and I had to act like it. I told him how Port-au-Prince worked and he listened. He obeyed everything that I told him. He was also very helpful to me. He used to wash my pants and iron my shirts. He didn't disappoint me and he liked going to school.

When he first moved in with me, I took him to Delmas 33.[6]

---

[6] Delmas is a large residential and commercial suburb in the northeast of

We lived there about two years, maybe two and a half years. Life in Delmas is more luxurious than life in Castro, which also means life in Delmas is more expensive. But the house I rented wasn't built very well. We couldn't stay inside when it was raining because water would get inside. We say *Kay koule twompe soley soley men li pa twompe lapil*—a leaky house can fool the sun but not the rain.

Rent at that time was about 800 Haitian dollars per year.[7] I could manage it. I was working in Mais Gaté at a school named Collège Jacques Desilien.[8] But in the end, Delmas just became too expensive. For example, in Castro, you could buy a pot of rice for 4 Haitian dollars. In Delmas the same pot would cost 5 Haitian dollars. So we moved to Cité Castro to save a bit of money. At that time our sister wasn't living with us. I already had Denis, and I couldn't afford to have Jeanette as well.

DENIS

When school was about to start, Johnny went to buy uniforms for me, and we went to the tailor together. Johnny used the money he made from teaching. I wouldn't say he was receiving a "check" because when you get a check it's for a reasonable amount of money. The small amount of money he was making from teaching was tragic. He also bought me a backpack and shoes. He didn't have the money to buy me all the materials, so I went to school with only three notebooks and two books.

Every day, when I came back from school, I would do all the homework I could and wait for Johnny to help me with the rest. I remember once that he helped me with homework and I got a

---

Port-au-Prince, adjacent to the city's airport. Individual neighborhoods in Delmas are referred to by number, since the suburb is organized around numbered streets that radiate out from a central road (for instance, Delmas 45, Delmas 18, et cetera).

[7] At the time of the interview, 800 Haitian dollars equals approximately US$90.

[8] Mais Gaté is northeast of Delmas.

10 out of 10. When I told him he said, "Bravo, keep getting good grades."

I really liked going to school and I did my best to get good grades. When the teacher gave us homework from a book that I didn't have, I would borrow the book from a friend, copy the exercises, and do the homework at the school. To be honest, I didn't have that many friends. My brother always told me that he didn't bring me to the city to have friends. He brought me here to go to school and work hard.

When I got the final report card for sixth grade, I got straight A's. After seventh grade, we didn't have money, but Johnny always told me that God would send us money. He went to the school and talked to the administrators so they wouldn't send me back home. And he told me something I will never forget. He told me that there are two ways to succeed in life—God and knowledge. To acquire knowledge I had to keep going to school. After God, that's what I believe in: knowledge.

I don't have the opportunity to go to the institute to learn English. But I learn. I'm trying to learn English from my books. In my free time, I take my books, I read, and I try to understand English. I have many books. My favorite books are stories, philosophy, Shakespeare, Schopenhauer, Voltaire, Jacques Rousseau, Descartes. After reading those guys from the past, you have a sense of what you're doing in life. By following them, you will also have a chance in life. Take Romeo and Juliet. Their story is beautiful. There's a lesson. They help us understand each other, how to live, how to respect one another. The power of love. You can do so much with the power of love.

Do you know Racine? When you are in a difficult situation, it helps you not to think with your head. I remember the father of Shemen hit the father of Robbie. The father of Robbie went to tell Robbie, "Your wife's father hit me. Do us justice." Then Robbie killed his father-in-law, and he went back to his wife, Shemen. And then there's this beautiful part. Robbie gave his wife a knife and said,

"I killed your father; you could kill me now." Shemen said, "You hurt me the first time by killing my father. Now you want to hurt me a second time by killing you? It's too much for me." I like to read stories that make you think, that give you faith to keep moving.

My dream is to become a big-time engineer. What really got me into engineering was the aftermath from January 12. All of those people died because of bad construction. I want to do a better job with construction. I want to build safer houses.[9] The first step to being an engineer is to finish high school. Now I have to figure out how I'm going to go to college.

JOHNNY

The day of the earthquake, I came home from work around 1 p.m. A few neighbors were playing dominoes. I wanted to play, but they refused to let me in the game, so I went inside to listen to the news on the radio. I love listening to the news. Especially sports news. I was listening to Radio Megastar when I felt the house shaking. Our house was just a regular box house, two stories high, made out of concrete and cement. I had experienced an earthquake probably four to five years before, but that one wasn't too bad. But with this one, the house was shaking and suddenly, from where I was on my bed, I was looking into the street—I realized that the wall had fallen down. I stood up to run, but then I remembered a neighbor saying that in case of earthquakes, one must look for a post and hug it. I went to the wall post and I hugged it. I stayed there until the end.

After everything was done, everything was broken. The aftershocks kept on coming every two or three minutes. We weren't the only people renting in that house. Some people in the house died. Many other houses built with concrete roofs in the Castro area collapsed as well.

---

[9] For more on urban planning and the 2010 earthquake, see Appendix IV, page 327.

I ran outside. The air was white with dust. I felt nauseous. Everything was spinning around and I felt like I was drunk. I thought the coming of Jesus was happening. I saw people running, with blood all over. Immediately, I thought about Denis, and started asking people if they'd seen him. Someone told me that she'd seen Denis walking around and that he was all right. He hadn't been inside when it happened. But still, I couldn't find him, and it seemed that he'd gone looking for me. I spent that night with a neighbor at the hospital. A pole had fallen on her arm and she didn't have anybody to help her. I used a wooden stick to try moving the pole, but it was too heavy. Luckily, another big guy came by and helped me, but her arm was already crushed. I took her to the La Paix Hospital.[10] I saw so many dead bodies. Before the earthquake, I was scared of dead bodies and blood. But after that day I stopped being scared. Cadavers became nothing to me, because I saw so many of them.

I went back to the neighborhood the next day and was told that everybody on our block had moved to the Pax Villa yard. I went there and found Denis, and was so happy.

DENIS

During the time when the earthquake happened, I was in class, in Seconde.[11] Imagine: You're walking around trying to find out if your brother is alive. And you see—walking in the street—you see a person with a foot cut off. And you see another person with a missing hand. And you want to give that person support. You would like to take them to the hospital. And you know that you can't because you have to find your brother. And after you finally find him, there's looking for food and trying to find where to sleep—and the mosquitoes.

---

[10] La Paix Hospital is located in the suburb of Delmas.

[11] *Seconde* is the Haitian equivalent to sophomore year of high school.

JOHNNY

The distance between where we were living and Pax Villa was about 3 kilometers. A lot of people went there because there wasn't anywhere else to go. Before January 12, no one would have thought to live there. The place is where they burn dead bodies. Sometimes we would see smoke rising from the chimney.

In the beginning, we didn't have tents. We spent two weeks sleeping on the grass with no covering. It rained sometimes, but just small drops. God saw that we didn't have anything to cover our heads, and he didn't let the rains come down. I remember something Denis did. It was quiet and we were lying on the grass with everybody, and Denis stood up and yelled, "Can someone lend me a blanket please?" The people started laughing and someone lent us a blanket. Some people still remember us because we asked for blankets.

Those were tough times. Everybody was hurt in different ways. Yet those were also some of the best moments in the camp, when we all took care of each other. Everybody was in need and everything we had was shared with as many people as possible. We lived like brothers and sisters, all together. We slept in the same area and nobody stole from each other. Unfortunately, after three months, things started to change.

DENIS

Pax Villa had a fence around it, but it didn't stop people from going inside. The piece of land was very large. When we got there, everybody was looking for blankets and other materials in order to build some shelter. Later, we went to the woods to get sticks to use with clothes to build a tent. After a while, some foreigners came and helped us—they brought plastic sheets and we used them to build better tents. But I do remember times when I questioned if we were still human.

JOHNNY

We think God had other plans for us. If we didn't die from the earthquake, there's something waiting for us. So we were living day by day. Whatever happens, happens.

DENIS

Even in the camp, I never stopped studying. A lot of people were affected mentally. A lot of people got into gangs. I didn't want to give up my studies, so my brother and I looked around to find a government school. I was going to Lycée Jean Mary Vincent de Caradeux, the public school. That's a far distance from the camp. Me being lightweight and not healthy, I couldn't walk all the way there. I had to pay 5 gouds for a ride. Then on my way back, I had to pay the other 5 gouds, and spend the whole day with nothing to eat. The days that I didn't have money, I had to force myself to walk the whole way. I left Pax Villa at 7 a.m. without breakfast, and then came back home at 3 p.m., my stomach still empty.

I graduated high school in 2011. We celebrated in our hearts. We had no money. But we were happy within ourselves.

The earthquake changed everything, dreams and plans. I'm still studying. I don't go to college. And I don't think it's going to be possible. I'm still hoping. I study on my own. I'm trying to keep it up.

JOHNNY

When I was living in the camp, other people there understood that my advice was helpful. I gave them advice on how to clean the place and they listened to me. They liked Denis and me because we had a good relationship with everybody. I started teaching the kids at the camp.

After the earthquake, when the school reopened, I was offered my job back. Before the earthquake they would often owe you one or two months' salary. Now, they would owe you four or five months back pay. If the parents don't pay the school, then the owner of the school doesn't have money to pay us. I went back for a month or two. We had fewer and fewer students. Because you get paid for the number of students that enroll, wages dropped lower than what I was paid before.

I figured it would be better for me to do side work and get paid immediately. That's when I turned to construction and other odd jobs. So that's what I do now. At least I can save for a plate of food every day. A plate for me, a plate for my brother.

My brother and I put our heads together. If my brother is working, when he comes home with money, I take the money to the market. We might buy little things of rice that will last for a while. If we're both working, we put money together to last more days. We always stick together. If it's a job that my brother can do, I let him do it.

I work any time someone calls me, especially people that are building houses. For example, somebody passes by and sees the work that we're doing and likes it and comes back and says, "Listen, I like what you did. I want you to do something for me." I give them an estimate of what they need to buy. I come by, do a couple of days working, and I earn money. And you see the tents here? I helped build, with my brother, most of these tents.

Whenever I get a phone call saying that I'm going to work tomorrow, joy jumps up into my heart. It stops me from sleeping. I get up in the morning and put my clothes on, go out the door with a smile, and I'm thinking about what the work is going to be like. While I'm working, I'm thinking about that pay and try to do a good job to get more work.

I never expected this. I'm a teacher. I'm used to teaching students. It hurts me to see them. Now, they're on the streets.

DENIS

I'd like to be a writer. I'm so attached to my books. I remember once I only had 100 gouds on my way home from school.[12] I saw this wonderful book that I liked and I just thought, *Forget it, I'm just going to buy the book*. And I spent the whole day with no food. I read the Bible. I read novels. I'll read any regular book I find. That's how I pass my time: reading.

We have to understand each other's stories. And it's not going to get better if we fight among each other. Sometimes, when you're in a camp like this, and living with many people, it gives you opportunity to learn how to live like a family with the other individuals that you don't know. That makes me feel good. When the sun goes down, we go to the field and play soccer or play a little dominoes among ourselves. That kills a lot of time.

But it's kind of brutal. So many people here are the lowest, the poorest. If they cause violence, they get kicked out. Then they're totally on the streets. We have to pull ourselves together to live among each other. Our personal problems that we might have between each other, we don't let that get in the way.

We have to purchase water from outside the camp. We treat it with Clorox and Aquatabs.[13] But sometimes the water dries up. Then you have to go further away to buy it. No money, no water. We buy charcoal wood to cook. Most of the time, people sell it in the yard. But if no one is selling it, then we have to go to the market downtown, very far, to buy it. We have outhouses made out of wood. They are overfilled. They're not clean. The international organization AID came up with this system of latrines. They used to clean them, but they don't come anymore.

---

[12] At the time of the interview, 100 gouds equals approximately US$5.

[13] Aquatabs is a brand name for water purification tablets that help prevent cholera and other water-borne diseases.

Hunger. The sun. Starving. The people. The heat. When it rains, there's so much mud it's hard to walk. Our things get wet. When it's sunny, it's too hot to stay in the tents. The trash smells very bad. The place we're living is a place where dead bodies are burned and buried. It smells like a cemetery.

I used to think I was alive, but I'm not. I exist, but I'm not living. This is not a way for human beings to live. Imagine you wake up in the morning and then you have to wait until when you're going to sleep to eat something. Just think about it. I'm a human. And I want to live like one. I want to be real. I want to live like a human being.

After four years in Pax Villa, Johnny and Denis have returned to Cité Castro, living in an apartment, a small square room in a cement block building. Inside, there is a small refrigerator, a bed, and a table. There are twenty-five or thirty books on a shelf that the brothers made themselves. There's a rack they made for their clothes and a blackboard they paint and write on. Under the bed, there are tennis shoes. The stairs to the apartment are still in partial rubble and dirt from the earthquake. There's a carpet on the floor where Denis sleeps because the bed doesn't fit two people comfortably.

CITÉ CASTRO, 2015

JOHNNY

I was getting tired of being at the camp. It had become very unsafe. People started stealing from one another: sneakers, blankets, and other things. Bad individuals established themselves in our midst. There was a chance that we would get caught in the crossfire one day. Cops used to show up at the camp and beat people up. It didn't matter who you were. When they were pursuing someone, they would beat up and arrest every young man and woman. They almost beat up Denis, but an old lady defended him. He was lucky that day. We really felt unsafe because we didn't know when the police would come looking for someone. We heard a rumor that the land's owner was receiving payment to let us stay there. So he was making profit, while we were being kept in those conditions. People started protesting in the streets.

Six months later, we were moved. I.O.M. told us to find a place anywhere we want.[14] They didn't find the place for us. We found a place and they came and investigated it. They gave us 26,500 gouds to rent an apartment, 1,000 gouds as relocation fees, and 5,000 gouds to start a little business.[15] Everybody that was in the camp was being relocated. In March 2014, we left Pax Villa.

DENIS

One day when we were still living at Pax Villa, my brother and myself were out working, and when we came back somebody had come with a razor and cut our tent. They'd stolen all of my books and all our valuables. Even my dictionaries. I haven't been able to replace the books that I lost because of money.

As I told you before, I really wanted to go to college to become a civil engineer. But it seems like it's going to be too expensive. So I thought to myself why not take a writing course? I took the 1,000 Haitian dollars we had left from I.O.M. and I enrolled in a journalism course in order to pursue writing.[16]

JOHNNY

I'm thirty-four now. There's no more Pax Villa. It's all over and it's a good thing. I keep in contact with people from the camp. We were

---

[14] The International Organization for Migration. I.O.M. is an international NGO based in Switzerland that assists refugees and internally displaced peoples.

[15] Approximately US$800 total.

[16] Approximately US$110.

together for four years. Though it was tough, we were a family. When we learned that we were leaving, it was bittersweet. We did have a party, but it wasn't all rejoicing, you know. We knew we were going to miss each other.

I've gone back to teaching. I teach sixth grade. I have fifteen to twenty students.

I still live with Denis. He likes studying. I do too, but since I'm a bit older there are certain things I can't do anymore. Now, my worry is Denis. He has two more semesters to go. Whenever I can, I buy him a book.

I'm doing my best to see if he can become a journalist. That's the main reason why I went back to teaching. I wish I could do more, but our means remain very slim. Sometimes, I go for three months without getting paid. If the students don't pay the monthly fee, then the teachers do not get paid. Do I think that when Denis finds a job he will help me as well? I don't know. I hope so. But I do it because he's my brother. And he'll decide what he wants to do with his money when he makes it. I still feel responsible for my brother and sister, but I know that they'll have to be on their own eventually. They see how I behave and maintain myself. I hope that they'll follow in the same path.

I have a girlfriend. We also have a newborn son, Johnsly. He's twenty-two days old. We're not living together right now, but she loves me a lot. She's living with her sister. She's working at a factory. She takes care of most of the bills for our son so I can help Denis with the little I have.

DENIS

I'll never forget the time my brother came to visit us in the countryside and played soccer with me. Then January 12 brought us closer, because we made our way to survive. We said brothers should stick together. In the camp, we played soccer together. We read the Bible together and talked about God. We talked about our future and what might happen in our life.

JOHNNY

I had all these beautiful dreams of going to the university but those dreams were shattered. I'm hopeful for my son. As a teacher, I'll be able to help my son and I have faith that God will help me provide for him. For us Haitians, we don't have any assurance that we can adequately educate our children. We only hope that we can. Nobody knows how long we'll be here in the world. We're all passengers. We could be here today and be gone the next. I don't know where this love comes from. My son comes first. However, my girlfriend or my child cannot decrease my love for Denis. As long as he can't find work, I will always help him.

One fight we had was about what language to use in the courts. Most lawyers use French in court, but now some are starting to use Kreyol a little bit. This is a fight I want to win. Most people in Haiti don't speak French. My clients are mostly poor and uneducated. So if I speak French in court, they don't understand what's going on. The first thing that I needed to do to get the legal system to change its language was simply to use more Kreyol in my practice. For example, beginning in 2004 I did a lot of advocacy saying that Kreyol should be spoken in the courts. There's no shame in speaking Kreyol, and I addressed the fact that it was complex to do legal work in two languages—Kreyol and French. After nineteen years of doing this work, I think some people respect it when I say we should be speaking Kreyol inside the courts as we do outside. And everyone knows that if you really need to express something, then you need to speak Kreyol.

—*Mario Joseph, human rights attorney*

LAMOTHE LORMIER

53, water expert/driver/law student/translator

Lamothe Lormier has lived in Port-au-Prince for decades and has held a number of positions, including literacy teacher and medical translator. His passion is the environment, and his special expertise is water. He identifies the major problems facing Haiti in the future as 1) scarity of water, and 2) lack of clean water. Lamothe is a former board member of an organization called the Gift of Water, headquartered in the U.S. He has traveled throughout Port-au-Prince and the Haitian countryside talking to local communities about water and providing instruction on practical solutions.

Lamothe describes himself as a kind of Renaissance man and is a constant reader of literature, history, and philosophy. Tall and soft-spoken, Lamothe loves to converse on an incredibly wide range of subjects. His love of his country is tempered only by his occasional bouts of despair over the future. We spoke for many hours on the porch of the Matthew 25 House in Port-au-Prince, a guest house in Delmas. We also spoke to Lamothe as we drove to various spots around Port-au-Prince. He pointed out garbage-chocked ravines, kids swimming in a polluted river, and other places of extreme environmental degradation. Following up on a lifelong interest in law, in 2015, Lamothe enrolled in law school in Port-au-Prince and is currently studying ideas of forgiveness in criminal legal theory.

I moved to Port-au-Prince when I was twenty. For me, coming from the countryside to Port-au-Prince was overwhelming. It's wild, it's big. I mean—the cars, the TVs, the everything. Here we have the Internet, here we have iPhones. But in the meantime, you see someone naked at Delmas 23.[1] There's a small natural spring there. People come and bathe, right in the street. You see a cow wander by. And the traffic? Sometimes on Lalue it can take two and a half hours to go two miles.[2] So there's contradictions everywhere you look in this city. And now with my computer I can communicate with anybody in the world on Facebook. But I look out the window and there's a child in the mud, a donkey. Two centuries in one spot.

They call it the Republic of Port-au-Prince. Everything flows from Port-au-Prince. If you need a driver's license, you need to come to Port-au-Prince. If you need a passport, you've got to stand in line in Port-au-Prince. If you need to change the title of your car, you need to come to Port-au-Prince. For a long time there used to be only one airport, that's Port-au-Prince. So much of the infrastructure of our society—the government, the universities, everything—is in the Republic of Port-au-Prince. And so naturally everybody wants to be in Port-au-Prince.

The city has the tendency to attract people from the villages because the city is perceived as a sign of civilization. If you are in the city, you are inside civilization, and if you are outside of the city, you are outside of civilization. In order to feel important, you need to claim that you are from the city. And I think that must be true not only for Haitians. Say you live in San Francisco or New York or

---

[1] Delmas is a large residential and commercial suburb in the northeast of Port-au-Prince, adjacent to the city's airport. Individual neighborhoods in Delmas are referred to by number, since the suburb is organized around numbered streets that radiate out from a central road (for instance, Delmas 45, Delmas 18, et cetera).

[2] Lalue is a nickname for John Brown Avenue, a major road that runs through Port-au-Prince and Pétionville.

L.A. You feel one way. You feel you live someplace important, no? I wonder if someone from Kansas feels the same way.

Port-au-Prince was built to house 500,000 people. Now the city has about 3 million souls. You could say that in some ways it began with Duvalier, the first one, the father.[3] Duvalier wanted to show that he was very popular, that his regime was strong, so he would send big trucks to the countryside and load them up with peasants. They'd come for celebrations in the city. And many of these peasants simply never returned home. That's one part of the big flow of migration. The other side of it is that agriculture is no longer enough to sustain the country, and so thousands of people in the countryside, because they cannot grow enough crops to survive, move to the city to find a job. People stay in Port-au-Prince because at least they can find something. I mean, you see people living in trash, but they still think they're living a better life than in the mountains. They chose this city despite the violence—despite everything.

Myself? I moved to Port-au-Prince because this is the only place where there's access to a higher education. At that time, there was nowhere else. In the whole country. I'm fifty-three. Things have changed a little bit now, but when I was twenty, options were very limited. And so I came here, to the Republic of Port-au-Prince, a place with a foot in two centuries.

AS A CHILD I WOULD DRINK THE
WATER FROM THE RIVER

I was born in the Artibonite Valley, which is in the center of Haiti.[4] The Artibonite is the big river that crosses the area. The river is polluted, and that is the river water that I used to drink as a child. I

---

[3] For more on the Duvalier regime, see Appendix I, page 293.

[4] Artibonite is the name of Haiti's largest department (administrative division) and makes up much of the country's northwest.

didn't know any better. So as a child I would drink the water from the river and, then, like all normal kids, I'd have worms.

My village is called Liancourt. I would say there are maybe 2,000 to 3,000 people in the village. It's a pretty rural area. Mostly we grew rice, but it was never enough. I grew up in deep poverty. Many, many children in my village lived the same life. Some days I would go to school. Other days I wouldn't.

I have four sisters and three brothers. It's a big family. My father was Catholic, and my mother was practicing Vodou, but she didn't want my father to know.[5] Sometimes she'd spend money going to the Vodou priest, for whatever reason—I don't know. So, I witnessed that. But early on my perception of not only Vodou but religion in general kind of shifted because we didn't have any food. My concern was survival. My mother would take me to these ceremonies where people would leave money on the ground. Without them knowing, I'd take some of that money and use it to buy food. If they had known that at the time, I would have been in major trouble. We were told that if you took money from a ceremony, after a year, you would go crazy. I kept taking money and, well, I'm not crazy yet. But these are the experiences that shape your thinking.

Education wasn't that important to my family. If it was a choice between me going to school and going to harvest, they would send me to the farm. It hurt me at that point—all I wanted was to go to school. Not necessarily because of the education itself, but because of the life in my house. I felt a kind of togetherness at school that I didn't feel at home.

You see, school boosted my confidence. I was perceived as smarter than the rest. I was able to memorize facts very well, and I've always been very good at solving problems. I'm very careful when I say this because I don't believe that some people are blessed with more intelligence than others. When you read all the theories about

---

[5] For more on Haitian Vodou, see the Glossary, page 309.

intelligence, you know that there are so many different types of intelligence. Emotional intelligence, social intelligence, et cetera, but it might have been that my brain was better equipped to adapt to the system that I was in, so I made it. Therefore my self-esteem was kind of higher than the rest of the kids, because they kept saying, "Lamothe is smarter." It makes you feel like you can explain the world, the universe. It gives you the fuel to continue. Of course, this can be a trap. Because you start to love the attention.

But the truth is that I have always valued education because of the color of my skin. As you can see, I'm very dark. This played a big role against me when I was little. I was bullied a lot. But education was a kind of therapy for me. I felt, *Here is a field where I can win and color doesn't matter as much.*

I left my village to go to high school. I went to live with my aunt in a small city on the coast. This was my first escape. Unfortunately there are so many people who get stuck because they didn't get the chance of an education. I was lucky enough that I had that opportunity.

When I went to my aunt's city, I didn't even know that there was this other language, English. This other language, Spanish. In the village there is no way of knowing something like that. My life began to change, to open up. I saw the ocean for the very first time.

Looking back, the education that I was exposed to was also very dangerous. You begin to think that education gives you power over the rest of the people. And you begin to believe that you have privilege over the rest of the people, that you deserve the wealth, because you have an education, and that other people—poor people—don't deserve anything because they're not educated.

After high school, I went to the state university in Port-au-Prince to study social service. This was under the dictatorship of Baby Doc in 1982.[6] It was a very scary time. It was like something

---

[6] For more on the Duvalier regime, see Appendix I, page 293.

out of Orwell's book *1984*, only two years earlier than he predicted. Vodou was being used to brainwash people, and to reinforce the fear. We all knew that Big Brother was out there watching us, so we had to be careful. There was no freedom of expression at all.

For instance, at the university there were certain topics you couldn't ask the professors. How could we talk about political parties when there's only one party of the government? The man was president for life. So there we were reading about the French Revolution, the Russian Revolution, our own revolution! But we couldn't talk deeply about any of these events. You see what I'm saying? It was like living in nonsense.

But things began to change. I was still at the university in 1986 during the fall of Baby Doc. I participated in the student protests. Like any normal twenty-five or twenty-six-year-old does anywhere in the world. I went out in the streets. Now I can see that I was naïve. You don't see things the same way when you are fifty than when you are twenty-six. Like so many others I envisioned a better Haiti. A Haiti where there would be a lot of trees. Where everyone had access to education. Where we actually had elections for president, for parliament. I dreamed all those things. But now I realize, *Wow, the system is bigger than I thought*. There's been so much frustration since 1986. It wasn't a revolution. It was only a first, small step.

EDUCATION IS NOT ENOUGH

After university I began working in a literacy program. Wasn't being paid. I just did it because I wanted to contribute. I was teaching reading in high schools, as well as math and social sciences. At that time there were some Americans working in our schools. Some doors opened for me. I began making a good living as an interpreter.

So yes, I was teaching people how to read, how to write, how to count, but here's the reality. When you live in an environment with

98.5 percent deforestation, providing an education is not enough.[7] An education won't feed a population. That's when I heard about an environmental program in California. How on one small farm you can grow a lot of food. I decided I wanted to learn some of these agricultural techniques and incorporate them into the curriculum of the literacy program. I went to Willits, three hours north of San Francisco.[8] This was in '95. It was such an experience. I studied intensive agriculture. And I came back to Haiti hoping that I would have a demonstration garden, where I could teach people about agriculture and everything, but it didn't work out.

EVERYTHING IS A CHALLENGE

I ended up working as an interpreter with medical teams and that's when I became involved in water. Because while I was working with all those medical teams, the issues that they were addressing, to me, were like putting on Band-Aids. They were trying to provide people with medicine for gastrointestinal diseases and other health problems related to bad water. I thought, *What a waste of time and money, when the real problem is water.*

Everything is a challenge here. I don't blame anybody who lives here and dreams about leaving. Many Haitians feel that in order to have a better life, they have to leave, to be outside Haiti. No, you can't blame them. And it's true that I could have stayed in the U.S. Many times I've thought about this. But I came back to Haiti. I felt

---

[7] In 1923, forests covered as much as 60 percent of Haiti. By 2010, forest cover had dwindled to less than 4 percent. Laws regulating the felling of trees in Haiti have existed since the mid-nineteenth century, and numerous laws requiring permits for felling trees were passed in the twentieth centuries. However, deforestation remains one of the major environmental threats in Haiti, responsible for erosion of arable soil and increased risk of floods and other damage caused by natural disasters. For more on deforestation in Haiti, see the Glossary, page 309.

[8] Willits, California, is home to the Grange Farm School, an institution that trains students in sustainable agriculture.

that I could make a difference. I have the education. This chaos must be addressed, and if someone with my knowledge doesn't address it, who is going to? So, it's in my blood now. If I could unlearn what I've learned, or unknow what I know now, that would be different.

It kind of reminds me of the movie *The Matrix*. I took the red pills, and I can't go back again. I can't just be silent. If I were silent now, I would carry so much guilt inside of me. There are so many battles to fight. You find one. I chose water. I saw people that are sick, and 80 percent of the diseases were the result of lack of clean water. That's how I got involved. I've been in charge of the Gift of Water program for over fifteen years now. I teach people about the importance of clean water, and demonstrate methods of purification. I also advocate for cleaning up our rivers, ravines, and water sources. The job is endless.

In a normal city there should be running water in every faucet. That's the bottom line. There's an area north of Port-au-Prince where there's a water source, underground wells. There's an eight-inch pipe tapping out water. Tanker trucks drive by, fill up, go, fill up, go. And then they take the water into the city and drive by people's homes and sell it. I'm talking about people with homes with water systems. They pipe it into the water system and it comes out of the faucet. But it's not drinkable. The well water is contaminated. There's a lot of *E. coli* in the water. The water is only for domestic use, like showers and washing, but you can't—or you shouldn't—drink it.

Our drinking water comes from the same aquifer north of the city, but it's treated through reverse osmosis. It goes to the UN and is converted. It makes safe drinking water. This began after the cholera.[9] Before, people would just get the water from everywhere and drink it. They got sick sometimes, but it was a very slow process. When you get sick from cholera, that's a different ball game. If you

---

[9] For more on the cholera epidemic in Haiti, see Apendix III, page 329.

don't get rehydrated right away, you are gone. You're dead. Seven thousand people got sick in the cholera epidemic.[10]

THERE'S ALSO LACK OF WATER

So, now, on every corner you are seeing these stands selling small plastic bags of water. That is the primary source of drinking water for the majority of people in this city. It's very heavy on their budgets. Every day they pay for water. It adds up. People here, as poor as they are, they pay so much for water. But let me tell you this—I won't drink the water from the bag. The BPA—bisphenol A—level in bags is too high.

And there's another problem that is even worse. They've been pumping water out of the aquifer for forty, fifty years now. At one point, the water they will get will be too salty to convert. I don't know how soon that will happen. I haven't seen any studies yet. But it is just a matter of time. It isn't an "if"; it's a "when." You can use pasteurization for salty water. For that, though, you need heat—and money. It might be possible to use solar energy to get the water from the ocean. But for how much? And it means that the money that you need for health care, for education, you must invest it in water. How can we take this option?

---

[10] Lamothe further comments, "When people talk about the UN and cholera, this is the analogy that I use: You have a brand-new car. The manual says that every 60,000 miles, you should change your tires. Every 5,000 miles you should get an oil change. Every 90,000 miles, you change the belt. That's what the manual says. So you go 100,000 miles and never did any of those things. Now, you lend your car to a friend and that friend took the car and ended up killing people. Okay, now, who should be blamed?

"The owner of the car is the Haitian government. It has been 200 years, and they have never provided clean water for those people. For so many years, they never did anything—they didn't change the tires. The driver is the UN. They came in the country. They should test somebody. They should know that there's a health concern. If someone is sick, this is a very fragile country and anything could happen, so they shouldn't come."

I often feel like a prophet with bad news. I'm trying to work to provide clean water, but if nothing is done, soon there won't be enough water at all. Haiti is 98.5 percent deforested. All the trees have been cut and used for timber. It creates drought. For years, we've been living in drought. Without trees, all the rainwater flows into the ocean instead of remaining in the soil. So, I'm addressing clean water, but there's also a *lack* of water. These are two different things.

Whenever I do my trainings, I always give the bad news. The next conflict between Haiti and the Dominican Republic won't be over immigration. It will be over water, unfortunately. We're going to run out. So we'll have to go there—the Dominican Republic—and find it. So that will be the conflict, like India and Pakistan, Palestine and Israel. I won't be around to see that, but this is where we are moving. I wish I were wrong.

PLASTIC IS A HUMAN PROBLEM

This river here—Bois Chene—this was a natural riverbed many years ago.[11] We used to have water in it. Where's the water? It's been dry many years. Only a little water in the rainy season or in the spring. This is the river of plastic, now—along with so much else. Laundry baskets, cans, shirts, egg boxes, bags, detergent bottles, everything. Pigs. You name it, you can find it in the river. And what you see right here is a microscopic look at a bigger thing.

Fifty years ago, it wasn't like this. It wasn't because people were more educated, but because Port-au-Prince didn't have so many people. And they hadn't yet introduced plastic into the environment.

Plastic is invading our lives. The stuff satisfies our needs for maybe an hour or two hours, but it causes problems for 500 years. When it's raining, all this trash will end up deep in the ocean. Some of it will make it to Cuba. Some of it will make it to Jamaica. We can

---

[11] The Bois Chene ("Oak River") is in Haiti's northwest.

solve this. Let me quote a French environmentalist, Albert Jacquard, who said that we need to live together as brothers and sisters, otherwise we are going to die together as idiots.

Of course plastic isn't a Haitian problem; it is a human problem. So this is a riverbed, but it is also a representation of human failure. It's impossible for me to imagine that with all the technology that allows us to recycle things, with the organic matters here that can be used for composting, and we still just let it all sit here before it goes out to sea. There are easy answers. Why not tax this plastic? Why not give more incentives for recycling?

Haiti is a leader. Ours was the first slave revolution in human history that succeeded. To me, that's a lot to share with the world. But, let's be honest, what came after that? After 200 years of independence, what? Albert Camus commented, I believe it was in *The Stranger*, that if you put someone in a box for all his life, always in this box, finally he'll be used to it. He will be used to that box, and then he will stay in that box until he dies.

This is what puzzles me about Port-au-Prince. You see people smiling, you see people laughing. And then you see, for instance, someone sitting near a garbage pile and eating. There is a certain sense of order in this chaos. Things have their place. Otherwise, we'd all go crazy, but, do you notice something? You don't see that many crazy people here. We've begun to accept our situation as normal.

And then we have an earthquake that kills 200,000 or 300,000 people, who even knows? And I saw people with one arm, with one foot, and they weren't complaining. The courage of the survivors teaches us a lot about the complexity of a human being. I've got two arms, two legs, and I still complain? It's hard for me to comprehend. We all have a lot to learn.

I was hoping that the earthquake would allow us to make a new plan. To say, this is a time, this is an opportunity to rethink Port-au-Prince. Look at Brazil. At one point they moved the capital to another place! The earthquake was horrific, but it was also a possibility to rethink the country in a different way—to change our education system, our environment. The whole world was focusing on Haiti. Even Hollywood had Haiti fever!

All that foreign interest, all that foreign money. Have the levels of poverty and misery changed? And even right now, today, we have a foreign army—the UN—in Haiti.[12] This is another occupation. The people call the UN *tourista*. It means that they are here like tourists who have little interest in what goes on here. They are supposed to be keeping the peace, but the United Nations, the United States, or any other foreign country can't come here and fix our problems. The solutions are going to be Haitian or there won't be any solutions.

I don't want to call what happened after the earthquake a failure. I mean, what would you expect? But I did have hope. You lose hope when you die. Hope will follow you to your grave, but at a certain point, too, you've got to be realistic. What are the conditions that need to change for change to happen? It makes me feel very sad to see countries, for instance, in Africa that have only been independent since the 1960s. Compare them to Haiti, and you see a big difference. Look at some countries in Asia, Singapore, South Korea, Taiwan. Seventy years ago you could compare them to Haiti. There was a writer, Gunnar Myrdal, who won a Nobel Peace Prize in Economics, who predicted in his book *Asian Drama* that those countries from Asia would never break the cycle of poverty. History proved him wrong. They broke the cycle and now you see they're very different countries.

WHY AM I SO LUCKY?

So I believe change is possible. And yet sometimes I feel like this life is not a problem to be solved, but a mystery to live with. I tend not to take things for granted anymore. When I go back to my village it's

---

[12] For more on the UN peacekeeping mission to Haiti, see Appendix I, page 293.

a kind of metaphysical trip, a trip inside of myself, too, and I can see, *Wow, this is where I would be stuck if I didn't have an education.* I look at my friends and relatives and I see how they are trapped in misery, and they have no power to overcome.

And then I wish that everybody who has been raised in the Western world should make a trip to Haiti. And a trip to Haiti won't be a trip to Haiti; it would be a trip inside of themselves. And it might lead them to question God, and ask, Why am I so lucky? I will appreciate the water that I'm drinking. I will appreciate the road that is so nice that I'm driving. I will appreciate the peace.

I have to believe that beneath every tragedy there's room for triumph, there's redemption. I've recently gone through a divorce and I miss my two children in the U.S. I miss them so much. I have all this negative energy inside of me now. I'm trying to put it into something positive. I've been focusing on law school and the environment. I've got some time left. Maybe I can contribute something. Maybe not. Who knows where the adventure will take me? All I know for certain is that when I go to bed in the middle of all this chaos, there's still a chance I can contribute something.

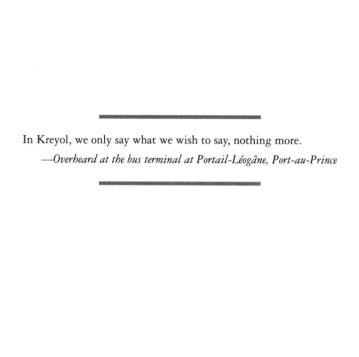

In Kreyol, we only say what we wish to say, nothing more.

—*Overheard at the bus terminal at Portail-Léogâne, Port-au-Prince*

ALINA

24, mother

We met Alina (a pseudonym) in the tuberculosis ward at the General Hospital in Port-au-Prince. The interviewer, a doctor himself, spoke to Alina about her condition. The ward was housed in a semipermanent shelter adjacent to the largely destroyed main hospital radiology building. Initial improvised efforts to care for tuberculosis patients at the General Hospital after the earthquake had evolved into an ambitious and deeply dedicated organization called Ti Kay Haiti, led by an American named Dr. Megan Coffee. The main TB ward was crowded with patients, caregivers, family members, oxygen canisters, and a nest of oxygen tubing; we tried to find some quiet and privacy. While Alina was being treated at the General Hospital for TB and H.I.V., she also had nowhere else to go, and was living in the hospital with her four-year-old son. As we talked, the boy darted around the hospital campus.[1]

I have two children. The oldest one, Reuben, is here with me. I was never married. Reuben's father is a jerk. He knocked me up, and then said my child isn't his, just because he is dark and Reuben is lighter

---

[1] Editor's note: This story and two others (Josil, page 235, and Christopher, page 255) focus on hospitals and medical care. We've chosen to leave some of the questions in because it reflects the intimate nature of the doctor/patient relationship here. For more on current health crises in Haiti, see Appendix III, page 317.

than he is. Reuben is four years old now. He'll be five soon. The youngest is nine months old and living with his dad in the Dominican Republic. He's not the father of my first son. I was never married with him either.

I was nineteen in 2008 when I was pregnant with Reuben. At that time, I took the H.I.V. test at Carrefour Center, Fort-de-Fou.[2] I was positive. I received some ARV medication for my pregnancy.[3] I received just one medicine. I took it in the morning and afternoon. I don't remember what it was. It was some big white pill.

Reuben was born March 30, 2008. The delivery was without complications. Reuben was tested for H.I.V. when he was born, and the test came out negative. They retested at three months and six months. His test at six months came out positive.

They told me not to breastfeed him. I didn't listen. I didn't think he could catch the virus through breastfeeding. I didn't have money to feed him other things. They said if I did, it wouldn't be good for him, but they didn't explain why. They didn't clearly say that he'd be infected.

I started getting sick at age nineteen, after Reuben was born. I started feeling pain in my chest, and I was coughing all the time. I went everywhere—spent a lot of money, and no one could tell me what was wrong with me.

---

[2] Carrefour, on the northwest edge of Port-au-Prince, just south of Port-au-Prince Bay, is a dense residential suburb of more than 400,000 and was near the epicenter of the 2010 earthquake.

[3] ARV or ART refers to antiretroviral therapy for H.I.V. It can also be referred to as HAART—highly active antiretroviral therapy. This kind of effective, combination treatment for H.I.V. was introduced in 1996 and changed the course of H.I.V. disease dramatically, from a near-certain death sentence to a medically controllable chronic disease. Living with or dying from H.I.V. is largely a matter of social forces—poverty, inequality, access to medical care, et cetera. The therapy became fairly widely available in Haiti beginning in the early 2000s. When used appropriately during pregnancy, HAART can lower the risk of passing the virus from mother to child to less than 2 percent.

I don't know how I became sick. I just started being sick. All of a sudden. It started with the coughing—it was the hardest part—and spitting. It made me lose a lot of weight.

In February 2011, I was following treatments at a hospital in Carrefour, but they told me that I had to come to the General Hospital in the center of Port-au-Prince.

I didn't want to come to the General Hospital, because there are so many things here that people shouldn't see, and the staff doesn't treat the patients well. However, they told me that I had to come. I was told that I would find a beautiful *grimel* with long hair who would take care of me.[4]

When I came to the General Hospital, the doctors paid for me to do a chest X-ray. When they told me that I had tuberculosis, I thought I was going to die. I started taking drugs for it. I stayed for twenty-three days. After taking the medications, I started feeling better. Then I went home.

I discontinued the treatment after five months instead of six, because I thought I was already healed because of how good I looked on the outside. I went to the Dominican Republic after the first treatment that I didn't finish. I spent the whole month of January there. Then I became pregnant in the Dominican Republic with my second son and became sick again. I didn't have medication for either TB or H.I.V. in the Dominican Republic. I didn't take ARV when I was pregnant with my second son. I didn't have money to take them. I knew that the baby could be positive. I was just hoping everything would be fine.

I came back to Port-au-Prince fifteen days after my son was born,

---

[4] *Grimel* is a Haitian term for a lighter-skinned woman, usually inferring lighter skin with African features. There is an entire lexicon of physical and racial descriptions in Kreyol—most dating back to the colonial era, some lost over time, but others very commonly evoked. What is interesting here is that Alina is referring to an American doctor with red hair, far from the Haitian meaning of grimel, but seems a term of endearment for Dr. Megan Coffee.

in April 2012. I've heard from my second son's father that he was not infected. The test was negative.

When I came back here to the General Hospital, they saw that I had active TB again. Dr. Coffee didn't want me to leave before finishing the six-month treatment like the first time. She kept me here until I finished it. I thought I was going to die, since I heard that you usually die after a relapse. But God looked favorably upon me and the doctor took care of me and fed me. I've been here for six months, going on seven, for the treatment. I'm done with the TB treatment. I'm now taking only ARV medication.

GOD KNOWS

Since I came back from the Dominican Republic, I've been sleeping here at the hospital. My older son is with me. I told the doctor that I was going to go back home to the place I know in the Dominican Republic. It's called Isabel. I liked it there. I had my Haitian friend with me to help me out. Here, I suffer. But the doctor said no, because I won't find the ARV there. But, I think that's where I'm going to go anyway because I have nowhere else to go.

Do you have hope?
Well, with this disease, only God knows for how long I will stay on this earth.

I'm waiting on God. All I can do is take the drugs and wait on Jesus. Only God has the last word. Whatever He wants for me, I'll go by this. Life or death. The best thing would have been for me not to catch the virus, but I did. So, I have to deal with it. I'm not afraid.

What do you want for Reuben?
I still can't send him to school. I don't really have the means. He should have gone to school at three, but now he can't.

What will you find happening in your life in the next few months?
I don't know. Only God does. I really don't know. Only God knows what He has in store for me.

Do you lose faith?
No.

Why not? What hope do you have?
For what?

In 2014, we returned to Ti Kay to get an update on Alina. She had left the General Hospital and was out of contact for more than a year. There was a rumor that she had died. We spoke with Margot Albert—a volunteer from San Francisco helping at Ti Kay—at their new location near the airport. They no longer had an inpatient space for treating tuberculosis or H.I.V. Patients were now supported in the community, often assisted by other patients who had been cared for by Ti Kay.

DR. MARGOT ALBERT

In February or March 2014, I heard that Alina had passed away. There was a belief that a nurse had seen her die, but then someone else said that she was in Cange.[5] We sent Josil, one of our workers, to Cange, but he didn't find her there.

I don't know what made her decide that she wanted to walk away from treatment and the community here. She was living in a house with other patients, Josil, Marlene, and another woman. It was people who had become support systems for each other in the ward. I think the relationships changed once they didn't have that ward structure. When she walked away, her son was in an orphanage. She

---

[5] Cange is a Partners In Health hospital in the Central Plateau, hours from Port-au-Prince.

was working there for a while. It's in Delmas 33. He was living there as an orphan, but she could still see him. That was the last arrangement I knew about. I don't know if Alina was living at the orphanage or at the house with other patients. I'm just not sure what made her disappear.

BAZILE BERMANTE

28, high school student

We spoke with Bazile Bermante on a bench in a public park in downtown Port-au-Prince. She wore a bright pink shirt, and she also showed us her school uniform, which was inside the plastic bag she was holding. Despite her difficult story of abandonment and chronic homelessness, she hopes, finally, to complete high school soon.

I was born in Port-au-Prince. My parents are from Jérémie.[1] They never married. I have two brothers and one sister, but we are not close.

Since I was eight or nine, I've lived in public parks. I sleep in alleys. I sleep behind cars. My sisters and brother won't take me in. They don't consider me their sister. They say our mother died because of me.

My father met my mother in school in Port-au-Prince. While in school they started dating, but my grandmother didn't approve because they were still in school and too young. My father wanted her anyway. So he got her pregnant rather than lose her. My mother got kicked out of her parents' house. She got pregnant a second time. But my father didn't take his responsibilities seriously. He left her with two kids. I don't know why he did that to my mother.

---

[1] Jérémie is the capital of the Grand'Anse Department at the western tip of the Tiburon Peninsula.

A little bit later he got back with my mother and made me. But when I was born, he said that I wasn't his child and wouldn't recognize me. He accepted the other two as his children but didn't accept me in any way as his child. That brought division to our home. Back then, I always saw my mother sitting and thinking. When I asked her what was wrong, she always said that everything was fine. But she was thinking about the things my father did to her. My father didn't give us food. Once he even kicked her out of the house, and she had to go live with other people in another house. These things hurt me and are engraved in my memory forever. One day my mother said, "Your life is going to be wasted." We both cried. From all the things she told me I remember that one. I didn't understand then, but growing up I started to understand.

One day, when I was four or five years old, my father locked me inside the house and said that I wasn't his child and that he hated me. That really bothered my mother. After he locked me up, my mom called him into court and they told him that he was doing wrong. After being forced to court he hated my mother so much that he killed her. Yes, he killed her with magic.[2] He killed her because of me. After killing my mother he went after me, but he couldn't kill me. He sent people after me but they couldn't kill me. I don't understand why they couldn't do it.

The day of my mother's funeral, my brother and sisters and I went to live with different people in different areas in Port-au-Prince. We couldn't meet with each other. We started looking for each other when we became older but that brought division between us. My sisters and brother still blame me for the loss of our mother.

My father died three years after my mother died. After my mother died, he had a lot of women. One of them was very evil and wanted him so she cast a spell on him so she could have him for herself. And

---

[2] Bazile is referring to the use of spirits capable of harm that is part of the Vodou belief system. For more on Vodou, see the Glossary, page 309.

later, after she realized that she didn't want him anymore, she killed him the same way he killed my mother.

I didn't like my father for what he did to my mother. But the way he did it, he wasn't thinking. If he thought about it he wouldn't have done it. If he was here I'd forgive him. I hated the things he did, but I think that evil spirits made him do that. I would never seek vengeance.

After he died, other members of the family on my father's side sold everything: the houses, and all our goods. They said that we couldn't possess anything because we were different. They took everything and we couldn't do anything about it.

After I lost my mother, I was left with the neighbors. They treated me badly. I had to wake up around 3 a.m. to go get water, and I worked until 8 or 10 p.m. In the beginning, I stayed because I was going to school. When they stopped paying for my school, I moved to another neighbor's house. When I was about eight or nine, I found myself sleeping in the street, in public parks. I was still going to school but when my friends wanted to visit my house it became a problem. I always told them that I would visit them instead and afterwards I would go back to a public park to study and do my homework.

It was very hard for me to find food. At a certain time during the day I would ask for money to buy food, or I would ask a person selling food to give me some. Sometimes I would spend three days without eating and drinking and even a week without taking a shower. I would just brush my teeth and wash my face. Sometimes the dogs and cats would give me hard times, but I just pushed them away and went back to sleep.

When it was raining I used to get under a car, but all my stuff would get wet. I would sometimes go inside a car if the rain was bad and wait for it to stop. If someone saw me, I'd tell them that I'd leave after the rain stopped. I didn't really have anywhere else to go, so I'd just find another car. Every month I would switch areas because it's not good when too many people know you from one place. I was always scared of being taken for a thief.

God always took care of me. I always found good spots. No one ever came to rob me while I was sleeping. During the night when there was something wrong, I always felt it through my skin. I usually slept all night long, but when something was going to happen, God always lets me know and wakes me.

Not all the dogs you see in the streets at night are real dogs. A *djab* is a spirit that dances in somebody's head. It transforms the person into many things, like snakes, donkeys, or other animals. I saw it with my own two eyes—the spirit gets inside a person and he crawls like a snake and turns into a real snake. One time, I saw something on the roof of a house and it had a hat on its head. Somebody told me that it was a *lougawou*—a werewolf—and I wanted to see it with my two eyes, but they told me not to do it. Another time, I remember I was coming from night watch at church. I saw a tall man and a short man—I thought that it was a kid walking with his parent, but before I came closer they disappeared. I was walking alone in the streets. But I don't really believe in the djab. I don't believe in them, because if I did I would think while I was sleeping in the street they would try to eat me.

Behind the cemetery there were some young girls who went to prostitute themselves. But I always stayed faithful to myself. I've always met people who were offering things and I would take them. But some other people would offer me things and I would say no, because I knew they would ask for something in return. I didn't want to add to my suffering.

I never got into a relationship with anybody, but I had many people who talked to me. I had friends. They were different than me because their parents were alive. Sometimes they would give me some terrible advice. They would ask me to go steal people's stuff or do prostitution. Things that would make me feel bad. So I told them no, I would rather ask people for money instead of stealing.

I didn't want to ruin my life. They would try to convince me by saying, "You'll make money." But my heart never wanted to do it. I also knew that if they caught me stealing, people would beat me, or eventually kill me. I told them that I would rather suffer now because I know one day things will change.

AFTER THE EARTHQUAKE, I FINALLY FELT EQUAL TO EVERYONE ELSE

After the earthquake, I finally felt equal to everyone else. I was already sleeping in the streets. Everybody joined me. During that time it was easier for me to get food, because everybody was sharing. They didn't care if they didn't know you. In the public park where I was sleeping there were so many people. I lost all the things I had. I had one of the best spots before, but during that time nobody could say that they had their own spot.

During the night there were people doing bad things. The men were attacking the women. Sometimes when I turned one down another one would try. I was always switching sleeping places. But I never really slept very much. I thought that Jesus was coming, or we all were about to perish.

I GOT THE NICKNAME "LITTLE POLICE OFFICER"

I got the nickname *Ti Polis*—little police officer—from Pastor Malette. He found out the way I was living from other people I was hanging out with. I used to sleep in churches, but I didn't go to a specific church. Then I met a friend who told me that she would take me somewhere, and this place turned out to be Pastor Malette's church, Shalom. I met the people at the church and many of them started to know about how I live, about my poor condition. I got converted. I started going to Shalom often.

The reason the pastor called me *Ti Polis* was because he asked me to give orders: for example, if people were disturbing the church, I would tell them to move on. He saw that I did it well. When he asked me to do something, I did it and I respected everything he said. He said that I was a good commander and that I could direct. After that day my name was Ti Polis.

When he said that, I smiled. I felt it in my skin. Pastor Malette treated me well. But gossip caused me to not be around him anymore. What happened was, there was a trap set and I didn't know it. There was a restaurant at the church. The pastor had made me the manager. When people went to buy supplies, I registered every transaction in a notebook. But one day someone wanted to go buy something and there wasn't enough money. That person told me that the pastor said to bring him all the money at once. I didn't know that it was a trap. When I brought the financial report, this person called me a thief. She said that I took some of the money, but I told everyone that if it was me, God would judge me. But if it was them, God would also judge them. That day, it was my turn and the next day it would be theirs, and the truth can't be hidden forever. They insulted me. They shouldn't have disrespected me like that. After I quit, I went back to the street.

When I left, Pastor Malette wasn't even there. He only found out I left when he came back. He called me and talked to me. He told me that it was nothing and people sometimes call you a thief—when you do it, they say you did it, and when you don't, they still say you did. If someone calls you a thief, just ignore them, because you are not one. I told him that I understood, but I have feelings. He told me that I shouldn't have left while he was not there. I know I made that mistake and I should not have left during his absence. I apologized to him. We're not enemies. When I see him, I greet him. And I still go to that church. The person who accused me is still there. When I see her I always say hi, even if she answers with hypocrisy. When church is over, I just go back to the street.

THEY HELP IN THE WAY THEY CAN

It isn't easy for me to earn money, because I don't have any profession. Now I work in people's homes. It's a job that is often full of humiliation. Sometimes people curse you. They look down on you because you are working at their house. They want you to know that you are not from their class. Sometimes you cook for them and they don't even give you food. But what I like about working at people's houses is doing laundry. It's hard, but after you're done the person pays you and you leave. When you're doing laundry, people don't find the time to insult you.

Now I'm struggling to finish with school. I'm in the junior year of public high school. One year left. The teachers don't know about how I live, my struggles, my private life. Only the students who sit next to me know. Some of them give me money, others give me food. Sometimes they even bring me clothes. They help in the way they can but they can't do much because they are living with their parents. But I always have good grades. I will find a way to pay for university. I'm ready to fight. I want to learn administrative sciences and find a job.

The fun times I have are when my school is having activities. One time, my school organized a trip to the beach. I enjoyed swimming with the girls. I felt so alive, because the girls welcomed me in a very good way. They brought food, fruits, things that I never eat.

My dream is to have a family. Not only to have a family but to find the right person. But eventually he will ask to see my mother and father. That's where the problem always starts. I have no family to speak of. I wouldn't like my children to go through the same things I went through. And if I do have kids, who is going to look after them while I am working? I think about these things. I don't want my kids to live worse than I did. These are the things that keep me from having a family. I hope that one day all the sadness will be gone.

This used to be the White House. It went down in the earthquake. Gone now. That rich blanc, the movie star from the States, the one that has a lot of interest in Haiti—Sean Paul? Sean Penn? Sean Penn. You see? I don't know anything about this guy! But I hear he's the one who paid for the bulldozers. Someday they're going to start building a new foundation.

—*Jean Pierre Marseille, while standing in front of the recently bulldozed remains of the National Palace, the official residence of the Haitian presidents. (The palace was designed by Haitian-born architect Georges H. Baussan and completed in 1920.) Seven years after the earthquake, there's an empty patch of grass where the building once stood.*

EVANS DÉSIR

50, coal vendor

Evans Désira, father of seven, sells coals in Delmas 33.[1] When we met Evans, he wore a baseball cap and white shirt that somehow stayed clean despite the fact that he routinely lifted gallon buckets of the coal he sold.

When I was a young man, I was a superstar. I danced, I acted, and I was a good comedian. I even played in the National Theater. I'm still a very good actor. In the '80s, I used to train people for plays. Many schools used to call me to help them produce theater and dance performances. The people from the schools used to give me money to do it. I'd buy the costumes, train the dancers, and prepare the stage set. I know how to do a lot of things, but I have to sit in a corner now because in Haiti all the theaters are destroyed. I can't make a living anymore in the arts.

I met my wife at a party at her house. I was a gentleman, and I always danced with the hosts. I danced with her, and we became friends. The next day was a Sunday. I was going to star in a play, so I invited her to come see me. Now, we have been friends for a very long

---

[1] Delmas is a large residential and commercial suburb in the northeast of Port-au-Prince, adjacent to the city's airport. Individual neighborhoods in Delmas are referred to by number, since the suburb is organized around numbered streets that radiate out from a central road (for instance, Delmas 45, Delmas 18, et cetera).

time. We started having kids in 1982. We are not actually married yet, but we'll do it one day. The way we're living, we don't have the time to make a plan. We're poor. We're struggling with the kids.

When I first got together with my wife, she was working at a factory. When she made a piece they would pay her 25 gouds, sometimes even 80.[2] She is working at an orphanage now. She doesn't make a lot of money, but the little money she makes helps us. She only comes home on Fridays and she goes back on Saturday afternoon.

I sell charcoal in order to get by. My nails get dirty because of it, but I know that my children's lives will be better. I'd love them to learn a trade and find good jobs. Right now they can't find anything. I can't even pay for their classes anymore. Sometimes people don't buy the coal because they don't have money to cook food in their houses. Things are so hard here that people don't always cook every day.

I also have one son who has been sick for eight years. It's his feet. He finished high school and now he's taking a class at a church in the neighborhood to learn about refrigeration. He also attends classes about electricity and plumbing. He forces himself to go because he wants to, but his foot still hurts. Sometimes there is some yellow liquid that comes out of his foot. One day it is healed, another day it gets bad again. I've been spending so much money at the hospital. I pay for all these tests and they always say that everything is fine. The doctors told me I should buy him fruit, juice, milk, and vitamins, but I can't do it every day. And I don't always have the money to pay for his medications. When he eats well and takes all his medications, he gets better. But when he stops, he gets worse. Now both of his feet have open wounds. Last night while it was raining, he told me that he felt that his ankle was being opened up. He was sitting with me and making faces. My son's foot was hurting, but I ignored him because I knew that I didn't have the money to buy medications.

[2] Roughly US$.50 to US$2.

Sometimes his eyes turn yellow, but when he eats well, his eyes look normal. The reason why I don't cry is because God gives me a little bit of strength. Some people tell me that if my son goes to another country he'll get better treatments. If I could find help to travel with him, his foot would heal.

MY OWN MOTHER WENT
THROUGH A LOT TO RAISE ME

My own mother went through a lot to raise me. I remember that she didn't have anything, either. She used to call me to her and tell me that she was hungry and I could hear sounds from her belly. She lives in Miami now. She doesn't have much money, but she still sends me some. Those times she doesn't pay rent on time just to be able to send us some money. That's how we pay for our children's school. My wife and I often prefer not to eat. I always do my best for my children because I know that they'll help me in the future. Even if you don't have many things, you should invest the little you have in your children, so tomorrow they'll help you. I don't know how God will do this, but I'm still hoping to go to the U.S. I know that the Americans can heal my son. My mother is so old and not living well. She is staying at her sister's house, but they neglect her sometimes. Her grandchildren and I should be by her side to take care of her. She needs us.

Before all this, I had so many good times with my wife. We used to go to the theater and to concerts. Now when we do have a little bit of money, we save it so we can buy food for the kids. I want to go sell some coal so I can cook corn for the kids. We have beautiful children. Our children, even when they are hungry, they don't go asking other people for help.

Dancing is still in my blood. I've always told myself that I have to have my own dance team. If I find the opportunity, I'll be a dancer again.

MINA AND EVE

Mina—16, student
Eve—34, lawyer

We spoke with Mina (pseudonym) and her lawyer, Eve Emanuela, at the Bureau des Advocats Internationaux (B.A.I.), a public interest and human rights law firm in downtown Port-au-Prince. Mina hesitantly told us her story. Eve provided additional context concerning prosecuting sexual violence crimes in Haiti. Eve, or Met Ev, as she is known to her friends, lives in Port-au-Prince and was herself a victim of sexual assault in her childhood.

MINA

I'm sixteen now and in tenth grade. I'm living with my parents, and I have two brothers. I'm the oldest. I was born in Carrefour in 1998.[1] My dad sells goods for a living.

It was November 2, 2010. I was at home with my brother. I was cooking when a man entered the house. I didn't know he was coming in. I knew him from the neighborhood, but we weren't friends. I was twelve years old. He was eighteen and taller than me. He grabbed me from behind. He took me to the bedroom, and he left when he was

---

[1] Carrefour, on the northwest edge of Port-au-Prince, just south of Port-au-Prince Bay, is a dense residential suburb of more than 400,000 and was near the epicenter of the 2010 earthquake.

done. I don't know how long he was in my house. At first, I wasn't sure what he was going to do, but I sure did know that he had no right to do it.

I felt strange. I usually tell my mother everything. My mother went to the police and they arrested him. My father agreed with everything my mother did. I was scared. His family started threatening me. The next day, I went to the General Hospital. They transferred me to Christ-Roi. Christ-Roi put me in touch with KOFAVIV who in turn put me in touch with B.A.I.[2]

Once I found B.A.I., I wasn't as scared anymore. I liked that the lawyers cared. They really knew our constitution and were pleading for me. Ms. Eve became my lawyer. I really like Ms. Eve. I laugh every time I see her. I love her very much. She's always smiling. She has an open face. I'm kind of scared of mean people.

I was scared in my own neighborhood. The man's family members were threatening to kill me or beat me. It doesn't sit right with me or my family that the man's family was harassing us. I never used to hear the things that I heard people calling me. Dirty words. I don't want to repeat them. They also said that my family went to the judge because we needed money.

The man was sentenced to six years in jail. He had already spent two years in jail before the trial. I think he should stay in prison for fifteen years. That's what the constitution says it's supposed to be.

His family stopped bothering me after the trial, but they did say to our face that they'd kill me. I still live in the same neighborhood with his family, and I see them in the streets. When I see them, I try to avoid them, but I don't feel safe around them. I especially feel unsafe when I'm alone. Before, I felt safe in my neighborhood. Now

---

[2] Christ-Roi is a neighborhood on the east side of Port-au-Prince, as well as the informal name of a hospital in that neighborhood. KOFAVIV is an acronym for *Komisyon Fanm Viktim Pou Viktim*, or Commission of Women Victims for Victims.

I'm scared, especially since all his family members know me and I don't know them.

I come to KOFAVIV every Saturday, and I have a great support from my friends. We do arts and crafts, sewing lessons. I am learning how to make sandals. We joke around. We sometimes sing or read poetry. I'm happy here. I love them, and I love my family.

I want to become a lawyer. I want to help other young girls like me going through this. I like arts and crafts and spending time with my little brothers. I like to read novels, but I don't read anymore. I used to go to the library to get books, but now I can't. My mother is not comfortable with me leaving the house after what happened. I don't want her to worry, so I don't go anymore. In my neighborhood, I don't have any friends anymore. Most young girls in the neighborhood moved away or are with child. I am different. My friends are the people who come to KOFAVIV on Saturday, so we have something in common.

I feel like he took a piece of my future. I worry about what my husband will think of me. I will not be a virgin on my wedding day. I try not to think about it.

EVE EMANUELA

I just wanted to point out how fast the assailant was. He walked in, grabbed her from behind, pulled her skirt up, and raped her. He was out just as fast he was in. He was wearing a pair of shorts that made it easier for him.

The situation right now is pretty bad for her since she lives in the same neighborhood as the aggressor's family. Family members usually think that the rapist is going to go free until they face trial. When they realize that the aggressor is going to jail, they start threatening the victim.

In our culture, the family doesn't consider the assailant's act, they only think that you put their own in jail. That's the worst thing you could do to a family. You become their worst enemy. They harass the victim with the unrealistic hope that the victim will get scared and release the aggressor. That's not possible. It's not up to the victim. Once the person is detained, he has to go through the whole process and be found either guilty or innocent.

An aggressor's family doesn't usually start with harassment; they sometimes first offer money to the victim's family. It's before the hearing. If the family accepts the money early enough, it is possible that they may find some police officer willing to take a bribe and release the person. But if the victim's family is adamant on pursuing channels of justice, then the harassment begins.

The law says the sentence is minimum ten years for any victims over fifteen years old and fifteen years for victims under fifteen years old. The judges never respect that. In this case, she was twelve years old when he raped her. He should have automatically gotten fifteen years to start with. He was eighteen years old then. Every judge interprets the situation differently. Since the rapist was kind of young, and though the victim was only twelve, she was physically well developed. This created a bias for the judge. He was thinking that maybe they were in a relationship and didn't tell anyone. That's why he failed to objectively analyze the case.

Some judges are really strict. They follow the law, but other judges give the law their own interpretation. We tried to refute the sentence, but the judge wouldn't listen.

The judge needs to enlighten people. He needs to say to them what violence is. Instead of bringing their own bias to a case, our judges need to apply the law.

One example is, with me, I'm helping the people who are sexually violated. The judge says to me, "Oh, you're too into that. You're too angry. You need to calm down. One day, somebody will rape you. You have to take it easy." They make a joke. They just say, "You might be raped." They don't say, "I will rape you." They make jokes about it. This happens often in the judge's chambers before we move into court. It's just the lawyer, the victim, and the judge. And the court reporter is writing. So they joke around a lot. If it's a little girl, they're not going to joke that much. But if it's an older girl, they will joke around like it's a fairytale, like it's like a story. Like it's something that's not real.

In history class, we learned about Haiti—about this country that I live in. My ancestors were slaves in the French colony. They decided that based on the French Revolution in 1789 that "everybody is born free and equal in rights." And so they fought for it. So many personalities emerged like Toussaint Louverture, who died in France, and the other soldiers such as Dessalines, Pétion, and Boyer. On May 1803, Dessalines took the French flag down, ripped off the white part which gave us this blue and red flag that we have today and which is waving on Haiti's soil. If Dessalines could live again, he would be very disappointed, because he didn't fight for *this* Haiti. Now we have social inequalities between Haitians. Instead he was fighting for a free and united Haiti. Today people say that if you live up in the mountains you are the son of light-skinned Pétion and if you live down in Port-au-Prince you are the son of dark-skinned Dessalines. Today we are occupied by the United Nations. Dessalines would have been ashamed to see it. And I even think that if Dessalines had the chance to come back to life again, he would have died immediately after because he didn't fight for this.

—*Winter, 31, social worker in Cité Soleil*

ADRIENNE PHATAL

48, jewelry maker and merchant

We first met Adrienne at the offices of the Bureau des Advocats Internation-
aux in 2012. She was accompanied by her then fourteen-year-old daughter,
Loutchama. We spoke with Adrienne on five more occasions over the course of
the next four years. The mother of three and the grandmother of one, Adrienne
is a small but extraordinarily forceful woman. When we first met, Adrienne
had her own jewelry stand on Lalue (John Brown Avenue). However, due to
depression and continued fears for her own safety and that of her surviving
daughters and grandson, she has since stopped working and remains essen-
tially in hiding in a small, two-bedroomed apartment in Carrefour. Adrienne
only leaves to shop and attend church on Sundays. However, the apartment is
only temporary shelter, and soon the family will have to move again.

I need to get this off my chest—it's packed up inside me. In spite of
God, things have never been easy for us. Things are hard in this city.
It's especially hard when you're a woman living with three kids and
no husband. For many years, I've sold jewelry, custom-made jewelry.
I design it all myself. I make necklaces for men, and I make earrings
for women. And I make bracelets for men and women.

I'm from the countryside. My mother and father worked on the
land. They died one after another—one month after my mother died,
my father passed away. My kids—they hardly even know where I'm

from. I was six when I came to Port-au-Prince. Back in my time, education was really low, and people didn't have money to go to school, so they'd send their kids to Port-au-Prince hoping they'd get a better station in life. There's something in our blood that makes us think it's going to be better if we come to Port-au-Prince.

When I arrived here, it was not sweet. I was living with my mother's cousin. He put all his own kids in school, and treated me like a restavek.[1] He enslaved me. He said, "Go and grab water, go cook food, go prepare everybody for school." Think of it—you're staying with someone you don't even know. They don't put you in school. This person I lived with, most of his kids have become successful. Some are doctors, one's an engineer, another is a nurse.

Eventually, I just started working and living my own life. I worked in a factory that made gloves. I also took a side course and learned how to read and how to write my name. Then I met my husband. He was in the Haitian army. He was a sergeant, not the type that was going out among the people. He stayed in an office. We had three daughters together. One day, years ago now, his leg just started swelling. The doctor could never tell us what was wrong, but me personally, I think it was something mystical. You know, during the army times, the police, they did more wrong than they did right. So who knows? Maybe somebody wanted to hurt him. We went to all the doctors and no one could help my husband. We couldn't find anything that could cure him, and finally he passed away. When he died I was pregnant with our youngest daughter, Loutchama.

Since I lost my husband in 1997, it's been like going up a mountain backwards. Even worse, like walking toward heaven backward. In 2000, two of my daughters were in a car accident. They were walking home. My daughter Tania is still in pain in the leg that was broken in the accident.

---

[1] In Haiti, children who are used as unpaid domestic servants are known as *restaveks*. For more information, see the Glossary, page 309.

I PUT BOTH HANDS IN THE AIR

Before January 12, 2010, I was living with my three daughters and one grandchild in the same small house, a rented house. During the earthquake, I was on the street, doing my business. Tania and Loutchama were both home at the time. Tania escaped. She says during the aftershocks someone grabbed her and pushed her out of the house. There was no one there. It must have been the hands of God because we never knew from this day whose hands those were. But my youngest, Loutchama, was in a little hallway study, and the house fell on her.

At the time, I'm thinking, *This is Jesus's time.* Jesus Christ, I'm telling Him, "Save my life, give me a chance, and forgive me for my sins."

Everybody was having their own problems. There was a lot of dust in the air, a lot of running up and down. It was hard to help other people. If someone needed help, people would say, "Wow, I have my own problems, I can't help you." When I got home that day, I put both hands in the air and saw the house was totally destroyed. At the time I didn't see anyone. At this time there were still aftershocks. I didn't even try to go for my things because I thought I wasn't going to need them anymore. I couldn't find my kids. I had faith in God that they were still alive, but I was also in doubt because I didn't see them. By then it was dark. I spent the whole night going back and forth between the house and my jewelry stand. I was thinking that my kids would go looking for me at my stand.

The next day I found one of my cousins who told me that my auntie had come to my house and taken my daughters with her. That's when I found them, Tania and Loutchama. My family had pulled Loutchama out of the house when I wasn't there. She spent the night in the rubble listening to all the people walking over her feet and hands. She was yelling but nobody could hear her.

I think God blessed me by saving my child. When I saw

Loutchama at my auntie's house, her head was still bleeding and her back was broken. I carried her on my back and began looking for a doctor, but I couldn't find one. I was carrying her and I fell. I didn't have any strength. I was hungry, I was tired. But you know, it's like the old saying—you fall, you just get back up. Loutchama was crying and she was thirsty. I couldn't find her water. One guy gave me the shirt off his back, and I held it to the deep hole in Loutchama's head. Since I couldn't find a doctor, I did the old medicines that I learned from my family. I got some bitter orange and salt and mixed them together. I got a razor and I cut her hair with it. I cleaned her head with the orange and the salt because that will kill infections.

We had no house anymore, so we just sat in the car, an old car that was around the neighborhood. After three days, we got a chance to see a doctor. The doctor said, "Hey, ma'am, you did a good job! We don't even need to put a Band-Aid on it 'cause it's perfectly clean."

But we still didn't have any food. It's only when the blonds[2] came that we started getting some food. And even then I couldn't get much because it was a war to get food. People were fighting, hitting each other. I don't know about other areas, but in my area, you gave your name and they gave out cards. If you didn't have a card, you would not be able to get food. But then you would bring your card and they would say, "Well, your name didn't come up, I'm sorry." I heard other things. Like some guys would trade food for sex. This was inside the camps. I didn't want to live in camp.

We stayed in the car and in the yard outside because we were still afraid to go inside any houses. Finally, we were given a tent. We lived there for months.

At first, Loutchama was walking normally. But as the days went on, she started falling. After a while, her body started drooping. She couldn't hold herself up anymore. She was like a humpback. And that's when I decided to take her back to the doctor.

---

[2] Common term for white foreigners.

When we got there, the doctor said her spinal cord was broken. So in December, they operated on her back. They put an iron rod in her spinal cord. After the operation, she couldn't do anything. She couldn't do anything else but stand just like this, or lay just like this.

They put an iron in her back, where the spinal cord is, I guess to keep it straight. Six months later, she had an infection and they had to re-operate. They took a bone from the side of her waist and used that to do the operation on her back. She had four painful surgeries. But after that, for a while, everything was fine. Loutchama was even going back to school.

WHAT WOULDN'T I DO?

It was seven months after this second operation, on April 30, 2010, when a young guy, a young teenage guy, came to my house while I wasn't home. He was a neighbor. His house was separated from ours by a wall. When he came to the door he asked Loutchama, "Where's your mother?" and Loutchama says she's not here, and he asks, "Where's your sister?" She says, "My sister went to meet my mother at the place where she sells jewelry." Immediately this guy entered, and locked the door behind him. And he did what he shouldn't have done. He raped my daughter.

My other daughter came and knocked on the door, boom boom boom. She kept knocking on the door, but he forced Loutchama to stay quiet. He said, "Shut up," and pushed her. He made her jump the wall to his house, and he jumped the wall also. Then he gave Loutchama 5 gouds and said, "Don't tell anyone." He gave her real, real, real hard pressure. "If you tell anybody, you know what's going to happen to you."

He was twenty-three years old. My daughter was only thirteen. Loutchama ran back to our house, to her sister. She was crying, and she explained what happened. And Tania took her and brought her where I was sent to my stand, where I was selling my jewelry. She said, "Momma, you're gonna die when you hear this. Pick up your things, let's go home."

You see, when I get upset, when I get shocked, when I get so mad, my whole body itches, and a rash just pops up.

When we got home, they explained to me what had occurred. I asked my daughter, "Do you know this young man who did this?" "Yes, I do." "Can you show me where he's at and where he lives?" "Yes, I can," and then we went together.

When we went next door, we saw him. He put his hands on his head like this. My daughters said, "Mother, here he is." I went up to him and I greeted him with kindness. I said, "Good afternoon, sir." Then he said, "Good afternoon, Mother." I said, "Isn't that shocking what I heard from my daughter." He said, "*Mamu*, this was my first time."

I held onto his neck. God gave me strength. And he was trembling. I sent Tania to go get the cops. While we were waiting, a friend of his came around and saw me holding him and said, "Why are you holding my friend?" He said, "Georges, what's wrong? Why is this woman holding you?" The man who attacked my daughter said, "Go ahead about your business. You just see two people talking, don't worry about it. You go ahead about your business."

Then another friend came. He said, "Hey Georges, what's wrong? Why is this woman holding your neck?" "This woman's accusing me of raping her daughter," he said, and the guy came to fight with me. So when the police came, they found my hands on Georges's neck, and the other friend fighting with me. I fought him. He broke my arm—you see?

The police said, "What's happening?" I said, "This guy raped my daughter." But the police arrested the friend, not Georges. He went back in his house. I explained the mistake, and the police went to Georges's house and they arrested him.

Was I afraid? No, I wasn't. Not at all. What wouldn't I do to protect my daughter?

We all went to the police station, my daughters and myself. Loutchama identified the guy. At that time she was in real pain. We hadn't taken her to the doctor yet. When we finally did take her to the hospital, the doctor gave her some tests to see if she had AIDS or if she got any infections—and this is the bad part. The doctor said the guy even had it with her in the rectum.

I'M GOING TO TURN INTO A FLAME OF FIRE

After we got home, the next day, Monday, I received a summons from the rapist's family—they were calling me to court. The family was trying to pressure me to drop the charges. They were trying to get him released from jail and so they came after me. Ever since that day, I've been persecuted by this family.

That same Monday, I went to go see Mario[3] at the law office. My friend introduced me to him. I showed him the copies of the medical documents from the doctor showing that Loutchama had been raped.

Later that same afternoon, the police came and arrested me while I was working at my stand. The rapist's family made the police pick me up. The police also went to my home and pulled a gun on my daughter. She was so afraid she fell in the street. They arrested her, too.

They were trying to pressure me into dropping the charges. But I didn't waver. When they took me and Tania to the commissary yard at the jail, we met the rapist's uncle. This uncle has friends in the police. And he started to pressure me. "Well, madam, I'm just wanting to ask you, what you going to do about my kid, my family member who's in jail?"

Another police officer came and he was talking hard. "Hey, I heard about you, woman. I hear you like to put people in jail." I couldn't understand what was going on. I said, "My daughter

---

[3] Mario Joseph is a human rights attorney and director of the B.A.I. For more on B.A.I., see Mina's narrative, page 115.

was raped. I want justice for my kid." He was really mad. He said, "What's the matter with you?"

So you see, any problem you have with people who have power in Haiti, they can just come and get you and arrest you. Sometimes it's worse—they kidnap you. People might think you're in jail, but you're dead somewhere.

I said, "Don't start on me. I'm going to turn into a flame of fire in your hand. Don't joke. When I get out, I'm going to go out to the streets. Then I'm going to every radio station and every television station and tell what happened to my daughter." I'm not kidding. I'm in jail and my young child has no mother—what would you do?

They put me and Tania in a cell. I made a lot of noise. I demanded water. I shook the gate. The police said, "Lady, just calm down." They wouldn't give me water to take a shower. I was about to go to court—I didn't want to go smelling bad. I'm not kidding. I'm shaking the gate: "Give me water. I need to take a shower." I made a lot of noise. Another cop came in, "Ma'am, here's a bucket of water." I grabbed the water, put it over my head, then gave it to my daughter. We toweled ourselves off. Finally, they took us to see the judge.

The judge said, " What's wrong? What's going on?" I told him I wanted myself and my daughter Tania released, that we'd done nothing. I offered to pay. The court took the money—2,500 gouds— and let my daughter go. But he wouldn't release me.[4]

It's all part of the game. It's their way of making money. I mean, this guy raped my daughter and I'm in jail. But you find strength. You have it in you. And when it comes to a point, you'll find it in you.

Thank God I had a lawyer, Mr. Mario.

While I was still in jail, I was allowed to go to court to see the trial of my daughter's rapist. I was there to make sure he was convicted. We were lucky. It was a woman judge. The judge almost cried because she had a daughter the same age. That judge loved

---

[4] At the time of the incident, 2,500 gouds equals approximately US$60.

Loutchama. In the end, my daughter's rapist was convicted and sentenced to fifteen years.

We had three trials. But it wasn't about winning. The justice system worked for me this time. The evidence was overwhelming. I was supposed to get compensation as well, which I didn't get, but the compensation couldn't have saved us.

After some months, I was released, but Georges's family was still pressuring us. Two months after the conviction, one of them met my daughter and pointed a gun to her head just like the police. He said, "Come on—I'll crush your shit head." Those are the exact words—excuse me.

Now I try to keep my family home. I tell them not to take the streets. Let me, a grown person, find food for you all. We try to stay in one place so there's less danger.

Loutchama comes into the room. She's a beautiful kid with a shy smile. It's clear that mother and daughter have a deep love for each other, and also a true friendship, since they've spent so much time alone together in the past few years. She's wearing a back brace. Very slowly she sits down on the bed beside her mother. The two speak in Kreyol to each other for a few moments before Loutchama speaks.

LOUTCHAMA

Some people don't like me. They say I'm handicapped. They call me "handigirl." They call me handicapped. I just want to be back to normal so I can walk and be like any other child—like I was before. I don't want to be just the handigirl.

We'd love to talk to you more. Could we talk again sometime?
Will there be ice cream?

Later, as we depart, Loutchama asked if we might all become Facebook friends.

Following Georges's conviction, the rapist's family continued to harass Adrienne and her family. The threats increased and Adrienne and the family were forced to move to a small, one-room apartment in Delmas. During this period, Loutchama's condition deteriorated. The pain in her back was becoming more extreme. Doctors in Haiti and Boston were in communication and attempting to arrange a visa for Loutchama to be brought to Massachusetts for surgery that would improve her condition.

On August 26, 2013, Loutchama died in Port-au-Prince. While the circumstances of her death are not entirely clear, we believe she died of an acute infection that was not treated in time. On our next trip to Port-au-Prince six months later, we went directly to see Adrienne. This time she was living in a new apartment near her church in Carrefour. She told us that the church was one of the few places she was able to find solace. For a long time, we all sat together in silence. It wasn't the time for questions, but Adrienne did tell us a bit about Loutchama's last day, as well as the story of what happened to Tania in the month after Loutchama's death.

LOUTCHAMA HAD A FEVER

The day she died, Loutchama had a fever. I bathed her and washed her hair. We went to the hospital. The doctors said she was anemic, but couldn't see anything else wrong.

I went downtown to buy stuff for juice. When I came back, her eyes went to the back of her head. I decided to take her to church. She died on the way. There was an abscess in her back. It never healed. But Loutchama wasn't sick enough to die.

Then, twenty-two days later, Tania died.

The rapist's family had been calling me anonymously to threaten me. They made animal sounds in a way to let me know that they'd change my daughter into one. I guess God didn't give them the power to take Loutchama's zombie, so they turned to Tania.[5]

---

[5] Here, *zombie* is used to refer to a curse that causes death.

I was at an all-night prayer meeting when I had a vision that Tania was about to die. I went home and had another dream about it. I heard the *bann chanpwel*[6] come to dance in front of my house that night.

I hate Vodou and do not understand why our leaders think they should get involved with it. But I felt a great pain all over my body. I yelled for Tania. Then I grabbed my phone and started calling some church members and pastors to come over. They came to help me pray.

When they came, they asked me for Tania. I had left her in the bedroom studying. When I came to the room to get her, she was already dead. That was early on Saturday. People were telling me to call an ambulance and put her in the morgue, but I refused to. There was no need. It's no stranger who was doing this to me. It was the rapist's family. Because their son was in prison, they wanted to take the lives of my family.

We took Tania to the church and over the weekend and we prayed and prayed and prayed. On Monday, she came back to life. You should have seen me then. I was as thin as a thread. Two lost daughters. But God breathed on me and gave me back one of my lives.

Tania has been through a lot—car accident, prison, death. But God woke her up the same way He raised Lazarus from the dead.

I SPENT EVERYTHING I HAD TRYING TO HELP HER

I'm not going to lie to you. I hate my country now. Why? Because of this justice system. It only exists on paper. I never found justice for Loutchama.

---

[6] Bann chanpwel is a musical band of evildoers who are said to dance in front of a victim's house when they are about to collect his or her spirit. After or during the dance, the victim will die unless the dancers are met with a higher, greater force than theirs—usually in instances where the victim or victim's family are praying Christians.

I spent everything I had trying to help her. Her schooling, the surgeries, the medications. If the earthquake didn't happen, my daughter would have not been hurt, we would have not moved, and we would have not met that criminal who raped her and cause me this nightmare. I want to leave Haiti and finally have peace. Peace for me and my other children.

I thought Loutchama would be out of the country in time. The physician explained that she needed another surgery, but I refused because it didn't seem like the four previous ones helped much. To me, the physicians and B.A.I. don't really care about the poor. But I don't blame the physicians. They did their job. I blame B.A.I. The organization should have never hired Haitian lawyers. Anyone in Haiti will always defend its own interests, not that of the poor. They're after food for their own families.

It helps when I read the Bible. I believe in it. With the Bible in my hand, I trust that God will take care of everything. He sees how much I'm suffering. My soul is not well. I really don't want to stay here. I am not free and I can't go anywhere. I'm scared all the time. We are suffering. But God always keeps His promises. God promised me that I'll stay alive and become a witness. If it is God's will, I'll leave one day. Maybe you coming back here is a sign. You may have something to tell me or me you. Maybe people will hear my story and listen.

TANIA JEUDY

27, nursing student

Tania Jeudy is Adrienne's daughter and Loutchama's sister. During our many visits with her family, Tania was mostly silent. Tania is a shy person, but once you get her talking she opens up and appreciates a good joke. We were able to speak with her in 2015, after Loutchama died. Shortly after she lost her second sister, Tania experienced an apparent near-death and resurrection.

I had three sisters. Two of them died. Leica and Loutchama are dead. My other sister is Mirlande Jeudy. My father is Deriste Jeudy. He died when I was six years old. My mother is Adrienne Phatal. I also have a good relationship with my sister Mirlande. She's older. I hope to help my family have a better life than what we had in my childhood. I dream of a nice life with family and friends.

I'm in my third year of college. I am studying for a bachelor of science in nursing. I hope to become a great nurse. I have one year left to finish. It's a private school. We ask around to come up with the money to pay for school. For the third year, I paid 3,500 gouds total as entrance fees and 400 gouds per month.[1] The previous pastor at my church and church members used to help us. I haven't

---

[1] At the time of the interview, 3,500 gouds equals approximately US$90. 400 gouds equals approximately US$10.

been to school lately because I can't find money to even pay the entrance fee.

I HAD TO LAY HER ON ME

I think I had a good relationship with Loutchama. She was a good child. She did well in school. She had some issues with learning after the earthquake. We understood because she was a victim of it.

On the day of the earthquake, I was at home with Loutchama. It was just the two of us. I had some beans cooking, and I was lying in bed. She was sitting in the hallway studying. As I was checking the beans, I felt the house shaking. I immediately ran outside, and as I turned around, I saw the house falling. Loutchama was still inside, and the house fell on her.

I thought that only our house was affected. It wasn't until I looked around that I saw the houses around also fell to the ground. I thought Loutchama had died. There were people coming around to help. I called them. It took a long time to pull her out. At that time, we didn't see that she had any broken bones. We didn't know that her spine was broken.

Around 2 a.m., my mother found us, and she took us to Lalue. She bathed Loutchama with bitter oranges and salt. The next day we went to a hospital. They shaved Loutchama's head to have better access to her wounds. Her head had holes in it. They treated her and sent her home. For Loutchama to sleep, I had to lay her on me, because she couldn't sleep on the floor. We were all praying for her. She cried, but sometimes she was in so much pain, she couldn't cry.

When we saw that she wasn't getting better, my mother went with her to a mobile hospital in Champs-de-Mars.[2] There, they referred us to the hospital at Diquini. When we arrived at that

---

[2] Champs-de-Mars is a park near the former site of the National Palace.

hospital, they said that she needed surgery in her back. We didn't really have any one person helping us financially. God spoke in the heart of many people, and at that time, my mother also had the jewelry business.

After the surgery, Loutchama seemed fine and started going to school. It wasn't until after the incident that she became worse.

HE NEVER ARGUED THAT HE DIDN'T DO IT

It was April 30, 2011, one year after the earthquake. That day, after I came back from school, I left Loutchama at home and I went to bring some food to my mom at the market. When I came back, the door was locked and Loutchama told me what happened.

The man locked the front door, and he forced her to go to the back and go over a wall and raped her. I think that was why her back broke again.

I took her and went to the market to get my mother. We came back home and went to find him. We found him standing in an alley. He told us not to talk too loud. He didn't want the passersby to hear anything we were saying. My mother told me to go get the police patrol car that was parked at the next street while she was made sure he didn't run. When I came back with the police, we found out that he and his friend had fought my mother and he fled. The police were able to arrest the friend. Then they drove us to the General Hospital. It was there at the hospital that the doctors told us that he raped Loutchama in her vagina and anus.

In order to free their son, his friend's family found him and brought him to the police. He never argued that he didn't do it. His mother was the one saying that he didn't.

All of that happened on a Saturday. The next day, we had to go to the hospital again. They did another rape test for her. She cried so much! She couldn't even walk after that. We had to call a friend to give us a ride.

We went to Pompier to give a deposition. Then we went to Parquet.[3] There too, they heard the evidence. After Parquet, they sent him to National Penitentiary. He switched his version of the story from what he had said to Pompier. They clearly saw that he was guilty. After that, we received papers saying that they were going to try the case in front of the criminal court. He was found guilty and sent back to the penitentiary.

We had to hide Loutchama at Carrefour.[4] Even before the case was tried at criminal court, we were receiving many threats. At one point, they said that they would kill Loutchama and me. They were looking for us. The man's mother said in front of us that she would kill Loutchama. We reported it to Cabinet d'Instruction.[5] One time, one of the man's family members accosted me on the street and told me that he would shoot me three times. I think that he didn't do it because we were on an open road. Even now, I don't feel safe. I only go to downtown if I have to.

The man's family served us a warrant two days after the incident. A few days after that, a police car drove up to my house and asked if I was Tania. When I told them yes, they pulled their guns out and arrested me. When I got in the car, I saw that my mother was also inside. When we reached Pompier, they took our cell phones and locked us in a cell. They didn't ask us any questions. When we were inside, I saw the man's cousin.

Loutchama was at the house by herself. A neighbor took her to her godfather's house.

We spent the night inside the cell. The cousin came back the next morning and asked to speak with my mother. He told my

---

[3] Neighborhoods near central Port-au-Prince, here the names refer to police stations in those neighborhoods.

[4] Carrefour, on the northwest edge of Port-au-Prince, just south of Port-au-Prince Bay, is a dense residential suburb of more than 400,000 and was near the epicenter of the 2010 earthquake.

[5] The Cabinet d'Instruction is roughly equavalient to a U.S. district attorney.

mother to drop the charges against his cousin, Georges. That's when we realized that they put us behind bars as a threat. My mother told the cousin that she didn't put Georges where he was, his actions did. After a while, they took my mother to see the judge. My mother said that she would not leave me behind. At court, they asked my mother to pay 2,500 gouds for bail.[6] She didn't want me to stay in prison, so she decided to pay. They held my mother and asked me to go get the money.

At the bank, I explained to a teller what happened. She understood and let me go first in the line. After we paid, they let me out and held my mother.

The next day, I went back to Pompier to bring toiletries for my mother. I brought some water for her to wash. I put some disinfectant in it since I knew how dirty the place was. They didn't even let me talk to my mother and rushed me out. That was a Wednesday. On Thursday, I went to see the same judge to ask why my mother was in jail. He told me that he gave authorization the day before to free my mother. He signed another form and sent me with one of the bailiffs. When we arrived at Pompier, they said they already transferred the case to Parquet prison, that there was nothing they could do. All of that was the doing of Georges's cousin. When we arrived to Parquet, we talked to the chief of police, and he was very touched by what happened. He ordered them to free my mother. That day, my mother went home. She'd spent four days in jail.

SHE WAS BETTER

Loutchama's back was getting worse. We went back to the hosptial. The doctor asked how it had happened and we told him. He said that the iron in her back came out of the bone and was now coming out of her skin. She needed surgery again.

---

[6] At the time of the interview, 2,500 gouds equals approximately US$60.

But after the surgery, the wound still wouldn't heal. At some point, it became infected. The bone was infected too. The doctor had to take a rib to replace the infected bone in the back. Through all of that, we couldn't take care of her as we should have because we were hiding from Georges's family.

In Haiti, one can pay very little to have someone killed. We were being harassed by Georges's family. They would call us on blocked numbers. They would drive by our house and have men on motorcycles take our picture. One of them called me and asked to meet with me. They tried to trick us into coming out of the house.

After Loutchama's surgeries, we went to live at Carrefour. Mario told us that there might have been a chance that she would travel to the U.S.A. to receive better care.[7] We were waiting on things to work out. In the meantime, I would wash the wound for her since I am in nursing school.

She was better before she died that week. She went to sleep that Sunday night, and on Monday she couldn't move. Since we hid from the family, they couldn't get to us, they used Vodou. When we told Cabinet d'Instruction that Georges's mother threatened to kill Loutchama using Vodou, they made it seem like they didn't know what we were talking about.

Loutchama wasn't feeling well. She couldn't sleep. She couldn't eat. She was just crying. We took her to *Médecins Sans Frontières*.[8] They prescribed some medicines and told us to go to General Hospital. Since we knew that we wouldn't receive care if we didn't have people we knew at the hospital, we went to Sainte-Croix at Léogâne. After they saw her, they said that it didn't seem like anything was wrong with her. We were happy to hear that, because we thought she would get better if nothing was wrong. We went home. It was a

---

[7] Mario Joseph is a human rights attorney and director of the B.A.I. For more on B.A.I., see Mina's narrative, page 115.

[8] Doctors Without Borders, an international medical NGO.

Thursday. We made some plantains for her. She didn't even have time to eat or take the medicine. She died.

We didn't have any money for the funeral. Other doctors helped us. People from church helped with the funeral, too. We called Mario. If we knew that was going to happen, we would have never tried the case. We lost more than we gained. Loutchama died, we spent a lot of money, we lost our home and our business.

Since Loutchama died, all is done.

I HEARD SOMEONE CALLING ME

Twenty-two days later, I became sick. I was in school, in the restroom, and I heard someone calling me. I went outside, but I didn't see anyone. I told my friend, and she joked that it was a zombie calling me.[9] I thought about it, and it troubled me. On Saturday, I went to a prayer at church. After prayer, I went home. I slept because I wasn't feeling well. My mom asked some members from church to come and pray.

So, after, I lay down. After I lay down, I lost consciousness.

Everything I am going to explain, I thought I was doing. It wasn't until I came back to myself that I was told I had never moved.

I see myself take my sandals and walk out. I walked until I reached Kafou Aewopo.[10] There, I saw a group of people. I felt like I was the only one seeing them because everyone else was minding their own business. There was a lady with long hair. She was really tall and everyone else around her was short. They were all looking at me intensely. That was when I realized that I was dead. The lady marched forward to meet me, and she slapped me. I lost consciousness. When I woke up, I was in a house. They beat me with ropes. We

---

[9] Here, Tania is referring to *zombie* as a reincarnated being that is calling her to curse her.

[10] Kafou Aewopo is a busy intersection near the airport on the northside of Port-au-Prince.

went to several places around the country. I saw myself at Jérémie.[11] I saw someone that I knew was dead. I don't remember everything.

People told my mother to call the morgue, but she refused. She said that it was only twenty-two days since Loutchama died. She wasn't going to lose another daughter. I came back after three days. After I regained consciousness, my mouth was sore from all the beatings. I had cuts inside my mouth. It took me a while to be better again.

When I came back to my body after those three days, I explained everything that happened. However, now it is very difficult for me. It feels like I'm reliving the experience every time I talk about it. Also, I know that not everyone will understand or believe.

I went back to school. One day, as I was in class, I felt a cramp starting in my head. I told my friend that my head was hurting. That's all I remember. They told me afterward that I ripped my clothes off. They didn't send me to the hospital because they figured that it wasn't a natural sickness. My family and church members spent the whole night praying. I returned to myself the next day.

That incident marked all of us. We know that Loutchama is dead. We are not living. We are scared. For instance, the other day as I was going to school, I saw Georges's mother. I had to stop and hide. I went my way after I didn't see her anymore. My mother isn't working. My sister Mirlande and I aren't working. My sister has a son, but he can't go to school. The pastor who was helping us, he lost his job. We can't work, and we have to eat and pay the rent.

I don't think it is a good living situation right now. I'm always scared. I always hoped that things were going to be better. Since we have God, we can't say that we don't have hope, but we do feel hopeless sometimes. I'm twenty-seven years old. I always dreamed to study oversees, but I don't have the means for that. It could happen.

Tout tan w'ap viv, gen espwa—my faith lives as I live.

---

[11] Jérémie is the capital of the Grand'Anse Department at the western tip of the Tiburon Peninsula.

GEORGE VALENTIN VALERIS

37, Vodou flag artist

We spoke to George Valentin Valeris in 2011 in his studio. He showed us the sequined flag he makes that depict Vodou spirits, or loas, and other Vodou themes. When we asked about one flag that showed a two-faced loa, he explained that one face is the loa called Baron Samedi, the other Erzulie. "They share the same head," he said. "They serve the same purpose. Baron Samedi represents death. And Erzulie is the spirit of love. So together, they represent love and death."

I was born in Port-au-Prince in Pétionville.[1] What they say is true: in Pétionville, you see a lot of the bourgeois. But you'll see people from the middle class and the lower class as well. I was born November 11, 1979. My dad is an artist. I can say that I know everywhere in this city. It's the city where I grew up.

It's not the same as it was before. Because of urbanization, everyone is coming to the city. The result is that there are too many people. In every corner you see people. They're coming from the countryside, from all over they're coming. And now everywhere you go, you see

---

[1] Pétionville is a wealthy, historic suburb of Port-au-Prince built into the hillside south of the city center.

people selling. They're selling on the streets and you see the streets are getting dirtier and dirtier. The city was not this dirty before. When I was growing up, certain parts of Port-au-Prince, there was nobody there. No construction. Now you can see it's only houses in Delmas.[2] You don't even see a tree.

In 1989, I became an artist. I started making Vodou flags. I really loved it. I was going to school, but I was very interested in art. At the age of twenty-five, I started my own shop. So like, this week, I had seven people working with me. And this is how they support their families, with the work they do for me. I work for a bunch of Vodou people. I make flags for them. When they need something they call me. But I don't have any relationship with Vodou because I don't serve any of the loa.[3] Sometimes I can say that the loa may use me to design something, but I don't serve them. I'm still a Seventh-day Adventist.

It's true that Vodou didn't start here in Haiti. Vodou came into Haiti when the slaves were brought here from Africa. The Africans were using Vodou a lot, but now Haitians use it more. When the slaves came, each of them came with a little statue of their loa. Each of them came with something. Some of them had the little Virgin Mary statue. They were always calling on their loa, and they were always praying. With the same spirit, they fought for independence. When they were planning the revolt for their independence, they had a big ceremony—it's called the *cérémonie du Bois Caïman*.[4] Most of the time there are people who misunderstand Vodou because we took our independence with Vodou.

Since slaves came from Africa, Vodou spread through the country.

---

[2] Delmas is a large residential and commercial suburb in the northeast of Port-au-Prince, adjacent to the city's airport.

[3] Loas in Haitian Vodou are intermediaries between people and a distant God. For more information, see the Glossary, page 309.

[4] The ceremony during which the first major slave revolt was planned. For more information, see Appendix I, page 293.

More people started doing Vodou. They started using the loa to treat people, to make remedies. They use Vodou to make treatment for natural diseases as well as unnatural diseases, something somebody might have done to you. For example, somebody might put a zombie on you.[5] Since Vodou gave you the disease, you have to use the same Vodou to cure it.

The *houngan*, the Vodou priest, can use limbs from trees or things that the loa give him, to treat people. What the loa tells him to do depends on the disease you have. The loa might tell the houngan to take the leaves from a tree, or to use oil to massage you—it depends on what you have.

A lot of people think that Vodou is the Devil, but that's not true. It's mystical, and it has a lot of good things. I'm not saying that Adventists should practice Vodou, but there's some good in it for them. And for Haitians, Vodou is part of their roots. Unfortunately, there are people who don't understand that Vodou is not here to do bad things, Vodou is not here to mistreat people. The person with the wisest loa is here to help people out. Somebody can use it to do bad things, but Vodou is not there to do bad things. It's the same way in other religions. They can use their religion to do bad things. You can use anything to do bad things.

Most of the Protestant religions, they have a relationship with Vodou because in order to have members come into the church, they have to do some Vodou. The pastor doesn't use a flag or music, but he does go to a houngan.

Not every religion has a rara band.[6] Every religion has a way to manifest, to show happiness, to show their feeling. Vodou has rara. But if you go inside a Baptist church, you can see they have a different kind of music but they still have music, and the people are

---

[5] Here, a *zombie* refers to a curse that causes death.

[6] Rara can refer to festival music or dance in general, though it's most closely associated with parades in the week before Easter.

dancing. They don't have the same rhythm as with rara, but they have their own way of manifesting. They each have different rhythm.

The head of the rara, he's in the front of the dance line. They wanted to make sure that when he's coming everybody could see him, so they started putting the sequins on his vest. Since the head of the line was wearing the vest, everybody saw it was beautiful. Then they started putting sequins on his hat. Everybody saw how beautiful it was, the audience liked it, so they say, *Okay, then we'll do the flag in sequins as well.* Since so many people like it.

I love what I'm doing, I love being an artist, I can see when I draw something or after I make something, I'm asking myself *What did I do?* It's not straightforward, like, *Okay, I'm going to draw something from the loas.* I'm Seventh-day Adventist, but I do Vodou art more than I do anything else. The Vodou is trying to take over.

How long does it take you to make these, with how many people?
About five days. Two people. Five days with two people. Eight hours a day, five days.

Ah, I see. So there are faces within faces?
Yeah, each big head is two heads. So these two loa, they share the same head. But they serve the same purpose. You can see that in that head, one of these two heads, one of them is smoking.

Baron Samedi. He represents death. Baron Samedi liked to smoke? And Erzulie is here.
Erzulie is the spirit of love. So together, they represent love and death.

You drew this whole thing in the middle of the night?
Yes, yes. I was sleeping, and in the middle of the night I woke up and designed it.

I HAD TO GET BACK ON MY
FEET AND DO THE WORK

After the earthquake, there was lot of stress, but I had a lot of demand, people were asking me for my work. So I had to get back on my feet and do the work. I lost everything, but after a few months, I started the shop back again. I made a big effort to pull together my soul and my strength, everything I had, to concentrate because I was working. I started forgetting about the stress. All I did was do this work until I forgot, about everything, the past, and then, you know, it was just my work.

The hardest thing is that normally you're doing great work. Not everybody gives importance to the work that you do. Sometimes Haitians forget where they're from. They say they will have nothing to do with Vodou. Few Haitians understand the importance of the work. Some Haitians who serve loa, they buy from me. And some houngan buy. Mostly the foreigners appreciate the work.

It's not easy work—not only to design everything—to sell it. The thing is, it takes a lot of time, a lot of days to work on a flag: to draw, to design, to put on the sequins and do everything, to teach other people to do it. It takes a lot of time, and you don't sell it right away. With the political problems that we have here in Haiti, the tourists don't really come. You have to ship the work to the United States in order for it to be sold.

The easiest part for a Haitian artist is to create.

FRAN

41, reporter

Fran is from Bainet in the southeast of Haiti. On the day of the earthquake, Fran was on an upper floor of a government building. We spoke to him in front of a church where a commemoration of the 2010 earthquake was taking place. When the quake hit, Fran was knocked unconscious as a government building collapsed around him. He then walked for miles to report from the quake's epicenter. As a choir sang inside a church, Fran talked to us about the day of the quake and its aftermath.

I'm a reporter, and my interest is in how people can climb out of the cycle of poverty. I came from the modest class. My parents were farmers. I have seven sisters and one brother. Because of my background, I'm on the side of those who don't have anything.

I've been with Radio Galaxie since 1996.[1] I started at the radio first, and then over time I shifted to TV. I do live news—live on the scene. Sometimes after gathering information, I'll also go into the studio and broadcast. Later tonight, I'm going to be doing a piece on the commemoration of the anniversary of the earthquake. The big question is, where is the awareness of the housing problem?

---

[1] In Haiti, radio remains the news media format that reaches the widest audience, and there are nearly 400 stations nationwide. Radio Galaxie is one of Port-au-Prince's most popular news radio stations.

On the day of the earthquake, I was at a government building to pay taxes for the radio station. I heard the noise, and I thought that it must be a thunderstorm. I was on the fourth floor. I suddenly felt that I was flying. I can't explain what happened because the next thing I knew, I was in a different part of the building. I don't now how I jumped or flew, or whatever happened. I was jumping up, and then I quickly lost consciousness.

When I woke up, I heard a lot of yelling and screaming. It was me. I was the one screaming, screaming, screaming, screaming. Yes I was. And then people around me were crying and there was all this smoke. Black smoke, black dust, everywhere. As a journalist I felt that I had to report what happened at this damaged building, but that was impossible. There wasn't any communication. My cell phone wasn't working.

My first reflex was to go and find my own children. I left that damaged building and walked to the school to see my children. I have two kids. One girl, one boy. My son is eight and a half. My daughter is seven. When I got there, my kids were scared, but once they saw me they were fine. My house in Port-au-Prince is in the south part of town. In this area there wasn't any damage because the structural support is very strong. I brought my children home to my wife. I told them that I would be back. They know that as a journalist, I have a passion, a need, to be where the events are happening.

I set out for Léogâne,[2] the epicenter of the earthquake. I didn't come home for three days. I didn't realize that distance was so far. I'd always driven there. In a big event like that, you just walk and you don't feel tired or anything. The only thing I remember is that I had to carry water. I took my water with me, that's all I remember. I was not the only one walking. There were people all over the streets and everybody was walking for miles.

---

[2] Léogâne is a coastal city 18 miles west of Port-au-Prince.

I knew Léogâne well. I'm a director of a network of journalists that meets periodically in that city. And even before the quake I knew that the houses in Léogâne were slowly sinking into the ground. I once interviewed a geologist, who is well known in Haiti, about this problem and what might happen in a possible earthquake.

When I got there, 70 percent of Léogâne was gone. It wasn't like in Port-au-Prince, where you could see still some houses standing. I couldn't call on a cell phone or radio or anything so I just got paper and wrote down what I saw. People were trying to pull friends and relatives from under the rubble. I heard people shouting: "Come and help, come and save me, come and save me." But because there was nothing to be done to save most of those people, I began crying. They weren't dead yet. They were under all that rubble. And they were asking us to come and save them, but we didn't have any tools or materials to pull them out.

You know, in the immediate aftermath, some people didn't call it an earthquake. They said that an enemy was attacking us. Some said this is the end of the world. There was a Haitian senator who said that there was a bomb, a big bomb that the U.S. was testing, and they dropped it on Haiti. People eventually received information about the earthquake through the telephone companies after the cell networks were repaired. They sent text messages to people saying that an earthquake happened. I didn't receive messages about where people could get water or where people could get food, but some people said that they received messages like that.

It took Radio Galaxie three months to be able to report news again. After three weeks, we started broadcasting, not giving live radio news, but we were able to put songs on the air.

At this time in the aftermath of the quake, I would give news flashes, or brief reports to foreign journalists, for instance to a reporter I know from Miami. But I wasn't able to do any local reporting. The little money that I made came from the outside.

Do you think that Bill Clinton has any real desire to help

Haiti?[3] He's dealing with a group of people who don't have any incentive to change. The reconstruction funds are doled out on the basis of nepotism and nepotism only. Clinton never asks, "Where is the reconstruction?" All those places that Bill Clinton said he's going to build. None of them happened. You've seen the city. Look at some of the bourgeoisie. They're the only ones who've had their houses fixed.

Those who have money get the help, not the poor. In many tent cities, people were given the deadline to leave, but they don't have the money to move. Clinton never asks why. But I can't say that on the air. I would be in trouble. I might lose my job. I'm not the owner of the radio station, I'm just a worker. There are certain things you can denounce, but there's a limit in the denouncing.

What else can I say? I can show the reaction of the people. I can say they give some people 1,400 Haitian dollars, and then they kick them off a property. Where are they going to go now? That is something I can report. But I can't say that it's been three years that they said they were going to build, and they still don't build. I can't ask, "Where has all the money gone?" I can't say that. I can say that Clinton and his committee didn't do the reconstruction they promised, but I cannot say that the bourgeoisie have somehow gotten all the money. If the bourgeoisie hear something like that, they will call the director of the radio station.

What we're starting to do now is to talk about these problems every day. If there is a fire in the tents or if someone dies for specific reasons, I can take advantage of that moment and say something that I wouldn't say in normal times. But after that, everybody closes their eyes. That's the system under which we journalists operate. We try, but we know our limits. Sometimes the radio owner will say, "I don't want to lose my advertising revenue."

---

[3] The Clinton Foundation has raised more than $30 million since 2010 for post-earthquake relief in Haiti.

BENITA MANDA

56, mother

We spoke with Benita in Koray, on the dusty outskirts of Port-au-Prince in a well-organized resettlement camp for those who lost their homes in the earthquake. She lives with her husband, six of her eight children, and one grandchild. Two of the children are severely disabled. Her home is one large room with a concrete floor and a tiny, tidy porch. There is space outside in the back for cooking and washing clothes. The walls are bare except for some Bible verses carefully written here and there.

In 2002, in my sleep, I saw an angel writing in the sky in big letters by the market in Pétionville.[1] Since I didn't have my glasses I couldn't read. When the people came and saw what was written, they started to scream, "Help! My God, we cannot bear this. All these comments on Haiti, no we can't bear this." In the dream the people did not say what was written. They were only screaming, "We can't bear this."

In my second dream, I was on the peak of a high mountain. I heard a voice saying, "I will destroy all the places where there are villains."

In my third dream, I saw that I was on top of that same mountain. I looked down to earth and saw nothing, nothing at all,

---

[1] Pétionville is a wealthy, historic suburb of Port-au-Prince built into the hillside south of the city center.

not even a tree. The only thing I saw was a sailing boat with a white sail.

In December 2009, before the earthquake, in another dream, across a yard I saw two houses. As I was passing through the yard to go in the street, I felt a big earthquake and the houses opened up and water was coming out of them. I saw all the caves in the cemetery open up and water was flowing. They opened up and closed. Then I woke up.

Also in December 2009, I had a dream that every single person on earth was running, all the authorities, everyone. I told everyone in my house that something was going to happen. They said, "You're always dreaming. You went to bed with your stomach full, that's all."

SIX YEARS, TWICE A WEEK

It's nine of us living in this little house. I have eight children, but only six of them live with me. Two of them are living in Delmas; I rent a house for them there so they can go to school.[2] My husband is a construction worker. He works in Delmas 37, making iron frames, building houses, preparing roofs for cement, tiling. But finding work isn't easy. He doesn't sit around. Every morning he goes up to Delmas in case someone asks him to do a little job for them. Me, I never go to Delmas because I haven't been able to go anywhere for four years—I have no one to leave the kids with.

My first child is thirty-three. I had him when I was twenty-three years old. He has a daughter who's here with me. I have Darling, she's here. She's in eleventh grade, and she was supposed to take the state exam. This year I should have two kids taking the eleventh-grade state exam. But I don't have money to send both of them. Only one is going.

---

[2] Delmas is a large residential and commercial suburb in the northeast of Port-au-Prince, adjacent to the city's airport.

Two of my children have disabilities. Nadine Manda turned twenty-two years old on January 7. Nadine was born normal. When she was three months old, she could sit. Once after giving her a bath, she started to play, she started to move her little hands. I had her sit, but then she fell over her face. Since that fall on her face she can no longer sit on her own. She became *mòl*,[3] I went to the General Hospital with her. The doctors watched her development until she was six months old. After six months, she still couldn't sit on her own, so they sent us to Saint Vincent.[4] The doctors at Saint Vincent say she had a *kriz menenjit*,[5] but I didn't see her having that. I only saw her fall on her face, no seizure.

I spent six years going to Saint Vincent twice a week, carrying her. I have two other daughters; one is twenty, the other is eighteen. While I was pregnant with them, I was going to the hospital with Nadine, carrying her down Rue des Casernes to Saint Vincent hospital. After six years without any solution, in 1999, I stopped going to Saint Vincent. I keep her at home with me.

The boy is Eli Manda. He is sixteen. He has a twin—Elizé Manda. Elizé is in eighth grade at a school in Delmas. Eli was born August 3, 1997. He was born normal. He was born on Saturday and got sick Sunday night. After he was healed and was released from the hospital, he put on some weight and became very beautiful. I breastfed him and everything was *byen pwòp*.[6] But it took him two years and six months until he learned how to walk. All my other children started walking around one years old. At age two years, eight months, he

---

[3] *Mòl* literally means soft, but here means something similar to a complete paralysis of the body.

[4] Saint Vincent's is an Episcopal Church school, clinic, and orphanage for children with physical disabilities, including support for the deaf and blind in downtown Port-au-Prince.

[5] Seizure due to meningitis.

[6] Literally "well proper," a phrase that describes when things that are expected to be well, are well/normal.

fell when he was playing with all the other kids, running, playing lago.[7]

He used to walk byen pwòp, by himself. Before the earthquake, he used to stand up and walk on his own. Now, I have to tie him up on the chair so that when he has seizures, he doesn't fall—that kind of makes him unable to walk on his own now. When he gets his seizures, he sometimes falls on the floor. If you hold his hand, he walks, but he can't stand and walk on his own. If he wants to stand up, I have to help him. Sometimes he tries.

He doesn't talk. He used to talk byen pwòp. He used to say "Mom," "Dad," and his twin's name, Elizé. He used to call, "Elizé." Even right after the fall he still used to call, "Mom." When the seizures started, that's when he stopped talking.

I went to a center where they put people with mental illness. They gave me carbamazepine for Eli.[8] Tomorrow will be eight days since they gave it to me for him, and he hasn't had any seizures. When he doesn't take that medication, he may have up to ten seizures in a day. He used to have seizures every day with no break. That's why I tied him down on the chair. If he has a seizure, he can fall. He stretches and stretches and stretches and moves and moves. His body becomes stiff, very stiff.

I CAME TO THE CITY

I was going to go to Italy. The hospital La Paix in Delmas 33 was arranging it. After the earthquake, they would take both of my kids, me, and all my other kids to Italy. The first group of people that went, they may have angered the *blan*,[9] because the blan stopped everything and didn't do it anymore. So I didn't go.

---

[7] Much like playing catch.

[8] Carbamazepine is used primarily in the treatment of epilepsy and neuropathic pain.

[9] *Blan*—literally "white person"—is best translated to mean foreigner.

OXFAM was also giving some money to the handicapped.[10] It doesn't matter how many handicapped children you have, they give everyone the same amount. They don't give us that money anymore, but it was very helpful. What they gave me helped me a lot.

There is a medical center close to here, but we can't find help there. Nadine has seizures. Today, she had six seizures already. The medicine that I have to buy for the seizures is expensive. I only find it in the countryside. I don't have money to go there. I need to buy it every month. When I give it to her, the seizures stop. She used to walk alone, but after starting to have the seizures, she lost the ability to walk alone. I have this prescription that they gave me at the center, but it doesn't work for her. I don't see any change. It's not strong enough.

Sometimes, looking at the kids and my situation, I feel that the burden is too much for me. This morning as I was giving Nadine a bath, and she had the seizure and broke the only bowl I have to bathe her with. It's like I am in a prison. Sometimes I say God take me. I don't want to offend God with these thoughts.

When I was seven years old, my father died. My mother was *malere*[11] I had an aunt who was mambo.[12] She doesn't have any kids. She took me from my mom. You'd think she would put me in school? She didn't send me to school. I worked and worked and worked very hard gathering plants for her to use in her remedies and treatments. When I realized she wasn't helping me, I left there to go to the city of Les Cayes.[13] I was sixteen years old and became a domestic servant

---

[10] OXFAM is a coalition of global charities that coordinate giving to alleviate poverty. OXFAM's support in Haiti following the 2010 earthquake has included providing access to food, water, and shelter as well as providing employment opportunities and other economic relief.

[11] *Malere* is a word for poor, in need.

[12] A *mambo* is a female Vodou priestess.

[13] Les Cayes is a city of 70,000 on the southwest edge of the Tiburon Peninsula. It is one of Haiti's major seaports.

for 30 gouds per month. That was a lot of money back then. I bought myself clothes, everything I needed with it. I started going to school in the afternoon.

In 1979, I came to the city so that I could find better work. I was eighteen years old. I found work here for 75 gouds per month.[14] In the same year, I met my husband. He courted me, we dated, and we stayed together. I had my eight kids with him.

Before the earthquake, I lived in Delmas 65. I rented. After the earthquake, my house was cracked. We couldn't stay in it. They put yellow tape surrounding it and asked us to leave. In the hills of Delmas 42, we made a little tent. I wanted a little place to stay with the kids. I can't go out, I can't go to work. I was looking for a little help then while I was up there, I.O.M. found this piece of land for us in Koray.[15]

I have been in Koray since April 24, 2010. There are six blocks in Koray; I'm in the third block. We're the very first people who moved here after the earthquake. There was nobody living around here. Many people said that they would not live here because it was only weeds and dust. The United Nations, many nations, and MINUSTAH joined together and brought us here.[16] They used to give us food, but not anymore. OXFAM used to give us water for free. Even though we were hungry, with this little piece of land, I felt good. Even though we were buying a bucket of water for 5 gouds, at least we have access to water.

---

[14] At the time, 75 gouds equals approximately US$15.

[15] International Organization for Migration is an intergovernmental organization made up of more than 160 member states.

[16] The United Nations Stabilization Mission in Haiti (MINUSTAH) was initially authorized following the 2004 coup d'état as peacekeeping forces brought in to stabilize the political situation and protect human rights and the rule of law after Aristide's ouster. They were given greater mandate following the 2010 earthquake to support reconstruction and stability efforts. For more on MINUSTAH, see the Glossary, page 309.

After a while, they built a well for us to get water through DINEPA.[17] We buy the bucket of water for 2 gouds. Before we had the well, we were buying a bucket of water for 5 gouds.

This house is mine. The World Vision organization gave it to me.[18] They said it's temporary, but I don't believe that they will take it back from me. They told us it's ours for three years. It's been about three years already. I hear I.O.M. is building permanent housing. You'll pay, but it will always be yours. After you are done paying it off, you can pass it along to your children, grandchildren.

THESE ARE MY PEOPLE.
DO YOU SEE MY PEOPLE?

I believe that with my faith, my kids can become "normal" again.

People say my handicapped children's problems arise from something mystic. They say my kids are like that because of *Dyab Rasyal*.[19] I don't believe in these things. I would never serve Dyab Rasyal. I accept Jesus. When my kids get sick I bring them to the doctor, then I pray.

I never asked why God puts me in this situation. God does no wrong. When I pray I tell God to have mercy on me because I don't do anything wrong. I've never lifted a finger to anything or anyone. I never abuse children. When I was young, I'd see someone who is handicapped and feel so bad for them that I would cry for them. Look at me now—I have two handicapped children.

I know God loves me because I have these dreams and I see them come true.

---

[17] DINEPA (Direction Nationale de l'Eau Potable et de l'Assainissement or National Directorate for Water Supply and Sanitation) is the Haitian governmental agency responsible for providing access to safe drinking water.

[18] World Vision International is an Evangelical aid organization.

[19] Dyab Rasyal is a manifestation of the devil in Haitian Vodou. For more on Vodou, see the Glossary, page 309.

After the earthquake, in my sleep, I was walking between a wall and a house, and there was a cliff in front of me. I heard a voice say, "These are my people. Do you see my people? They don't want to be aware of what is going on. After everything they've seen, everything I have done, they'd rather live in their imaginations. I will throw them down the cliff."

It's only prayer that's holding Haiti together, a lot of prayer. The poorer people pray the most. After everything Haitians have seen— all these diseases like cholera—they don't want to be conscious.[20] My children and I were not infected with cholera. Chikungunya fever came, my kids had it, but I didn't get it. If I had it, who would take care of Nadine? Who would bathe her? You see, God loves me. He protects me from everything that's happening.

This is how the story is. Sometimes I feel too wicked, I can't talk to God. I'm asking you to remember me in your prayers, lift me up before God and ask Him to continue to take care of me.

---

[20] For more on Haiti and cholera, see Appendix III, page 317.

MARITZA

22

We also spoke with Benita's niece, Maritza, while visiting Benita's house in Koray. Maritza stays at Benita's house when she needs to visit a psychiatric clinic nearby. Maritza lives in Les Cayes with her mother, father, and brother. She most likely has schizophrenia and told us that her illness started when she was twenty-one. Before she started treatment at the clinic, she was taken by her family to a houngan, *a Vodou priest.*

My family should have brought me to the doctor a long time ago. They never did. I believe in doctors, very much so. Doctors can find something to alleviate it for me. The medicines help me.

At the clinic, they give me pills, medicines, they give me shots. The shots make me dizzy. I can't sleep at all. I have a sleeping problem. I'm waking up around 3 a.m. I need to wake up at 4 a.m., even when it's hard to wake up.

The medicine, it's not good, it's not too bad. I'm a little calmer now. Sometimes I'm worse when I take it. Sometimes when I take it, I become very difficult. Yesterday, I made a big spectacle here at Benita's house. I made a lot of noise.

When people want to talk to me, I can sit and talk like normal. They say I'm crazy, but I know I'm not crazy. In the name of Jesus, I know I am not crazy. Sometimes, I don't know what I am doing.

Sometimes, I tell you, Dyab Rasyal comes.[1] When you are in public, in society, that's when it wants to come to put you to shame. Do you understand?

---

[1] Dyab Rasyal is a manifestation of the devil in Haitian Vodou. For more on Vodou, see the Glossary, page 309.

LOUIS ELIAS EZAUS

58, pastor and mason

When we spoke with Louis Elias Ezaus, he sat in a chair with plastic netting stretched across the metal frame amidst fruit and flower trees in front of his simple home of cinder blocks. Yet he's not a man accustomed to sitting. Sunday is the only day he's home. Every other day he walks dozens of kilometers to spread the gospel to the isolated mountain communities. After being educated in Port-au-Prince, he settled in Furcy, a beautiful village an hour or so up a mountain road from Port-au-Prince.

I remember my parents were talking one night and I overheard their conversation. My father said to my mother, "You're going to be mad with me because I'm unable to come up with enough for Louis's schooling. We're going to have to figure out a second plan. Try to figure out somewhere else he can get an education." It was 1961. One day a pastor, a friend of my father's, he came down to my neighborhood to buy some things that he needed. As the pastor was leaving, my father said, "I think you should take my son with you." My father bagged my stuff up to send me to Port-au-Prince with the pastor.

We went by boat. There was a big wind all of a sudden and the sail came loose, and the boat started rocking back and forth. They had told me not to stand, but I forgot—I wanted to see what was going on, so I stood up. And when I stood up, the sail spun around and struck me. I fell into the middle of the boat, on top of a water pump. I was badly hurt, but I was lucky because it would have been worse if I'd fallen into the sea.

The boat I was on made a U-turn to go back to a place called Miragoâne.[1] They paid a car for a couple hours to bring me to Port-au-Prince. I was in such bad shape that the driver didn't want to take me because he didn't want carry a dead body in his car. By the grace of God, I made it to the city alive. When I realized where I was, I was at General Hospital in Port-au-Prince. I couldn't see. It was like I was totally blind. And there were scars on my face. Everybody thought I was going to be permanently blind, but by the grace of God, I soon could see again. After thirteen days in the hospital, I was back on the street.

After years of working as a mason back up in the mountains, Louis Elias was called to the church and began work as a volunteer pastor.

I always do the best I can in God, I always put something in my pocket, even if it's not a lot, so when these desperate people come up to me while I'm walking, I can give them at least 25 gouds to get a drink of coffee. I might bring a pack of cookies to give out to the kids. Sometimes the people that come to this mission give me personal things for my family and I often give these things to someone else that might need them more. That's how I do it.

Whenever you're working for God, or you have a belief in God, you have to be fair and work toward fairness. You can't act like everyone else. You have to be a shining star in front of everyone, and you have to overlook some things. You're not doing man's work, you're

---

[1] Miragoâne is a coastal city of more than 50,000 and the capital of the Nippes Department. It is located 60 miles west of Port-au-Prince.

doing the work of the lord, and the lord uses all his niceness to do whatever he has to do. People feel I work too much, but when you want to do something, you have to put in the effort. I'm not doing this out of ambition. I'm not doing this job for myself.

JOCELYN

62, basket maker and farmer

While in Furcy, we also met Jocelyn. From the edge of a ridge, we could see Port-au-Prince and the ocean shimmer in the distance. Jocelyn was sitting in the shade of a church awning on a quiet Saturday.

My brother taught me how to make baskets. He's been dead fourteen years. I use bamboo. It's such a long process for me to make a basket. I cut the bamboo with the machete and dry it. This is how I make my basket—I put my foot on the piece of bamboo, and I begin to braid it. I start it on the ground, and then I hold it between my knees and continue to braid until I finish.

I have eleven brothers and sisters, and I have seven children, and eleven grandchildren. Some people, like my uncle, they help their family when they have so many children—an uncle can help with one or two. Six of my children don't want to leave me. And I have to work hard to survive with them because they want to stay here. They don't want to go to any other family.

The older one is twenty-eight, the second one is twenty-five, the third one is twenty-two, and the fourth one is nineteen. The fifth one is eighteen, the sixth one is seventeen, and the last one is fifteen. These children here now are not working because of Hurricane Sandy. We lost everything. They were at school before the hurricane. And in summertime, when there is no school, they work with me in my garden. Now we are in dry season, and it's difficult for the people who are living here to water a garden.

There's a little spring right down here, but only when we are in raining season.

We drink the water, but it's not safe. Sometimes we put some bleach in, like Clorox, and there is another pill I used to put in named Aquatabs, but we have no more.[1]

The roof of our house flew away in the hurricane. Now we just sleep in there at night. It's not comfortable for us to remain, but I don't have enough money to repair the house, and we're obliged to stay. We're ten in a house of four rooms without a roof.

I work every day, every night. With these baskets, with my basket on my head I go everywhere. I make baskets from bamboo, and I'm always looking for someone who has bamboo to buy. I sell my baskets in Port-au-Prince. Sometimes I sell my baskets to vendors, because they use them as containers. I also sell to the tourists, when there are tourists. Sometimes the Americans buy my baskets.

---

[1] Aquatabs is a brand name for water purification tablets that help prevent cholera and other water-borne diseases.

CHARLOT JEUDY

30, founder of Kouraj

Charlot Jeudy is an L.G.B.T. rights activist in Port-au-Prince. He lives in the neighborhood of Martissant where he was born. Martissant is a dense neighborhood close to the city center. Charlot created Kouraj, a safe space for gay, lesbian, and transgender individuals in Haiti to congregate and celebrate. Before our meeting, the Kouraj office had recently been relocated after threats of violence at their previous location. We were met by a Kouraj activist on the main Delmas road and taken by motorcycle through a maze of narrow streets to the unassuming office. Before the conversation began, we were scanned with a metal detector wand.

My mother is a fervent Catholic, so I was raised as such. I was born January 1, 1984 in Martissant. My siblings and I were raised there, and I still live there. What saved us was education. My mother made sure we all went to school. That's all I have, and that's what helped me realize that it wasn't fair for people to be attacked because of their sexual or gender orientation.

I was sixteen when I realized I was gay. I noticed that I was interested in other teenage boys like me. I started hating myself for it because everything I knew or believed condemned it. I prayed about it, but nothing happened. So I started faking being heterosexual.

When I turned eighteen, I confessed to my mother that I liked men. She responded that the most important thing for me was to finish school. Nothing else mattered. Until now, my parents have never questioned me about it. Maybe that's where I learned to be so strong and positive about this.

At twenty-two, I was in a relationship with a girl. I told her that we should stop because I was gay. From then on, I've been openly gay. Like me, my parents are true Haitian citizens. If they can accept it, maybe others will too. It was hard, but I was lucky to have a father who was a sergeant in the army. He was an authority figure in the neighborhood, and we were one of the first families to move in there. They respected him and couldn't attack me because of my dad, which wasn't the case for some other homosexuals in the neighborhood. But I did suffer. I suffered for my friends. So I started to think about how to change this.

One day in 2009, a friend was having a birthday party. He was also gay. Everyone at the party had such a good time! It was good to be with like people in a safe environment, so my friends and I started thinking about organizing L.G.B.T. nights. I was already involved in many other local civic engagement committees in my neighborhood, so I had the skills necessary to start an organization that would advocate for an issue that affects me personally. In 2009, there were a couple of organizations in Port-au-Prince that were looking at homosexuality from a medical standpoint, since the L.G.B.T. community is said to be more vulnerable to S.T.D.'s and H.I.V./AIDS. But we wanted something new, a safe environment for our community, and so we started with L.G.B.T. nights.

We named our organization "Friend to Friend," and it mostly existed to plan social events for the community. The first event we held was at a private home in Tabarre, which is a quieter, safer neighborhood than Martissant.[1] We also had an event called "Homo-naval" during Carnival time. Carnival is one of the most dangerous places for us to be, so we decided to have our own carnival.

---

[1] Tabarre is a neighborhood within Delmas in the northeast of Port-au-Prince.

We started talking about ourselves as the "M community" because all the L.G.B.T. words start with M: *Masisi* (gay), *Madivin* (lesbian), *Makomè* (trans), and *Mix* (bisexual). They are offensive terms, but we've turned them around and decided to own those terms instead. It makes us stronger. The term "homosexual" is usually only used by intellectuals. So we came up with the M community as a united entity and so people can understand exactly what we're fighting for in our debates. That's how Kouraj started.

IT'S NOT MY CAUSE, IT'S SOCIETY'S CAUSE

After the earthquake, the Haitian society started seeing us in a bad light. Haitians were hearing homophobic speeches everywhere. There were some preachers, mostly from the United States, who were teaching the people that the earthquake was the result of our sins, especially homosexuality.[2] We thought it was nonsense. But people were so scared of us that they started persecuting us. We couldn't even be under the tents. Some of us had to convert to Christianity to stay safe. The goal changed from social to policy. We decided the best way to do it is to start a dialogue. We started being more vocal—we use the media a lot. We have our own Web site too. We encouraged people to speak out about hate crimes. We became a voice for our community. It is unacceptable that people are attacked because of their sexual/gender orientation. Haiti shouldn't accept such things. This is a democracy.

We started going to towns outside the city and dialoguing with L.G.B.T. people. We organized them into groups and encouraged

---

[2] On January 13, 2010, the day after the earthquake, Pat Robertson blamed the tragedy on something that "happened a long time ago in Haiti, and people might not want to talk about it." The Haitians "were under the heel of the French. You know, Napoleon III and whatever. And they got together and swore a pact to the devil. They said, 'We will serve you if you will get us free from the French.' True story. And so, the devil said, 'Okay, it's a deal.' You know, the Haitians revolted and got themselves free. But ever since, they have been cursed by one thing after the other."

them to speak out. It's not my cause, it is society's cause. If we want to progress as a society, we have to start by changing our way of thinking. These erroneous beliefs don't do us any good.

You have to understand that in Haiti, religion holds a big place in our society. Even non-Christians have some religious beliefs. That is the reason why homosexuals are seen with suspicion. They're misunderstood. That sometimes leads to psychological abuse from their community. Even in politics, they use the term to denigrate their opponents. All the abuse forces some people to never assume their identity. They stay in the closet. They can't even have their family's support.

For example, let's say a young man admits to his parents that he is gay; they will throw him out of the house. He's not going to get any type of support from anyone. He won't find a job. It's really bad. And since religion, or should we say, the Catholic Church, controls in part our schools, our children's sexual education is not done. Thus, the population is ignorant of many things when it comes to sexuality.

Let's talk about the social and cultural aspect. Here, we have Vodou. Sometimes, Christians try to show that homosexuals are possessed by loas and bad spirits.[3] A lot of people believe that. Even certain homosexuals themselves. They use it as an excuse for who they are.

I have to tell you that I don't practice Vodou, but I participate in their ceremonies if they invite me. I don't really attach myself to one religion, but I've always liked the loa ceremonies. I first started practicing folklore dance and attending loa ceremonies around the time I came out to my mother. It was a way for me to show everyone who I really was. I liked the loa ceremonies. It was the only environment where as a man I could dance like I wanted to with no judgments. I could express myself how I wanted to. Haitian society sets the

---

[3] Loas in Haitian Vodou are intermediaries between people and a distant God. For more information, see the Glossary, page 309.

norms, but the Vodou religion is different—Vodou is the most toler-ant religion in Haiti to homosexuals. Vodou suggests the possibility of possession by loas, becoming inhabited by another spirit. There are certain loas that when they possess you, you behave like them. For instance, when Ogou, who is a male loa, possesses a woman, that woman behaves like a man.[4] When Erzuli Dantor, a woman, pos-sesses a man, that man acts like a woman.[5] These cultural beliefs create some sense of security for homosexuals, and I would see many other homosexuals participating in Vodou ceremonies from the time I started attending them.

But the evangelists have had a great impact. The churches have a coalition. They talk about it in their sermons. They use Sodom and Gomorrah as their example to show that homosexuality is bad and that God condemns it. They make us look like beasts. Those evan-gelists met with other Haitian evangelists to persecute homosexuals. For the first time in Haitian history, an organized religious group took the streets of Port-au-Prince to protest against homosexuality, on July 19, 2013. Forty-seven homosexuals were attacked that day. That wasn't the only protest there was. That same group protested all around the country. They even had the support of a state official who said that the south is the most immoral part of Haiti because of homosexuals. Can you believe it?

We work a lot on H.I.V./AIDS awareness. We talk to the youth about prevention. We distribute condoms and lubricants. We do things like that. We also sensitize the people about human rights in

---

[4] In Haitian Vodou, Ogou is a warrior spirit associated with a number of personae, with most manifestations closely bound to notions of masculinity. Ogou is frequently channeled in Haitian possession performances. For more on possession performances in Vodou, see the Glossary, page 309.

[5] In Haitian Vodou, Erzuli Dantor is a scarred maternal spirit that protects women and children and punishes those who harm the innocent. She is the patron of independent women and is strongly associated with the origins of the Haitian inde-pendence movement.

general and pressure the government to provide justice where justice is due when there is a case.

We've created a network. We help each other. We report the hate crime cases. We try to connect to many organizations that can help us in this fight. We need to eliminate that stigma, and I feel like it will also help against the stigma against H.I.V./AIDS. Some people have a double life because they can't come out to their wife. Since they will not use condoms, if they become or were infected from a male partner, they bring that into their marriage.

In our constitution, it's clearly stated that the government has the obligation to protect everyone, with no exceptions. Our government also ratifies many international laws as well. Are they upheld? Now, it is going to take a lot of work for that. Even the media that is supposed to be independent refused to play our commercials, even though we offered to pay. The best way to educate the population is through radio, and we don't have access to it.

There are no specific laws that discriminate against homosexuals; we have "social laws" against it. The last law about adoption that was passed was very discriminatory, though. It stated that homosexuals couldn't adopt. The pretext was that the child will somehow have a one-sided upbringing. That's bogus. We have so many single-parent families.

Madivin is the Kreyol word for lesbian. There are not organizations like Kouraj for them, but we also provide the same space for them. Even the women's rights organizations here do not really accept those women among them. They don't feel too comfortable working with us. The discrimination is not really different for them. It's about the same, and those women are sometimes sexually exploited because of who they are.

I think that if society becomes more sensitive about our case, if more gay people join the fight, things can be done. Kouraj is just a link in the chain. We need more people. They have to understand that other entities are trying to shut us up from many avenues.

They're trying to control the justice system and our press. Poverty is also making things harder. Even the discrimination problem is different based on your social status. I have a friend from the higher class who told me that his father is okay with him being gay as long as it's quieted. He told him that he will fly him to the U.S.A., Canada, or Dominican Republic whenever he has certain needs, but he should never get involved with anyone here. It's just a way to protect his reputation. I wasn't that lucky. As we say at home, *kote mare bourik se kote li sevi bezwen li*—where you keep the donkey, that's where it takes care of all its needs.

It's clear that society is made of different types of peoples and that they don't always think alike. It is our responsibility as individuals to overcome those barriers. If the community is engaged, things will get better. However, if the community stays passive, nothing will work out. We have to work to change things. The same way we're fighting against child slavery, we must fight for homosexuality. We do all we can to continue this fight. If we're talking about human rights, we have to talk about all of them. Someone cannot pick which one they like and leave the others.

All *pèpè* is good pèpè. Pèpè is hand-me-down clothes Americans don't want anymore. Another word for it is Kennedy, after John Kennedy. He was the president when the first export of old clothes was delivered to Haiti. They said it was a gift of the Kennedy family. Now you can find it all on the streets. You just got to find the look that is good for you. Because the shirt you might not like, somebody else is gonna love it. Who cares if somebody might have worn it first? Nobody's going to come up to you and say, "Yo, that's a pèpè shirt you got on there." That's not going to happen. Why? Because they're wearing the pèpè too. Even the bourgeois, they wear pèpè. Big-time shops in Pétionville, you'll see them selling pèpè. They even take a pèpè, clean it up, and put it in their big-time shops. I used to sell boots to the American soldiers here back in 1994. Some of these guys, they said they'd never wear secondhand shoes. After I showed them some pèpè boots, I had them buying boots—American boots!—from me every day.

—Jean Pierre Marseille

JOHNNY

30, L.G.B.T. rights activist at Kouraj

Johnny is a gay rights activist from Jacmel in southern Haiti. This often takes the form of keeping safe houses for gay men and women who are physically threatened or ostracized in their home communities. Openly gay, Johnny was assaulted on the street. Gay rights advocacy in Haiti includes living openly. Johnny has taken this much further and is speaking out, becoming publicly visible, and trying to educate people about gay rights.[1]

I was born gay. I was born at Tabarre, then my mother moved to Jacmel when I was six months old.[2] I moved back to Port-au-Prince when I was twenty to study. After some university studies in Port-au-Prince I went to the Dominican Republic for a modeling contest and won a scholarship to continue my study in Puerto Rico. I stayed there for four years and seven months. I returned to Jacmel in 2010.

I do the same things that Charlot does at Kouraj and we work together. Right now, I have a lot of people staying at my house. I can't provide for all of them, but I'm trying. Since I am a bit more educated than others, I try to take responsibility for them. People

---

[1] A note on language: *Masisi* is the word for gay man. This might best be translated as "faggot." The M community is working to reclaim this language, much like queer communities in other places and in other languages.

[2] Tabarre is a neighborhood within Delmas in the northeast of Port-au-Prince.

threw them away when they came out of the closet. Some people may think I am doing this for money. I am not; I'm a professional. I have a job. I am an economist. Any embassy or bank would be glad to hire me. Other people in the M community don't have that luck. I'm now very well known. Charlot is already well accepted, even in the international community. Any country would be glad to invite him over. I'm not at that point yet. They need to know that no matter what they do, I am and will be a *masisi*. Yes masisi is an insult, but to me it's not. I don't take it as such. To me it's a compliment. I thank anyone who calls me "masisi." They won't repeat it because it doesn't affect me. And they're telling the truth. That's who I am.

Growing up we were Baptists. Oh, it was really hard. It was hard everywhere—school, church, home. I couldn't sit with the kids in school or at church. On the buses, people used to make fun of me. I couldn't sit with the kids or be on the stage because I was effeminate. They used to kill us in Jacmel, but not anymore. They accept me now. Even people who were rude to me, I tried to talk to them and explain who I was. In Jacmel, they think that gays are outsiders. God destroyed Sodom and Gomorrah because of them. They also think gays are usually rich. What they don't get, before being gay, I'm human, and I tell them that. Every time someone would make a comment about it, I would tell them that they got on my nerves. That's how I feel comfortable in my skin. I have to make feminine gestures, otherwise I'm not okay. I always tell my fellow gays, they need to treat everyone with respect. They need to understand that not everyone accepts them. When they finally understand that, life will be easier for them.

You know, home is where the heart is. When I returned to Jacmel in 2010, there was some uproar and they were attacking gays. One day I was walking with a friend. Some people were standing there and started making derogatory comments about my friend. They attacked me and asked me to deny that I was gay. When I refused, they hit me in the head with a bottle. Charlot and my lawyers came to help me, but we didn't have enough proof to convict the attackers. However, the story gave some of us strength. When I was studying in Puerto Rico, it was very different. Men were kissing on the streets. I was surprised. I couldn't believe it. I was thinking about all the ways the L.G.B.T. community back home could enjoy that same freedom.

When I decided to fight for my rights, I became stronger. I wasn't afraid anymore. I decided that it was time to organize ourselves and teach the community about who we are. It's been four years since then. I was twenty-six years old. I was really afraid to walk the streets before. Before the incident I was not that outgoing, but now I am. They can attack me anytime at my house. I don't really care. I told them that if they're throwing rocks at me, I can do the same—I have both my hands too! They can kill me if they want. One time they were surprised to see me fight back. When the police came, people were asking me how did I fight, where did I find that masculinity in me. Can you believe it?

I don't need asylum. My family live here and in the U.S. My mother and brother live in Queens in New York. I've never been in the U.S. I want to visit my mother, but I also want to stay in my country to fight. My mother was trying to sponsor me for a visa, I said no. I am not done yet. If I abandon those people, they'll have nowhere to go. I want to stay in my country. I want to work for the M community.

My mother accepts me for who I am. She sees me like her son, not like someone who's gay. My father and brothers are against it, until now. I want to succeed my life and show them that I made it. At the beginning, it wasn't easy for my mother, but when she realized that's how I was born, she told me that she loved me like I was. But the rest of my family, no. My mother suffered for me a lot. It has been two long years since I saw her last. I told her that I have to see her before another two years. I have to touch her, then I will be fine for another two years.

Walk? Too far to walk! We're going to take a tap tap or a minibus if we can find a space on one. *Parque lai gon* is our destination— our destiny? Anyway, it's where we need to go to get to the graveyard. We'll take Rue Nazon, which is also called Martin Luther King. They're the same road. Nazon, I think that's the original name. Or maybe the board gave it the name Nazon, and the original name is Martin Luther King? Anyway, that's the best way to get to the cemetery...

—*Jean Pierre Marseille*

JEAN CARRASCO

55, cemetery worker

Jean Carrasco maintains graves and tombs at the Grand Cemetery in Port-au-Prince. The cemetery holds many of Haiti's most famous and infamous dead, including François "Papa Doc" Duvalier. Originally from Jacmel, Jean moved to Port-au-Price as a young man. He has five children, including his son who was visiting him the day of our conversation. The general Jean refers to guarding was an army chief of staff during Papa Doc's dictatorship.

SON

My name is Carrasco. That's my last name. Carrasco. It's like a Spanish name. I'm here visiting my father. He's worked at the cemetery for thirty-five years. He started before I was born. He builds tombs. He rebuilds the ones that collapse. And he cleans them, too. And the owners pay him to guard their tombs so he's here most of the day. Sometimes when I'm on vacation, I like to come down here just to see what my father is doing. It's peaceful here, so peaceful.

FATHER

What do I call myself? I call myself a gardener. I'm also a mason, as well as a guard. I watch over the tombs. I've seen a lot of things here.

Yes, a lot of things. See that tomb over there? Twins are buried there, both brothers. See that one next to it? It's crumbling. That tomb has no family to take care of it. And this tomb here? Notice the beautiful tree. This is the tomb of a Haitian army general. His wife used to pay me, but since she left for the United States, she stopped paying me. So fifty-five years in section 17. Yes. This is my base. I have a home, but often I sleep here by the general. His tomb didn't collapse in the earthquake. No, it didn't. Others fell, but not this one.

JANE WYNNE

69, environmentalist

In 1956, Jane's father established a piece of land as a nature reserve near Kenscoff in the mountains south of Port-au-Prince. We spoke to Jane during an Earth Day celebration. Jane and her family try to maintain their family house and land as a reserve, despite efforts of a local official, neighbors, and others to claim at least a part of the land, demanding proof of ownership.

At home my father's conversation—morning, noon, and night—was about the soil. I was the youngest of six daughters. My older sisters weren't interested. So my mother would say, "Go sit with your dad." That's how I learned about being connected to the soil.

I was born in in 1946 in Carrefour, on the outskirts of Port-au-Prince.[1] My mother was from Gonaïves; and my father was born in Utica, New York.[2] He came to Haiti in 1925 as a civil engineer and also a geologist. After they got together, my parents decided to leave Carrefour and find a place up in the mountains. There was a lot of erosion going on at that time, and my father wanted to show people how to protect the hillsides.

---

[1] Carrefour, on the northwest edge of Port-au-Prince, just south of Port-au-Prince Bay, is a dense residential suburb of more than 400,000 and was near the epicenter of the 2010 earthquake.

[2] Gonaïves is a city of more than 300,000 about 90 miles north of Port-au-Prince.

My dad had a vision, to teach people about "the runoff." Every day of my life, he was always talking about the runoff. We have to stop the runoff. Runoff is the water that runs off the mountains, the hillsides, and causes the erosion of the soil. He used to say the topsoil goes off the mountains, into the ravines, into the plains and down into the ocean in the same way that the youth will travel. Downhill! Because they'll always go down to the the city for jobs. From the mountains to Pétionville to Port-au-Prince.[3] But what happens? When they get to Port-au-Prince there aren't any jobs. So what did they do then? They'd take a boat to Miami to look for a better life. Some drowned on the way. Others were sent back to Haiti. It's been like that since 1987—the country became very poor after the Duvaliers left.

Under Duvalier, there were Makout all over the country.[4] It was a militia-controlled state. I remember in 1956, or maybe '57—I was very young—the Makout attacked a nearby house. I can't remember why. But there was a lot of shooting, and later on we heard there were people who died. Another time when Jean-Claude was kidnaped, they went around people's houses trying to find out what happened, and quite a few people were killed.[5] Yes, the Makout would overuse their power. But in general, there was more order in the country. Now everybody has a gun. You don't know who's killing who. At that time you knew if somebody got killed, it was a Makout or the government. But I also remember once we had a flat tire and a

---

[3] Pétionville is a wealthy, historic suburb of Port-au-Prince built into the hillside south of the city center.

[4] The *Makout* were a feared paramilitary group under the Duvalier regimes during the second half of the twentieth century. For more on the Makout, see the Glossary, page 309.

[5] In 1963 President François Duvalier's political enemies attempted to kidnap his children, including his young son Jean-Claude, in order to force him from office. The crackdown that followed the unsuccessful attempt left many dead throughout Haiti. For more on the Duvalier regime, see Appendix I, page 293.

Makout was the first one who came to help us. It's true, because they were the ones who were always on the road.

I TRY TO PROTECT THE AREA MY
PARENTS STARTED IN 1956

As I grew older, I learned more about the environment. I studied in the States for six years, two years of high school and four years of college—Anna Maria College, in Paxton, Massachusetts. It was a very small college. I took a course in Introduction to Plant Biology. The day after I came back home, my dad said, "Put on your boots, let's go up the mountain." I was twenty-six. Ever since, I don't think I've ever come down from the mountain. I go down to the city, of course, but my heart is always up there.

I try to protect that area my parents started in 1956. The reserve has over thirty acres of land. Now people say, "Something should be done up there." But they don't understand, it's a reserve! A reserve doesn't have to have big buildings, hotels, or whatever. My parents wanted to create a special place, a place where people can come and find different species of plants that are disappearing, like tree ferns, species of plants, and certain indigenous birds like the crossbill. You know the crossbill? It lives in the pine tree. It has a crossed bill because when it eats a seed, part of the bill lifts up the cone and the other part will push it down. The bird's tongue takes out the seed. Whatever seeds he fails to swallow fall down. These are the seeds that grow new trees.

There's a bird that's called the solitary bird—they call it the musician bird. It whistles like a human being. So beautiful. He lives up there, in those tree ferns. And in the other trees too—but he loves to nest in the tree ferns and in the pine trees. We want to protect all of those not only for our indigenous birds but also migrating birds.

The other day something happened which was very, very special. My daughter and her partner were driving up to the farm, and they saw a bunch of boys pulling a string with a bird attached at the end. My daughter and her partner stopped and offered them some money to let the bird go. When they took the bird home to our house, we called our friend, a bird man, an ornithologist. He told us it was the petrel that comes from North Carolina. It's like a seabird, and has webbed feet like a duck. He told us that there are very few left on planet Earth. So this very special bird is coming to Haiti to nest in our mountains.

The Audubon Society has been to the reserve many times. The Audubon Society sent a specialist and he found twenty-two different species of birds from Port-au-Prince, Pétionville, and Kenscoff village. But when he stayed at the farm for one night he found twenty-three more birds in one spot. Some are just migrating, but our place is the path where they all travel.

They used to consider the pine forest the "lungs of the Caribbean." But now we've lost so much. They say we have 2 percent of the forest in Haiti left.[6] There are so many causes of deforestation in Haiti. Number one is the need to have a space to grow vegetables like corn. And so they burn hundreds of trees at once, because they need land to plant. You will find many patches of cornfields, right in the middle of a forest. And they also need trees to make charcoal. But this deforestation started way back in the 1800s, when they used to export precious wood to France, to Europe. But now people don't care if it's precious or not, they'll use it for charcoal. And without trees, you know, the water won't remain in the soil. It's like my father used to say. We used to have waterfalls all over Haiti all year round. Right next to my house, there's a stream that goes down to a waterfall. It used to be so beautiful. There are about six terraces, six basins, natural basins where people could fish, things like that, but it's all lost.

There is a part of the reserve that's very special for us. We call it the center of the farm. Past the second set of pine trees, you find

---

[6] For more on deforestation in Haiti, see the Glossary, page 309.

a little house my dad built. That's where you find big, big trees, eucalyptus, we used to call it mèt lakou. *Mèt lakou* means "master of the yard." They were the biggest, oldest trees that were there on the land. We would need six people to hold hands together around the diameter of the tree.

It's very spiritual place for us. That's where we buried my dad.

If you hike up a little more, you find the most panoramic view of the south of Haiti. The farm's up to 6,000 feet high. You get to the very top and you have a living map of Haiti. You see the Bay of Port-au-Prince; you see the north of Haiti; you see the lake that separates Haiti and that we share with Dominican Republic, Lake Azuei. You can also see flamingos. And if you turn around, you see the whole south of Haiti, where right behind the mountain is Jacmel.[7] You can see Gonaïves. And you see, of course, most of Port-au-Prince, from far away. At night, it's gorgeous with all the lights. The reserve is a special place; you see almost 360 degrees, all of Haiti. I like to choose one spot to meditate. I used to call it "my little Tibet" because it was so high, when you look at it from far away. It would take me far off, far from planet Earth.

THEY'LL BRING IN SOME PEOPLE
AND SAY THE LAND IS THEIRS

But the way things work now is that if somebody wants somebody's land, they'll bring in some people and say that the land is theirs. You'll see young children shouting, "That's my land. You took my land!" That's how it started in our region—now this way of doing things has spread all over Haiti.

Someone from the younger generation told a man, a senator—I will not say names—that there was land in the mountains for sale.

---

[7] Jacmel is a city of 40,000 on Haiti's southern coast, approximately 40 miles southwest of Port-au-Prince.

Part of that land was ours. And then recently this senator came, and said to me, "If it's your land, where are your papers?" He had about a hundred people with him, and a carload of police officers with guns—and a lawyer, and a surveyor. The lawyer was a crazy guy—making lots of noise—and the surveyor was from Carrefour. He didn't even know the land up here. I was there with my son-in-law, and with a couple of friends. After one hour of disputing, all kinds of words were being thrown up in the air, he told the people he had with him, "You know what, why don't you go mark off the land that you believe is for the Wynne family, and the rest of this is now your land." They started dancing and screaming, "Yayyyy, Senator, this is our land, we're going to take it all." The senator said, "I'm not staying," and he left us in the middle of all those people with machetes—some of them had guns.

Later, the people the senator had left behind beat our horses. One of them had a miscarriage, a beautiful horse—she lost her baby. We went to get the policeman and he said, "No, you have to go get the judge—you know, judge de paix."[8] So my son-in-law went to get judge de paix. After that my son-in-law went with the judge and two security guards we have through U.S.A.I.D.[9]

My son-in-law had a gun and so did the security guards, and they took the judge down to the center. At the center, there were policemen who took the guns away from the security guards. I don't think the police had realized that my son-in-law had a gun too. When they got to a certain point, they saw the mob coming, and my son-in-law told them not to come further.

The mob came closer and started throwing stones, and my son-in-law said, "Do not approach." When they kept approaching, he shot up in the air. Somehow the mob grabbed one of the security guards

---

[8] A *judge de paix* ("justice of the peace") is a local legal authority in the Haitian justice system.

[9] For more on U.S.A.I.D. in Haiti, see the Glossary, page 309.

and beat him with a stone. They almost killed him. The policemen were there and did nothing.

The same week after the invasion, we were sitting in the yard and we heard a big thump hitting the gate. Our gate is made of tin, and we were wondering, *Who's knocking?* But it wasn't a knock, it was people passing by throwing stones.

A couple of months later, two friends from the neighborhood, a husband and wife who used to come and have coffee with us came and told us that, today, it's not a visit, they were coming by with an announcement that our house was actually owned by one of their great-grandfathers a hundred years ago. They said they weren't sure how it was sold, and that they needed to see our papers.

Some weeks later we realized this couple were going around doing the same thing to other people in the neighborhood.

I don't fear for my safety. No, but people can be threatening. A guy on a motorcycle came and he made a sign at my son-in-law and said, "I'm watching you."

My dad used to tell us, every square foot you are standing on, you have to protect it. To me, the reserve is a place apart. We had a stairway that led to the big eucalyptus tree, we used to call it "the treehouse." One day, I went to write something. I climbed up, and I spent some time up there. I was alone. When I went down the stairs, some sunlight went through my body, a sandwich between the sun and the earth. It was like the earth was the feminine unity, and the sun the masculine; and the sun was sending rays making love to Mother Earth, and I was in between them! This is when I really felt one with Mother Earth. One, just one. I opened my arms and my whole body just went. I let myself go on the grass.

The music is what calls all the kids. People hear the music, they know it's me. They run and say they want *krém*, give me *krém*. I have chocolate, vanilla, *mayi*—that's made with grits. Not white grits, yellow grits. They're 7 gouds. I've been selling ice cream for seven months. It doesn't work well. At the end of the day, I hand the distributor the money, and he gives me back a little bit out of it. The distributor has a lot of people selling. A lot of people. He's a cop.

I've lived in Port-au-Prince three years. I'm twenty-seven. I don't have money to do anything else, and I don't want to just be sitting around. So I just live with the little profit. Until I can find something else. If I had something else to do, I would do it. I do mason work besides this. But I don't have any special trade.

—*Ice cream vendor on Rue Nazon*

Ice cream man's going to make it. He's not doing so well, but he's able to eat, maybe even every day. Let me tell you a secret, too. We can go to 1,000 merchants. None of them is going to tell you, "My business is doing good!" Never. Especially if they're talking into a microphone. They're always going to tell you it's doing bad, you know? Because they're looking for any angle. That's the hustle. The hustle is part of the work.

The ice cream man, he's gonna be all right. Because he's resilient. He's used to the suffering. But somebody who's going hungry for the first time, it's the most painful shit ever. Like when I first came here. I couldn't take the hunger.

—*Jean Pierre Marseille*

GINA AND LIANS

Gina—41, codirector, SOFALAM
Lians—34, codirector, SOFALAM

SOFALAM is a center focused on supporting young street girls and their children in Port-au-Prince.[1] Many of the girls Gina and Lians work with have been restaveks, an informal system of de facto slavery that involves the importation of young children, mostly girls, from more rural areas of Haiti to work without pay or protection in Port-au-Prince homes, often in exchange for education.[2] Restaveks regularly run away from their host homes, or they are kicked out when they are no longer needed or become pregnant. Whether as refugees from a restavek situation or otherwise, the girls who end up on the streets of Port-au-Prince are often young, uneducated, and likely to turn to prostitution to survive. Gina and Lians try to help.

GINA

We work with homeless girls. There are two categories of those girls. Some of them are from the streets. That's all they know. They grew up there, and ate and slept on the streets. There are others, restaveks,

---

[1] SOFALAM stands for *Solidarite Fanm pou yon Lavi Miyo*—Women in Solidarity for a Better Life.

[2] In Haiti, children who are used as unpaid domestic servants are known as *restaveks*. For more information, see the Glossary, page 309.

who are only recently in the streets. The restaveks are children that someone—an aunt, a friend, a stranger—took from their home in the province promising them a home and care. But once they get to the city, the child becomes that person's personal and free maid. Sometimes they run away and live on the streets. There really isn't much difference between the ones who grew up on the streets and the kids who ended up there.

We take the girls and bring them to SOFALAM. We have specialists, like psychologists, who work with them. We teach them for three years before putting them in schools with other children outside of the center. We have a small school inside the center where we work to get them caught up before they go outside to school. The work varies by whether they went to school before or not. We help the ones who didn't go to school at all to learn a few things to increase the likelihood of them getting registered to school. In Haiti, the older you get, the harder it becomes to get into school, even if it's night school.[3] When we're done teaching them, we register them to a public school since our funding isn't enough for private school. After they finish sixth grade, we look for their biological parents in the province they came from and try to reunite them.

In 1994, the lady who started this project, Kettely Marseille, realized that among the many centers they had in Port-au-Prince, none of them were for girls, only for boys. The other centers used to say that they didn't want girls because they're more difficult, and they could get pregnant while at the center. However, Kettely was touched by the state these girls were in and decided to create a center for them, the first one of its kind. It was an open center at the beginning. The girls could come and sleep, and the center's workers would be paid extra to stay overnight with them.

The first center was CAFA[4] and we have SOFALAM founded in

---

[3] Night school in Haiti is typically school for adults.

[4] CAFA stands for *Centre d'Appui Familiale*—Family Support Center.

2002. Kettely said that she wasn't going to be there forever. So when she started getting old, some of the girls who benefited from CAFA created SOFALAM to continue with her work.

LIANS

I was at CAFA. I was in the streets. My family didn't have much when I was a child. My mother was very poor and my father died when I was six. There were five of us children, my two sisters, my two brothers, and I. When my mother died, we became orphans, and the parks near the presidential palace became our home. We stayed alive because of the good graces of people. There were many girls like me at those parks. We were divided into clans. I didn't have anyone to talk to me and guide me, so I fell into some wrong crowds.

In 1994, Mrs. Kettely opened her center and asked some of us to come and help keep the place clean. We used to go every day, Monday to Friday. What most attracted us in the center was that it was better than where we were in the streets. The police used to come and arrest us all the time at the park. They used to ask us about street criminals —if we told them we didn't know anything, they would beat or molest us before letting us go.

At CAFA, we received classes on manners, and it helped us in our situation. After that I said to myself that I would never raise my children on the street. When I became pregnant at sixteen, some of us decided to create the SOFALAM center. We approached Mr. Peterson about it—he used to help Kettely and he agreed to write projects and grants for us. He helped me find a place to rent at Carrefour-Feuilles.[5]

We chose to do this work because we know some young people like us who, after leaving CAFA, went back to the street. They gave birth on the street, and their children are growing up on the street.

---

[5] Carrefour Feuilles is a neighborhood in south Port-au-Prince unconnected to the larger suburb of Carrefour, which is further west of the city.

So SOFALAM decided that we would maintain a cradle for these children. We keep these children so their mothers can have time to either have a little business or look for a job without sending their children to work for another family.

The restavek system is real slavery.

GINA

The economy is the main reason. Most of the time what feeds the restavek system is the difficult times that many people encounter in the provinces. Their house is overpopulated with children, and they can't feed them. I must say, however, that's what people in the provinces think, but many times, they are better off than a lot of people in Port-au-Prince. They can find any roots or peas to eat, but they think that if the child doesn't come to the city they won't go to school. The government is to blame for this. Often when a child finishes the sixth grade at school in the provinces, her parents are unable to find any public school to continue the education.[6] So they send her to the city. Sometimes, it's with a family member, but I'd say 90 percent of the time it's with a stranger. It can be confusing because when you meet them and ask them who they live with, they often say an aunt, which should be their mother or father's sister. But when you ask, you find out that this aunt most of the time is not even related to the child.

LIANS

For example, say I live in Port-au-Prince and I want a restavek. I would take the bus to Jérémie, or Cap-Haïtien, or Bouvier. These places have many children whose parents would be willing to give them away in order to make sure they get an education.

---

[6] Little public education exists in Haiti, especially in rural areas, and most families must pay for private schools.

GINA

You'll find children also in Saint-Michel.

LIANS

Yes. So many places. And if you take a bus to Jacmel, not far away you'll find a little town called Seguin. That little town contains some of the poorest people of the country. And so many children! And when they see someone in a pretty dress coming into town, they don't even care who the person is, they'll start giving their children away.

GINA

They are usually promised school and food.

LIANS

Yes, and most of the time, they don't get either one. They wake them up at 2 in the morning when there's electricity for them to iron clothes. If they have babies, they will wake up the child to take care of the baby instead of taking care of their own child. They have to also cook. They have to mop. They will get spanked if they don't do these things even if they don't know how to do them. They usually don't go to school. You see, the parents, they think that their children are better off, but they are in a far worse situation. When the girls can't take it anymore, they run off to the streets. Some are as young as six, seven years old and others are as old as fourteen, fifteen years old.

LIANS

Here's an example of a common problem. If I'm a woman, I may get a child to help me out in the house. However, I'm not always in the house, and the man I live with, if he's a bad person, might molest or rape that child when I'm not home. It could also be my brother or my son—or all of them.

GINA

We have a lot of cases like that at the center. A lot of them become pregnant and then they send them away.

LIANS

Some of them also catch H.I.V. or syphilis. And when they don't have anyone providing for them, sometimes they become prostitutes. When they come to the center, they immediately get tested for H.I.V. Some of them have children who also are infected. We take those children and get them cared for. We also educate them on the disease. We let them know it's not as bad as they think it is if they get treated.

Some of them think that they'll never get out of the streets, but we share our stories with them. We show them that there's a way out. We saved many of them like that. A lot of them decided to go back home or to a family member. We always go visit them after that. I have some of them in La Saline near me. I always go visit them and talk to them.

GINA

Unfortunately, we're going through a financial crisis right now. We don't receive the resources we used to receive anymore. We're not sure if they stopped because of the new government in place. Right now, we can't even feed the children. It's hard. That's why we're looking for other sources for funding right now. Emaner Suisse helped us before. UNICEF used to help a little when it comes to health. Save the Children used to help with education.[7] However, they all stopped. We've had to reduce to fifty children because of the situation. We try. We write grant after grant, but still the money isn't there anymore.

---

[7] Emaner Suisse, UNICEF, and Save the Children are all intergovernmental or non-governmental aid organizations working in Haiti.

I would love to just get up one day and go to work and get a regular paycheck and have everything done like nice and dandy, like a lot of people that's living in this world. But that's just not my case. Thinking about my kids not going to school after I've spent a whole lot of money trying to keep them in school. And these are cheap schools. If I had the means, I would rather send them to the States or somewhere. My little son, Diego, he's in his first year in school. I haven't paid any money for him. The woman at the school knows me because my kids have been going to that school for years. I had owed her over 5,000 Haitian dollars for last year. So I went there and just paid her for last year. So she automatically gave me credit for this new year.

—*Jean Pierre Marseille*

DENISE DORVIL

43, mother, former housekeeper, and former sex worker

Sent to an orphanage as a young child, Denise has survived on and off the streets for most of her life. She's given up two children for adoption, later taking on the care of her grandchildren. She introduced us to her grandson—a little boy named Mickenson. After the earthquake, Denise found temporary reprieve living within a Haitian community in the Dominican Republic, but she returned after three months in order to vote in the presidential election. Some names have been changed.

I sleep in cars, I sleep in the street, I sleep on the sidewalk. People should see where I sleep. Tonight, I am sleeping under *pwela*.[1] Not a shelter, just a tent. I made the tent myself with two pieces of wood. It's in the back of the orphanage where I was raised. When it rains, water gets inside because the covers are worn out and the wood pieces aren't good anymore. For a bed, I sleep on a pile of wood from herring boxes with my children. During the day, I put the wood under the light of the sun so it can dry out after the rain. At night my body hurts.

I've been struggling since I was four years old. I'm now forty-three. I have no mother, no father. I don't have anybody to help me. Churches don't help me. I don't have a family member who wants to help me. My siblings and I don't have the same father but we have

---

[1] A *pwela* is a plastic tarp used to make tents.

the same mother. When I call them to tell them that I have problems and I need food or to borrow money, they say if I'm not working, how am I going to be able to pay them back? I tell them that even if I don't have the money, God will help me find someone who will give it to me. They don't agree.

All the ways I tried to succeed didn't work. I gave birth to four children. I gave two of them to an orphanage. Right now I have four children with me here. Two of them are my children and the two others are my grandchildren. The three-year-old is really suffering. I can't pay for her school. I can't even get her birth certificate.

I only see men loving me in my dreams. Last time while I was sleeping, I had a dream about a Haitian artist hitting on me. I told him that I was not interested in married men. People's husbands are trouble.

I always knew how to sing. I always said that I wanted to become an artist in my country. That dream didn't happen. I'm still young, but in order to pursue my dream, I have to know what to do—what decisions to make and which way to go. Sometimes poverty almost makes me go insane. Poverty has made me old. I can't dress myself well, and people laugh at me. They insult me and call me *grann nana* —shameless grandma. They call me homeless and tell me that I have no future. They insult me and I get hurt. But today, I believe in life, and one day, God will say a word for me.

A voice tells me to go do things, but I always ask God to keep me from doing them.

When I slept with men, it wasn't because they forced me. It was me who offered them my body. I slept with men to get money so I could eat. I don't like doing it, but the situation in my country, in my city, caused me to do it. Sometimes the men promised that they would give me 100 or 250 gouds, but afterward they wouldn't give me anything.[2]

---

[2] Roughly equivalent to US$2.50–US$6.25.

When I see the men who refused to pay me, sometimes I tell them that they will pay for what they did. I tell them that my vagina costs money and that they would never have done it if they knew I was going to hurt them. I tell them that God will judge them. It hurts me when I think about it. Sometimes I feel like dying. But I know the Bible says that we shouldn't ask for death, because God is the one who decides.

So I stopped sleeping with men. Men still want to sleep with me, but I don't take their offers because of the risk of getting AIDS or tuberculosis. I just rely on God now.

I ask people for money, 5 or 10 gouds so my family and I can eat. Sometimes we go to sleep hungry. Sometimes when I help a friend, they give me some food and I give it to my children.

MY PARENTS PUT ME IN AN ORPHANAGE

I'm from Jérémie, and I was born on November 6, 1971.[3] When I was young, my mother didn't send me to school. My parents couldn't take care of me, so they put me in an orphanage. When I was living at the orphanage, I used to eat and drink well. They sent me to school, and I got to sixth grade. When the white people used to come to the orphanage, they would take pictures and stay with us. Sometimes they would laugh with us and take us to visit Champ de Mars.[4]

The orphanage was run by Germans and French, directed by Rodrigue Ben Bichotte. When Bichotte was there, I was very comfortable. He was Haitian, and he founded the SOS Children's Village.[5] The director after Bichotte was Paul Beauvoir. He kicked

---

[3] Jérémie is the capital of the Grand'Anse Department at the western tip of the Tiburon Peninsula.

[4] Champ de Mars is a park in Port-au-Prince near the former site of the National Palace.

[5] SOS Children's Villages International operates orphanages and provides family services in hundreds of countries across the globe.

me out of SOS Children's Village. One day they were beating me for peeing in bed. I was crying so much, and I said that it was because I didn't have any parents that they were mistreating me. Beauvoir told me that I was a child from the street and humiliated me in front of the other kids. He put me in a foster home in Carrefour.[6] He did that to many of us. The kids were mad and said that we were in SOS before he came, and he shouldn't be the one kicking us out. I was the only one from Jérémie in the orphanage. The other kids were from Artibonite, Liancourt, Pont-Sondé, different areas in the country. Some of them had parents, so their parents took them back. Some of the kids got married and others have houses. But for me, there wasn't another life, only the foster home life.

So I was living with some people in Carrefour. They are dead now, but they treated me very badly. One of them saw that I was eating well and became big. He tried to rape me. I was eight years old. But the man didn't have time to rape me because I yelled. He slapped me, but the neighbors heard me yelling so they came to see what was happening. I told them that while I was sleeping, I saw the man getting closer to me. The neighbors invited me to come sleep at their houses.

The people who welcomed me into their house and were feeding me were Tonton Makout.[7] I began working for them, doing laundry and housekeeping so I could eat every day. Later, I fled because these people also began beating me. I went back to the SOS Children's Village, but they kicked me out again. After that I was alone.

I went back to the Bichotte family. They said they could help me continue with school. I went grocery shopping for them, went

---

[6] Carrefour, on the northwest edge of Port-au-Prince, just south of Port-au-Prince Bay, is a dense residential suburb of more than 400,000 and was near the epicenter of the 2010 earthquake.

[7] The *Makout* were a feared paramilitary group under the Duvalier regimes during the second half of the twentieth century. For more on the Makout, see the Glossary, page 309.

to get water for them. They didn't see an education or a future for me. They just wanted me to help them in the house. Every time I saw children going to school it hurt me. I asked them when they would send me to school, and they told me to just wait. I waited for years.

I KNOW THE CONDITIONS

I met my boyfriend on January 1, 1990. I was nineteen years old. He was older than me. I got pregnant by him and gave birth on April 16, 1991 in Carrefour. He took me to the hospital and he left me there and never came back. I haven't seen him since. Strangers were helping me and feeding me. The room cost 25 gouds, and I didn't have it.[8] They didn't treat me bad at the hospital because they saw that I didn't have money. They gave me a last chance and allowed me to leave the next day.

I never saw the father again. He left me for another woman. That means he didn't want me. I thought that I was going to spend the rest of my life with him. He's never asked about me. Even after the earthquake, I never heard from him. Now his child, Jessica, is twenty-two and has two children of her own, and I am the one taking care of them. He never gave me money for the child.

I had the other kids with other men, each child with a different man. None of the men stayed. They just got me pregnant, left me, and went to marry other women. Jessica is my first child. My second child, Gerard, turned eighteen this year. My third child, Dieuny, will turn fourteen in October. And my last boy just turned seven. His name is Dwight Phillipe.

I gave the two youngest ones to an orphanage. While they were in the orphanage, white people came and took them out of the country. I'd love to see them, but I can't. I don't have money. I had a visa but

---

[8] At the time of the interview, 25 gouds equals approximately US 65 cents.

my passport expired. I have no one to contact. I'm like a dog in the street. The white people used to write me pretty often. Mrs. Jane is a good white person. Mrs. Kathleen is as well.

Mrs. Jane used to send me good money, $73 each month. She is the one who has my boy, Dwight. Mrs. Kathleen—who has Dieuny— used to send $48.58 and the government would take $1.50 on each money transfer. It's not easy for someone who is working hard in another country to send you money. It's a big thing because they have bills to pay. Mrs. Jane sent me some money once when my older daughter, Jessica, was sick and I took her to the hospital. Later Mrs. Jane sent more money because my other child, Gerard had *djòk*.[9] I had to go to Jérémie to have it removed by a Vodou priest. Mrs. Jane doesn't send me money anymore.

I know the conditions when you give your kids to an orphanage. My children are not under my care anymore, but sometimes people with good hearts will keep contact. I searched on the Internet for these families that have my children and they reached out to me. They really liked me. They told me about the kids and how much they love them. But for now it's difficult to get hold of them and talk to the kids.

Mrs. Jane told me that she would help me travel to Guyana in October 2011. But I don't know what happened. Mrs. Jane sent me to the Social Welfare office to get a paper. She sent me all the information via Facebook. I was very happy about it. But the trip didn't happen, and I don't know why. Mrs. Jane told me that she was going to pay for school fees but I think that the school fee was too high for her. And I understand because she is already taking care of one of my children and she loves my child very much.

---

[9] An ailment believed to be caused by magic.

I DIDN'T KNOW IT WAS AN EARTHQUAKE

On Tuesday, January 10, 2010, while I was sleeping I had this dream where I saw two people who came and took our spot at the church. I told my daughter that we would not let those people stay next to us because they aren't humans. I saw my daughter telling the people to pray. Then I saw that the people turned into zombies.[10] The next day, I told my friends about the dream.

When the earthquake happened, I didn't know it was an earthquake. I was in a rented house and was going to night services at a Catholic church. I saw that everything was shaking. I couldn't understand. Dogs were running, the roads were moving. I thought it was because of the electricity. God protected me and didn't let me die with my children. At that time I had a house. The house collapsed, but we were all outside.

Even though I didn't lose many things, the people who lost everything are my brothers and sisters. We are one family. I went to see what was happening in the hospitals and everywhere. I saw so many people dying. I saw all the collapsed houses. Some people just disappeared and were never found. Everybody in Cazeau was sleeping in the street.[11] We slept up the hill on Bettany Street. So many people were sleeping on the ground there. The people there let me stay, and when they cooked, they gave some food to me and my children. We would take a shower one after the other and go to sleep around 6 p.m., because we didn't want people to steal our spot. During the night, we didn't care about mosquitoes or anything. I just brought my kids closer to me.

All the other nations came and helped. I saw people passing by with things that were given them. Some people in Cazeau received help, but not me, because I didn't want to get into the crowd and

---

[10] Here, *zombies* refers to people who have been cursed causing death and reanimation as undead servants.

[11] Cazeau is a suburb on the eastern edge of Port-au-Prince.

fight. I could have died. My children were crying of hunger, but I told them that I was not going to put my life in danger just for some food. If God didn't let me die from cholera or the earthquake, there was no way that I was going to die just to get the things that white people give away.

Because things were going really bad, a friend paid for the three-month visa for me to go to the Dominican Republic. While I was there, cholera was a whole story in Haiti. They said that the white people brought cholera to Haiti by contaminating the water.[12] I didn't see it that way. I cannot say that it was them because I didn't see them doing it. The bacterium that causes cholera is hidden. When it rains, the bacterium meets with trash and other bacteria and it gives you cholera.

When I was in the Dominican Republic, I stayed in a house with some Haitians. There were so many Haitians living around me. Life was good for me there. These Haitians treated me very well. They didn't even want me to clean the house. They told me that I was their guest and that they wanted to take care of me, because I would have done the same thing for them. I told them that I'm from an orphanage and that I'm used to working at people's houses. But they told me that people don't do that there. I would wait for them to fall asleep and I would do the dishes and clean everything. After I finished, I would take a shower and go to sleep. The next day when they woke up they were shocked. They thanked me.

I would do people's hair for a little bit of money. When I was a kid I learned how to do hair using mango butter and combs. That helped me buy food.

Before I went to the Dominican Republic, people used to tell me that Dominicans are killing Haitians over there. But when I went there, I saw that most of the buildings were built by Haitian workers.

---

[12] For more on the international response to the earthquake and the cholera epidemic, see Appendix III, page 317.

The truth is that Hatiains helped the Dominicans get their independence, but afterward they started to feel different about us.[13] When we travel there, they insult us by saying *peligros*—dangerous—and other words. Haitians are a people who get mad easily, so when they say words like this, things always go south. They don't want us to go to their country, but they cannot forbid us to go there. And after the earthquake, I was lucky to live there for a while.

I HEARD THAT THE PRESIDENT WAS GIVING HOUSES TO PEOPLE

When I first got back from the Dominican Republic, I stayed at a pastor's house. His name was Pastor Marco. I was sleeping at his church in Cazeau. I came back to vote for my president. I heard that the president was giving houses to people. So yes, I voted for Michel Joseph Martelly, but I didn't vote for him for fun.[14] I voted for change and for the country to get better. But when I see what has happened since, I regret voting for him. I know that he couldn't have done things for everybody, but as president he could have created jobs and many people could have been working now. Even myself who is not doing anything, I might have found a job. Each person who becomes president always says that their government will help Haiti progress. But I believe now that the only person who could change the country is God.

MINUSTAH is still here and they do work. They came to our country because of the violence.[15] MINUSTAH doesn't bother me,

---

[13] For more on the history of Haiti and the Dominican Republic, see Appendix I, page 293.

[14] Michel Martelly was the president of Haiti from 2011 to 2016. Before becoming president, he was a musician and businessman.

[15] The United Nations Stabilization Mission in Haiti (MINUSTAH) was initially authorized following the 2004 coup d'état as peacekeeping forces brought in to stabilize the political situation and protect human rights and the rule of law after

they didn't beat me or do anything bad to me. Sometimes bandits will come and beat people, but when they hear that MINUSTAH is coming, they run. I don't know how long MINUSTAH will stay. I could say ten years, twelve years, fifteen years, twenty years. I don't know.

WHEN I WAS BEAUTIFUL

My oldest daughter is a young lady now. She found a guy and got pregnant, and I didn't even know the guy. He died, and Jessica found another man and got pregnant again. Now she has two kids. Things aren't going good for her. She already looks like an old woman.

This child here is my grandchild. He has no father and his mother is not working right now. She has lived in the countryside since the earthquake. She can't take care of him. I'm not working either, but I can't leave him in the countryside. When he is in the countryside he gets a rash all over his body. I had to bring him here, but that doesn't mean that things are good for me.

My dreams aren't over. If God didn't want my dreams to come true, he would have never let me live. Now, I would love for God to give me a man who will marry me and get me out of my sinner life. I want someone who will understand when I'm sick and hungry, someone who can help me take care of my children. Men were only interested in me when I was bigger. When I was beautiful and fresh.

Sometimes I spend the night crying. I have so many problems. My grandchild sometimes wakes up in the middle of the night asking for food, milk, and most of the time I get irritated.

If God gave me a husband who would help me have a business, I would want a food business. I would sell barbecue and plantains. I've never worked in food service, but I saw how the Dominicans do

Aristide's ouster. They were given greater mandate following the 2010 earthquake to support reconstruction and stability efforts. For more on MINUSTAH, see the Glossary, page 309.

it. Over there they fry, but here we barbecue. The Dominicans have many cooking tools we don't have. Here we just use *pikliz*,[16] onions, good acid, and pepper. We boil the chicken, we add seasoning, and finally we put it on the grill. I can fry it as well. Fried is good, but barbecue is better.

I have dreams that God will make me travel. They say that foreign countries are beautiful: nice beaches, nice pools, and nice roads. Even if I'm not going to stay abroad, I would like to visit. I want my kids to visit other countries so they can say that they traveled and saw the world. I have visions, I have dreams, and one day what people didn't wish for me, they will see it.

I always had a dream that my kids would write a book about me. When I die, I want them to share my story. I've struggled a lot, and I don't like poverty. Poverty made me look old and caused people to make fun of me. Sometimes I ask God, "What did I do wrong?" But I always pray for everybody.

I've heard that an earthquake will happen in the U.S., so every night I kneel and ask Jesus to protect them. I would tell the people in the U.S. to have courage, especially President Obama. President Obama is doing a great job. I saw President Obama went to South Africa to talk about AIDS and cholera. He is a good citizen and a real president in the world. I like what he is doing. Even if I don't know everybody's name from the U.S., God knows them. Two of my children live in New York City. I always pray for God to protect the United States, Canada, France, Chile, Italy, Argentina, and all the other countries.

Don't say that Haiti is not a safe country and that you won't go there. You need to visit Haiti and see how people live here. You have to come, and God will protect you the same way he protects you in your country. I love everybody in the world. I love the people suffering at the hospitals. I love the people who are in prison. I love the

---

[16] *Pikliz* is a Haitian hot sauce.

homeless, I love the handicapped, and I love the old people. I love everybody, because we are one family.

Look, I am not a *kokorat*—a bum. It's just a hard period in my life where I'm not working, so when people insult me, I accept it. But I'm not a vagabond and never will be. There is no dumb job. Even jobs like cleaning the streets, cleaning houses, or even picking up dogs feces—those aren't dumb jobs. I would do anything because work is freedom.

When we returned to visit Denise in 2016, she and her grandson were living in a one-room house constructed from bright blue metal siding, just off the streets where she used to live. A local pastor built the house and gave it to her.

BONHOMME PETERSON

29, refrigerator mechanic

Bonhomme Peterson lives in a house in Ti-Place Cazeau[1] that his mother left for him. After the earthquake, U.S.A.I.D. gave him the opportunity to learn a trade.[2] He has a girlfriend and two children. He has found his dream job, and he hopes that one day his child will find what he likes to do, too.

My name is Bonhomme Peterson. I was born in Baradères, and I was raised in Delmas with my mother.[3] My mother was Mona Theodore, and my father was Andre Jeudy. Life was good.

My parents did everything they could so that I could go to school. I went to school on time, and I was provided for until I lost my parents. I lost my mother first. She had diabetes and a heart problem. It greatly affected me. She probably would have lived longer if she

---

[1] Ti-Place Cazeau is a suburb on the eastern edge of Port-au-Prince.

[2] The division of the U.S. government responsible for foreign aid, U.S.A.I.D. has had a presence in Haiti for over 50 years.

[3] Baradères is a city of 30,000 in the Nippes Department, west of Port-au-Prince. Delmas is a large residential and commercial suburb in the northeast of Port-au-Prince, adjacent to the city's airport. Individual neighborhoods in Delmas are referred to by number, since the suburb is organized around numbered streets that radiate out from a central road (for instance, Delmas 45, Delmas 18, et cetera).

had received proper care. My mother was with me, but my father was *andeyo*.[4] I had a good relationship with my father. He was a farmer. He grew roots, sugar cane, and coconut. He used to sell the cane to the wine-press. My mother used to have a business and she used to sew. I don't have my father's last name. My stepfather adopted me. My stepfather was nice too. We didn't see each other very much. He lived on an island near Baradères called Boukan. He had a big boat and used to fish for catfish and sell them to other countries. We used to go during the summer. He had money. He was killed. I'm not sure how, but I know that it was a conspiracy. People hated him because he was successful.

I lost my stepfather, then my mother, and my father.

I have three siblings. Jean-Gardy, Mardochee, and Cherline. Jean-Gardy is the oldest. We have a good relationship. He's my brother. We help each other.

This house is mine. It was left to my mother after my stepfather died, and now it's ours. It's a small house. I live with my girlfriend and our child. We are not married, but we live together. These houses in Ti-Place Cazeau were built in the years '83, '84 by Duvalier. The houses were given to factory workers by the Duvalier family. Some people didn't like the neighborhood and sold their houses. Back then, it wasn't a developed place, so some left it to live in Carrefour or somewhere closer to the city. My stepfather bought that house in '82, I think he bought it for 4,000 gouds.[5] I was raised here, and my child was born here; I have no other choice but to love it here.

My mother died when I was fourteen years old, but I was able to keep going to school. I went to school at SOS Children's Village, Ti-Place Cazeau.[6] I went to public school, and after I graduated I

---

[4] *Andeyo* means "outside" in Kreyol. Haitians use the term to refer to everywhere outside of Port-au-Prince.

[5] In 1982, 4,000 gouds equals approximately US$130.

[6] SOS Children's Villages International operates orphanages and provides family

wasn't able to go to college. I didn't really have tuition to pay. It was a public school. Nonetheless, I had to eat every day and provide for myself. That is what was hard—food, laundry, shoes, clothes. My girlfriend at the time's father encouraged me to learn a trade. He told me that if I couldn't provide for a woman, she would leave me to be with someone else. I am not with his daughter anymore. However, it was because of him that I can even be proud of who I am now.

I tried once to find out how much it would take me to learn my trade but it was very expensive. I needed to pay 3,000 gouds upfront and 2,500 gouds every month.[7] Fortunately, after the earthquake, I was able to learn few trades because of a program run by U.S.A.I.D. I enrolled in that program when it started. It is a nonprofit. We didn't have to pay. I was twenty-six years old. I learned to fix refrigerators and tiling. We came to class every day, and after each session, we received free lunch. We also had rotation hours. That was a great initiative. I wish I had the opportunity to help others like that.

These trades help me to survive. Even if I don't have a job every day, I have something to provide for myself. To work, one needs to learn how to do something first. If not, how would one find a job?

My first job was hard. I had to make a cold room. I had to call some of my classmates who were more advanced than I was. I knew what I needed for the job, and I was able to write a quote for my employer. I was taught how to do that, but I didn't know how much electric charge it would need to keep it cold. I asked my teacher for help. I made 4,500 gouds.[8] I took 1,500 and the rest was for my teacher and classmates who helped me.

I think I am living my dream. I always loved fridges. My mother had one. I would see how she would beg the technician to fix her fridge. After she died, I ended up selling the fridge, but I always

---

services in hundreds of countries across the globe.

[7] At the time of the interview, 3,000 gouds equals approximately US$75.

[8] At the time of the interview, 4,500 gouds equals approximately US$112.

wanted to know how to fix them. My other dream is to have my own fish business. I want to sell fresh fish in the neighborhood. I love fish. I am from Baradères. I love fish and the sea.

I do masonry and carpentry as well. You know that there isn't always electricity, so sometimes I can't find jobs fixing fridges. During my two years at the center, I used to pay attention when teachers were teaching students about masonry and carpentry. I picked them up that way. They have been very helpful. My girlfriend has a little business, but it can't help much. So my trade is what helps me. After the earthquake, I found a government job, rebuilding the public school of Ti-Place Cazeau. It was 50 gouds per day.[9]

Because of the earthquake, I was able to learn my trades. The earthquake was a disaster. I never thought that something like that could happen. I've seen many things that I never thought that I could have seen in my life. I've seen people buried alive. I've seen police officers losing their life trying to help. There was a fraternity and solidarity among Haitians. They loved each other. There wasn't color or social class among us. I thought that life was going to be good after the earthquake. Some people found jobs with those NGOs, even though they lost them after the nonprofits left from the city. I thought that the Haitian mentality would change. However, now, things are going back to how it was before.

My family slept in the street for two to three days after the earthquake, then we moved back in our house. The people who stayed in camps were people who lost their houses. Many of them didn't have houses to begin with, but they said that they lost houses. You can see that there are still people in camps. Even after some nonprofits tried to help them and give them money to rent houses, but they would take the money and move to another camp. Some people even rent tents in those camps. I'm sure some people will forever stay in camps because it benefits them. Some of those people don't even need the help.

---

[9] At the time of the interview, 50 gouds equals approximately US$1.25.

We have the youths, and they need to be proud of Haiti. They can't go to school, so they spend their daily life drinking beer and talking nonsense. Every youth wants a job with the government or a visa to the U.S.A., but they don't try to make things work here. They should try to stay here and work and build a future here the same way everyone does it in their country. Most of them don't even know how to speak English, and they think that life will be better there. How would they live? They should stay home and learn something and find a job here. I have friends and family members who left. Some of them had parents who sponsored them. Others left on a visa, and now they are illegal. They always say that they would be much better off in Haiti, but they never come back.

This government is not working for the youth. The youth need to stay in school. That's young people's only hope. They used to say back then that the youth is the strength of the country, but now I think that it is money. I think there should be a plan of retirement for every child that starts the day that child is born at the hospital. Imagine that old people don't even have retirement. Let's say that the parents die; how would the child survive? The government should think of a program like that.

I have two children, one from a previous relationship, and I'm ready to do everything to take care of them. I send them to school and I do my best to keep them on the right path. I learned what I liked, so I want my children to do the same. They are still babies, but I ask God to give me guidance and strength to take care of them. Religion doesn't save—it is faith. I have my experience to tell to my children and hope they learn from it.

Haiti is a great country; the government is what is bad. They make it hard for young and old. If I found money, I would help. The earthquake was a disaster, but I benefited from it and I wish I could help young people learn something to protect them in the future.

CHRISTOPHER DERAGON

20, medical assistant

We spoke with Christopher twice: in 2013 at the General Hospital and in 2014 at the Ti Kay office. After the medical staff at Ti Kay introduced us, Christopher met us with a warm, open smile that faded as he told his story, which includes contracting H.I.V. at birth. The virus can be prevented from passing from mother to child during pregnancy and delivery, but access to appropriate medical care to prevent H.I.V. is not available to all even in Haiti, which has excellent H.I.V. care in many settings.[1]

2013

My name is Christopher Deragon. I'm eighteen years old. I have TB and H.I.V. I was eight years old when I first got sick. I was in the third grade. I had to leave school because I became really sick. I didn't want to go to the hospital because I was afraid of needles. My dad first took me to the General Hospital. They didn't want to take care

---

[1] Editor's note: This story and two others (Josil, page 235, and Alina, page 97) focus on hospitals and medical care. We've chosen to leave some of the questions in because it reflects the intimate nature of the doctor/patient relationship here. For more on current health crises in Haiti, including the prevalence of both H.I.V. and TB, see Appendix III, page 317.

of me. So we went to Cange.[2] Then we went to Petit Saint-Joseph. We also went to another Catholic hospital. No one knew what was wrong with me. I used to cough a lot, and my eyes were swollen. I couldn't eat and I was really weak. I had a fever, and I had diarrhea. My stomach was hurting too. Then one day I was in the kid's ward at the General Hospital, and Dr. Coffee saw me there as she was walking by. She said that I was her son and took me with her. When I came here to the main TB ward, Dr. Coffee took care of me. She put me on some IVs. I was eleven when I first found out I have H.I.V. A doctor told me. I was really sad. Then Dr. Coffee told me too. She told me not to worry, she would help me.

I was born in Pétionville.[3] My mother died of AIDS when I was one. My dad took care of me when I was a kid, but he doesn't come when I'm here. I don't want him to catch the disease too. If he does, he might resent me for it. I don't live with him anymore. I went to see him this week. I gave him some money because he was there for me ever since I was a kid. He tried any hospital he knew of, so that I could get well. He said he couldn't do anything for me anymore. I would like to be placed in an orphanage. I don't have a mother, and my father doesn't want to help.

I take one pill each night, a big white pill. Only my father knows I have H.I.V. If I tell other people, then they stay away from me.

You look sad. What's wrong?
(Crying) When I talk about it or hear people talk about it, I feel like committing suicide. People say that I'll be humiliated.

You see that the treatment is working.
Yes.

---

[2] Cange is a Partners In Health hospital in the Central Plateau, hours from Port-au-Prince.

[3] Pétionville is a wealthy, historic suburb of Port-au-Prince built into the hillside south of the city center.

But you still want to commit suicide?
Yes.

Do you think about it a lot?
Yes. A lot. Because I don't want to get humiliated. I don't want people to tell me to get away from them or don't play with them. That's why I don't tell anybody.

2014, EIGHTEEN MONTHS LATER

My name is Christopher Deragon. I'm twenty years old. I'm still taking the pills, and my doctor is paying for my rent and my food. I live on Aviation Road with three other people. They all follow the same treatment.

I'm still discouraged with life. I don't like it when people are looking at me and ask what's wrong with me. I tell them to mind their own business. Sometimes people from my neighborhood mistreat me. They don't want me to touch them. I have to stay away from them. I have one friend that supports me. And I have my dad. He still lives in Pétionville. I don't see him often, but we talk on the phone. I wish I was somewhere where I would not be able to hear any noise. I do not like noise.

I work with Dr. Coffee. When she goes on her rounds, I go with her. I buy stuff that she needs and I help her around. Dr. Coffee is taking care of me. When I tell her I am hungry she says she knows. If God didn't send us Dr. Coffee, many of us would die.

Dr. Coffee said when she has her clinic, she'll give me a job there. But I don't want to depend on someone for the rest of my life. I would like to have a trade. I would love to read. I don't really want to come to this hospital every day. I wish I had something else to do. I am not doing it for anybody but for God and Dr. Coffee because she helped me a lot.

Last Friday, I went to GHESKIO for a blood test.[4] It was positive. That was hard to hear. Other people took it, and it was negative. I knew it was going to be positive, but still, people were looking at me. I was talking to a girl whose results came negative. It was tough. The doctor at GHESKIO said that they will change my pills. I agreed because I want to be healthier. He told me how important it is for me to take the pills. He said my CD4 was low, but I don't know what that means.[5] They tell me that I will stay alive as long as I take the pills. But you may come next year and find out I am dead.

I don't think so. Is that what you want?
I'd like to die right now.

How long have you been feeling that way?
Since 2010.

With your treatment, you can live until you are old. Do you really think that when I come back you won't be here?
I do think so. I asked God to let me die in my sleep. I don't pray about it. I would go to church, but I don't have any shoes. I don't like going to church in just any way, with my sneakers. I want to wear slacks and shoes to go to church.

---

[4] GHESKIO (The Haitian Group for the Study of Kaposi's Sarcoma and Opportunistic Infections) was "the first institution in the world dedicated to the fight against H.I.V./AIDS," according to its Web site, and "has provided continuous medical care in Haiti since 1982—never once shutting its doors or charging fees." The test that Christopher is talking about is a viral load—to check the activity of the virus in the body. With proper treatment it should be undetectable, or negative. He also had CD4 cell count testing, to measure immune status.

[5] CD4 cells are also known as T-cells, one of the body's major defenses against infection. Untreated H.I.V. destroys CD4 cells, leaving the body vulnerable to infection.

JOSIL JUNIOR[1]

24, medical assistant

Josil is a soft-spoken and extremely thoughtful young man, pausing frequently as we spoke. We met twice over two visits to Port-au-Prince, at the General Hospital and later at the Ti Kay clinic near the airport.

I didn't get far in school after my mom died. I can write my name and read a little. I can't do anything in an office, but I would be able to do other things. There are some guys here working for Dr. Coffee—I could do some of the things that they do. They help the patients eat or take medications, because some of them don't want to. I see Dr. Coffee talking to them all the time. Me, I try to understand. I talk to them, too, when they don't take their pills. We don't pay for the pills. People are trying to help us out. If Dr. Coffee wasn't here with those pills, they wouldn't know where to find or how much to pay for the pills. Some people throw them away. I tell Dr. Coffee, and she tries to sweet-talk them into taking the pills.

I became sick after the earthquake. Before the earthquake, I used to have my own little business. My little business was to sell Pap

---

[1] Editor's note: This story and two others (Alina, page 97, and Christopher, page 215) focus on hospitals and medical care. We've chosen to leave some of the questions in because it reflects the intimate nature of the doctor/patient relationship here. For more on current health crises in Haiti, including the prevalence of both H.I.V. and TB, see Appendix III, page 317.

Padap. They're quick recharge cards for cell phones. I was on the wharf of Jérémie.[2] It was sometime after 4 p.m. After I bought some Pap Padap to sell, I was on my way downtown, and I had a feeling not to go. I listened to my gut and didn't go. So I came back and sold the Pap Padap in another area. I was talking with my little cousin while helping her make water packs to sell when I felt the earth shake. I started running—the earth was shaking as I was running. It felt like I was running backward. It stopped after a while. I went back home to get my shoes, because I ran barefoot. It wasn't until I was running to my aunt's house that I noticed that it was worse than I thought. I saw people injured. I saw houses on the ground and people dead on the street.

When I first started getting sick, I went to a hospital in Carrefour. I was suffering from TB. It was after my medical tests that they told me that my case was too much for them, and that I had to be transferred to General Hospital. That day the hospital transferred me to General Hospital, I didn't even know what was going on because I was unconscious. When Dr. Coffee saw me, she rushed to me and gave me some oxygen. I was given a bed and didn't really feel like myself until after a few days on medication. I started walking again. That's when I asked the doctor to let me go home.

When my family came, they signed my release form, and I spent about two to three weeks home. At home, sometimes I would skip some pills if I couldn't find anything to eat. Because of that, I relapsed. I came back here, and Dr. Coffee took me in and started treating me again. She paid to have food made for us. When I'm here, I eat better and take my medications on time. You know, when I'm home, I have to do everything myself, and since I'm sick and out of a job, it's a little hard.

I spent a year doing the back-and-forth: I come for a while, I'll

---

[2] Jérémie is the capital of the Grand'Anse Department at the western tip of the Tiburon Peninsula.

feel better and go home. Then, I don't eat well, don't take the drugs properly, I relapse and come back here. I never stopped taking the medications, I just didn't take them how I was supposed to. You have to take them properly before the test can show that you're treated.

The doctor was giving me a bunch of drugs, but no one told me what I was suffering from. So I asked her about it. She asked me, would I be surprised if she told me what I was suffering from? I said no. She leaned and whispered to my ear that I had "the virus." I asked her what it was. I didn't know back then. She told me AIDS.

I thought I was about to die. I thought there wasn't any treatment for it, that there weren't any pills available. I didn't know that it could be treated, not until they explained everything to me. I know other people who also have the virus. Some people here. I don't think they know I have it too, though. I've seen people who look really healthy. My only problem is that I'm weak. I can't run. When I try to run, I feel heavy.

I think the doctor said it can't be treated. Meaning that you'll always have it. You can't have sex without a condom or be careless about your body anymore.

Okay. That doesn't mean it's not treatable. It means that you won't completely heal from it. You can't erase it from your system.
You can treat it?

Yes. You're on treatment now. Right?
Yes.

Do you know the name of your pill?
I usually take a big pill. It's called Big White.

No, that's not its real name. You call it that. What's the name? Do you know it?
Wait a sec. I know it. Let me remember. ARV!

Right! What is ARV?
I usually take it at night around 7 or 8 p.m.

Okay, but what is it?
It's medication. It works against the virus.

Great! This is the treatment!
Okay. Yes.

You are on treatment. If you follow it, you'll be fine. You need to be careful like you said when having sex.
My girlfriend and I haven't had sex since 2008. She knows about the TB only. Only I know that I have the virus. Let me tell you why I didn't tell anyone. I don't want to tell people and they humiliate me for it. You understand? I don't know their heart. We have a son together. It's not like I have a headache and can take a pill to make it go away.

DJENANE SAINT-JUSTE

35, dancer and choreographer

Djenane Saint-Juste is a dance instructor and teacher of Haitian culture. Djenane was born in Port-au-Prince, the third generation in a line of dancers. During the fall of Papa Doc in 1986, her mother's house was riddled with bullets while her mother attempted to protect her. They soon abandoned Port-au-Prince for the country.

As a young adult, Djenane attended college in Cuba and lived for a while in Venezuela before returning to Haiti. She and her young son became the target of violence during unrest that occurred in 2009. Fearing for their safety, Djenane left Port-au-Prince for the diaspora permanantly, in this case, California. The diaspora is often referred to in Haiti as the eleventh département *(the country has ten* départements, *roughly equivilant to states in the U.S.). We spoke to Djenane in Marin Country, California. She recently moved to Minnesota with her family.*

My grandmother was a Rara queen in La Gonâve, an island that is off the coast of Port-au-Prince.[1] Rara is when a group of people gets together and gives prayer and song to the spirits around Easter time.[2]

---

[1] Gonâve is a large island in the Gulf of Gonâve, about 40 miles northwest of Port-au-Prince.

[2] Rara is a form of festival music that originated in Haiti; it accompanies street processions, typically during Easter Week.

A Rara queen dances in the street and challenges other people to dance. My grandmother gave birth to my mother during one of these street processions. "Just get my baby out," she said, and everybody who was there helped her. The story goes they grabbed the baby and kept on dancing.

Then, when my mom—who my grandmother called Fofo—turned one year old, my grandmother got pregnant again, and she sent my mom to Léogâne[3] to be with her godmother. Léogâne is *the* Rara town in Haiti. There's always a lot of dancing and music. Nobody taught my mother how to dance. She became a dancer by herself. She saw her mother the Rara queen dancing in the streets with others and my mom danced along with them in the ceremonies. She didn't know the names for the rhythms or steps. She danced them naturally.

When my mom turned fifteen, she traveled to Port-au-Prince to Viviane Gauthier because she wanted to study and learn the names of the steps. Viviane Gauthier's school is one of the most renowned dance companies in Haiti. They do traditional Haitian dance. There were other schools, but they are gone. Most of the dancers emigrated to other countries in Duvalier's time, so we lost so much.

After two years, my mother became a teacher at the center and started to travel to dance internationally. She went to the Balé Nasyonal of Haiti and became a renowned dancer there, too.[4] When she was twenty-three, she had me.

Things were tough economically. My father was gone, and she had to quit school and find a job in order to put me through school and to give me everything that I needed. She wanted me to go to private school, and private school in Haiti is expensive. We had to

---

[3] Léogâne is a coastal commune directly across from La Gonâve in the Ouest Department. Léogâne is known for its Rara festival. It was also situated at the epicenter of the 2010 earthquake.

[4] The National Dance Theater Company of Haiti.

travel from town to town, from space to space, to find a cheaper house to stay because she had to cut costs. From the year I was born until my sixteenth birthday, we moved at least eight times.

As a child, I knew it was hard for my mom. If I wanted something, and she couldn't give it to me, that would hurt her. But the only thing I wanted was to be with her.

Each time I picture my mom performing, I see an amazing human being. On stage, she was so free. She was so happy. She could be dancing eight, nine, ten hours, and she always had this big smile on her face. I thought, *I want that happiness*. That is the way I started dancing. They tried to put me in the kids' company, but I wouldn't go. I learned with the adults' company. Viviane was a tough lady. She didn't permit any mistakes, and she would tell you to your face, "You're not good enough. Get out." So I would do the steps until exhaustion. I would do it over and over and over until Viviane would say, "You're good."

At five, I had my first big show at the National Theater in Haiti. Viviane asked my mother if I would be able to dance onstage, and my mom said, "I think so." They tested me, and I introduced the show. That's maybe where I get my confidence.

After that, dancing was the only thing I desired. I never desired candy or what other kids wanted. It was the only thing I asked my mom for. "Can I go onstage? Can I go with you? Can I dance more?" I always wanted to feel that moment again on stage.

It was a good and bad time. My mom was also an activist and really involved in politics. Besides dance, she did poltical theater. They had shows that criticized the government and told people about human rights and how things should be, and I was always with her. That was how I met a lot of activists in my early life. I missed school sometimes because we had to hide. The Tonton Makout were after us.[5]

---

[5] The *Makout* were a feared paramilitary group under the Duvalier regimes during

Often we went to Jacmel to hide.[6] Everybody went to the ocean to have a big bonfire and to sing and dance. I remember saying, "Well, we'll die tomorrow, so let's celebrate now." The activists' kids would play, listening to the conversations the adults had about how this country and its people should be and what we could do, even though we were beaten up a lot by the Tonton Makout. A lot of my mom's friends got killed. A lot of them were separated from their families, exiled.

I skipped school to be there, but Jacmel taught me something. From my mom's friends, I learned Haitian history. Most of the history books at school were written by Europeans. They weren't really the true stories of our home. The books said that we needed to celebrate Christopher Colombus, somebody who committed genocide, and we have to celebrate him?[7] Makes no sense. If not for my mom's friends, I would never be aware of the struggle we have gone through, the fact that we were colonized many times, and we had to pay for our freedom.

I became a secret girl. I never knew who the parents of other kids might be; they might be Tonton Makout. I had to learn to not tell my friends what my mom was doing or where we went when I missed school. It's a small country. Whatever you say could put someone else in danger.

The scariest part for me was when Baby Doc was leaving the country in 1986.[8] We were living in a small house in Port-au-Prince. The house wasn't well made, but it was a colorful one. My mom knew I loved color. Inside, she painted it pink and yellow and green, and she told me, "Here's your castle." I loved it. I remember

---

the second half of the twentieth century. For more on the Makout, see the Glossary, page 326.

[6] Jacmel is a city of 40,000 on Haiti's southern coast, approximately 40 miles south-west of Port-au-Prince.

[7] For more on Christopher Columbus and Haiti, see Appendix I, page 293.

[8] For more on "Baby Doc" Duvalier and his exile, see Appendix I, page 293.

it was not even the size of an average bathroom, but we were actually happy with what we could afford.

But one day, my mom grabbed me and threw me to the floor. She lay on top of me and put the mattress on top of her. There was shooting all night long. I couldn't sleep. All I heard was shooting and felt the weight of my mom on top of me, shaking, and me shaking on my own. It was the longest night of my life. When we woke up the next day, there were bullet holes all over the walls. Since our house was so close to the street, it was hit by many bullets. We moved after that night. Then we moved to another house, then another one. From then on, I was never able to sleep through the night. Never.

WE BUILT A HOUSE AND WE BUILT A STAGE

We saved up to buy land in Thomassin.[9] We built a house and we built a stage. It wasn't a fancy stage. Basic. Some people came and said, "Oh, you need a light." They brought lights and put them on the stage. "Oh, Fofo, you need curtains!" They brought curtains. It's nice to see people collaborate. For a while, we didn't buy food because the neighborhood was bringing tomatoes or carrots or milk, everything.

On Sundays, we would have a big performance. Everybody in the neighborhood would bring their chairs, and all the kids performed for their parents. People would dance, have fun, and talk. We would teach the young people how to dance, sing, and drum.

We were happy in Thomassin. I always woke up with a big smile on my face. My brother ran wild in the neighborhood. We had our own garden of corn in the front of the house. We also had teas and different herbs. I remember every night we used to get our corn and have a bonfire in front of the house. To everybody who was passing, we would say, "Come!" We would have some rum going around. That's it. No electricity. But you can see the stars. They were so bright. You

---

[9] Thomassin is a neighborhood of Pétionville in the mountains south of Port-au-Prince.

felt that you could touch them. And when it was a full moon, it was like heaven. There's nowhere else you'd want to be. Ahh, Thomassin. But you can't be at two places at the same time. Now, I'm here. I have to embrace it.

I HEARD THAT CUBA WAS GIVING AWAY SCHOLARSHIPS TO HAITIANS

I heard that Cuba was giving away twenty scholarships per year for Haitians who wanted to go to college. I applied, passed the test to get in, and got the opportunity to go. I studied physical education and sports, not something I really wanted to do, but it was available and all that we could afford. I'm very glad I went, because I met a beautiful community there—people with big hearts, people who know what community means and are not thinking about profit or anything material.

In Cuba, I met my son's father, Javier, who is from Venezuela. I got pregnant. I asked for a year off of school and went back to Haiti to have my baby. I was twenty-five years old. His name is Hassen. It means "good thing" in Arabic.

Javier and I married in Haiti, and then flew to Venezuela to start living. Things just weren't right. He wasn't the right person. But we have a beautiful son. We're all meant to make mistakes. If something doesn't work, that doesn't make us a bad person, so I got on an airplane and went back to Haiti. I left Hassen with my mom in Thomassin so I could start school again in Cuba. By that time, Aristide had left Haiti for the first time, and the country was in trouble.[10] There was a lot of anger, kidnapping, shooting. No food. Everybody was afraid. It was a civil war in Haiti. In December, I went back to Haiti and

---

[10] Jean-Bertrand Aristide was elected president of Haiti in 1990 and removed by coup in 1991. He returned to the presidency in 1994–95 and then was again elected in 2000. For more on Aristide, see Appendix I, page 293.

took my son with me to Cuba. The director of the university said, "I'm sorry, but you cannot have a baby with you on the campus." That hurt my heart. I was like, "I want to study." The university said, "Well, we understand, but you can't stay in the country as a student with a baby." One of my friends said, "Write to Fidel." And I did.

A couple weeks later, I received a letter that they would give me a place to stay with the baby to finish my studies. They gave me two tutors and a lab with a computer. I had a place to stay close to the school, and the bus would pick me up. The community took care of my son. Every day, people fought about who was going to take care of him. They fed him, gave him a shower, and played with him until I got back. When I finished my thesis and graduated, I went back to Haiti and thought, *That was the most amazing experience.* My time in Cuba has stayed with me.

PEOPLE COULDN'T FIND WORK

I started working in Port-au-Prince teaching Haitian dance. There was less work for the citizens, but there was work for foreigners. They had big cars, big houses, big money. The local people who were called "uneducated" couldn't work. They had no house and no food, and things were very difficult. People couldn't find work even if they were qualified, so many organized together in the ghetto to kidnap, abuse, or rob people in order to be able to live. If you were a young person doing well, you were the first target to be abused, robbed, or kidnapped in order for those people to be able to feed their families.

My mom said, "Move in with me. It's not safe. You're at your house with a child. You're not safe by yourself." So I moved back with my mom, and two or three weeks after, a couple of people kidnapped a Canadian woman who was living a block from our house. A lot of people were disappearing. The gangs were sending young kids to ask for information about people living in our neighborhood. You're not scared if you see kids in the neighborhood. You might invite those kids to your house and give them a plate of food, but there were a lot of kids asking and looking—who has a healthy life, who has cars, who is working, who is traveling a lot? Some people in our neighborhood advised us to be very careful. We always struggled to put things together, but we were moving forward. I was able to work and provide more, and my mom, too.

There was real violence. Some people in the neighborhood struggling for food came and stole my pig, but that wasn't related to gang stuff. They were just trying to live. One time, I got out of work and people were throwing rocks at my car and into the street because there was something going on in the country. I couldn't get out for a few hours, and my son was in school. I was in Pétionville, and my son was in La Boule.[11] Luckily, the director of the school kept him until 7 p.m. that night.

I couldn't do it anymore. I thought someone would try to kidnap Hassen. What would I do if somebody came and took my son? Would I be able to kill that person? I'm not a violent person, but I need to defend my son. That fear was inside me. I talked with my mom, and she said, "Well, you have a visa. Go and stay in the U.S. for a couple years." I'm like, "Okay. I don't see myself killing anybody. I better go."

I knew people in San Francisco, California. When I came the first time in 2008 to teach and dance, I had a lot of friends. Everybody in the dance community wanted to meet me. But as soon as they knew that I came with my son to stay for good, many of the friendships weren't the same. People weren't willing to help or understand my situation. I met people in the city who said they had Haitian roots and were always talking about Haiti, about doing things for Haiti, Haiti this and Haiti that. They put the flag out. They wore the flag all over their bodies. They even changed their names to say they had

---

[11] Pétionville is a wealthy, historic suburb of Port-au-Prince built into the hillside south of the city center. La Boule is southwest of Pétionville.

relatives in Haiti. They felt they were more Haitian than I am! But I was here struggling, and there were people who didn't even answer my phone calls. One Haitian woman with a child, and there were people who wouldn't even give her a hand. That was very hurtful.

Everywhere I went, they wouldn't give me a job, because I had no work visa. I was teaching anytime anyone would let me. I was doing Vodou blessings of buildings. I was doing cleaning, any job just to survive.

I began staying with Hassen with different friends who would open their house to us. I didn't have a car. I was living day-by-day. I had to walk miles. Because I couldn't leave my son to find work, I had to carry him on my back. Sometimes he was so tired. He would cry on the street, "Mom, I can't anymore. I'm hungry." I had nothing to give him.

People that were there for me were students who barely could afford to pay for a class. Sometimes my students came with a bag of groceries to give to me, or they would pick up Hassen and take him somewhere.

I found a lady, a good friend, who was opening a dance studio in the Mission neighborhood, and she said, "Do you want to teach there?" I said, "Yes, I'd like to, but I have no papers." But she said okay. The way we did it, she got a percentage of cash from whoever came to the class. That's the way I started to have income. I built a dance company with the people who were really there for me.

I rented a room in San Francisco. It was a garage that they had turned into a room with a bathroom. But I loved it. The couple that was living there had two kids. One son was the same age as my son, and the husband was born the same day as me. Those people! It was supposed to be a relationship where I paid rent, and that's it. They were feeding my son and me. All the time. They said, "Don't buy anything. Eat as much as you want." When I had a late-night gig, they kept Hassen. They gave him a bath and put him in the same bed as their son, like he was part of the family.

I'm so grateful for that couple. I left their house when I didn't have enough students to be able to pay them rent. I told them, "I don't want to stay here anymore. Someone offered me a place to stay." They said, "Why?" I didn't give them more details. They treated me so good, and I knew they needed money, too. They struggled, but in their struggle, they had a space in their hearts to help another family.

My experience in the United States has been strange. The people I thought would be willing to help were not the people I expected. The people I met randomly on the street became my family.

I THOUGHT MY WHOLE WORLD WAS DESTROYED

Hassen and I moved in with a student in December 2009. It was on Church Street by the trains. I was struggling so much I was thinking about moving back to Haiti. Then the earthquake happened. I had just come out of a dance class. My friend called me and said, "Djenane, are you home? Something just happened in Haiti." I said to my friend on the phone, "Now you have me scared. What's going on?" She said, "Go. Turn on the TV."

I saw the earthquake. I thought my whole world was destroyed. I just sat down and started crying. Then, I'm like, *No. I cannot cry. I don't know. I need to know first.* I called my mom. She said, "Hi! Hi!" I said, "Are you okay?" "Yes." That's it. The phone cut out. There was no more communication with Haiti.

I called a friend in the Dominican Republic who studied with me in Cuba. I said, "This is my mom's phone number. This is all her information. Please do your best. Bring her there. Keep her with you." My friend called her mom, a very smart lady who was living at the border of the Dominican Republic. I never saw someone so resourceful. She somehow got in touch with my mom and told her if she got to the border she would get her across. But all the streets were destroyed. People were suffering. My mom and my brother Jeff didn't want to leave people like that.

Because of the aftershocks, my mom and my brother were sleeping outside the house. Nobody was sleeping inside. Everybody was on the street in tents. My mom, all the children who used to dance for her, and their parents were under the tents until there was no more money and no more food, nothing to eat.

So they left. A police guy gave my mom and my brother a ride to the border. My friend's mother fed them and called me. That's when I finally spoke to my mom. I said, "I'm gonna find the money to bring you and Jeff here." My mom said, "Okay, but I'm not going to stay."

The student I was living with called the rest of my student community. People that I don't even know sent money and clothes, and the student who helped me find the dance studio asked her parents if they would pay for my mom and brother's plane tickets to come to the United States. They sent money for both of them to come and didn't ask for anything in return. That's how I brought my mom and brother to the United States.

But my mom never wanted to stay here. She mostly stayed for my son because I was working all the time, and she said, "He needs love. He needs stability." We were all living on Church Street by the trains. Each time the train went back and forth, the house shook, and my mom and brother thought it was an earthquake again. They knew it was the train, but they were very traumatized by the earthquake. They couldn't sleep.

By that time, the U.S. government offered T.P.S., temporary protected status.[12] It is a status that the United States gave to all Haitians living in the U.S. a year before or after the earthquake.

---

[12] Temporary Protected Status (T.P.S.) is a form of residency in the U.S. granted to citizens of other countries who have fled certain natural disasters and other crises. For more information, see the Glossary, page 309.

You have to pay for your T.P.S. I had four people: my mom, brother, son, and myself. It was around $400 for each person. My mom wasn't working. I was working under the table, doing whatever I could—a gig at the park, dancing at a party to entertain guests, taking care of kids, watching an elderly person, cleaning a restaurant—all for cash money. I had no day, no night. I never had a schedule. Whenever some work came, I went. "I heard somebody needs their house cleaned, can you?" "Yes." "I liked what you did at that party. Can you?" "Yes!" Finally, we applied for T.P.S., and we got it.

We thought the protected status covered a lot of things, but it only gives you the possibility of working in the United States. You don't have insurance or help to pay your rent or for food. They don't even offer you a range of work opportunities. You need to find your own work and pay taxes. Besides that, you pay a higher rate of taxes than anybody else in the country. I thought I could go to school. I applied to graduate school and got accepted, but then I found out that I had to pay with my own money because you are not eligible for scholarship or financial aid under T.P.S.

I got my first apartment ever in the U.S. Every day, we found things on the street. My mom and I would carry chairs or mattresses on our heads, or people brought us furniture. Finally, the whole house was full of things, and we didn't pay for any of it. That was our first start in America. We were legal and able to work.

I'M NOT A CITY PERSON, EVEN THOUGH I GREW UP IN THE CITY

I ended up in Marin County because the rent is cheaper. Also, I love trees and water. I'm not a city person, even though I grew up in the city. I like to stay close to nature.

My mother and I teach dance and music and drumming together. We go to different public and private schools in San Rafael, Petaluma, San Francisco, and Oakland. She still doesn't want to stay.

When she got T.P.S., she still couldn't work because she didn't know enough English. Wherever she applied, they said, "No, you don't speak English. We don't want you," or "You're not that young." She felt frustrated as a woman who had been working all her life and never depended on anybody.

One day, one of the children we teach came up to me and said, "Djenane, my father said that Haiti's the poorest country in the world." I said, "Yes. Your father is right. Haiti is the poorest country in the world." He looked at me. I felt like he was going into his emotions, you know, thinking. "But what do you think?" I said.

And he said, "I really love that song your mom teaches. I like the drumming. I learned that Haiti fought the best army in France. I think Haiti's a rich country that has a lot of culture. I love Haiti."

I said to myself, *The kid gets it.* His father is the most important person in his life. He listened to his father. But he has his own opinion after the work we did together. He's questioning now, and not only saying, "Haiti's a poor country." Haiti is a poor country. I cannot lie about that, but what else? He had the answer for me. I just listened.

For many years, all over the world, they have been feeding ideas about Haiti, that the Vodou is bad, that the people are bad. Even Haitians tell their children to not associate themselves with Haiti. Haitian people are scared of their own culture. The brainwashing tells you that your culture is no longer good. That's the same thing as telling you that your color is no longer good, the shape of your face, your hair.

That is why wherever we go, we teach dance and music. That is what we must do as part of our journey in the world. Wherever Djenane and Fofo go, we are supposed to give back and transmit that culture to others.

Now I'm moving to Minnesota. I think I offered California what I had to offer it. Now it is my time to go to Minnesota. And when it's time for me to go somewhere else, I will go. Maybe from there, I'll go back to Haiti or to Africa, who knows. For me, as I was telling you, the most important thing is to live life fully and to be able to build something completely. Not halfway. Not just an inch. Maybe I'm too ambitious, but I want to be able to develop myself and give as much as I can until I cannot anymore.

It's like this game in Haiti where you sing and pass this seed from one palm to another in a circle. You're sitting down and looking everybody in their eyes, which can be very intimidating, but you are building something together. The song goes, *Bag la soti nan men manmanin/Men li rive nan men papa'l.* It's like, "The seed or the rings came from mother and go to father and make it go around and around." Between mother and father there is a whole generation. The meaning is that you're going between generations as you pass the seed. It's an exchange. You get to be you, and I get to be me, but at the same time, we're part of the circle. When you pass the seed, sometimes it isn't so smooth, but that's life. Nobody came with a book that told us exactly who we were. We're on that journey to discover who we are and to be a part of the world. But at the same time, we have to be aware of the person next to us and make as much good as we can. It's hard trying to be the best human being you can. Everybody makes their mistakes. That's life. Being human.

Maybe me coming from Haiti, going to Cuba, Venezuela, and now here, maybe there's meaning behind it. Maybe right now people don't understand, but in a few years, the next generation might be powerful enough to understand and take action and be proud to say, "I'm from Haiti," or "Haiti is a poor country, but what else?" Who knows, huh?

PATRICE FLORVILUS

37, attorney

We first met with Patrice in his busy law office in downtown Port-au-Prince on Rue Lamartiniere. Across the street looms the large statue of Jean-Jacques Dessalines—one of the pivotal and controversial heroes of the Haitian Revolution—on a rearing stallion. Patrice's time was tightly scheduled. Still, in our brief conversation, Patrice covered a considerable amount of ground. A passionate believer in defending human rights, Patrice told us of his work representing the poor, the violent political climate in Haiti since the time of his birth, and the prospects his country faces since the earthquake.

We were fortunate enough to speak with Patrice again in 2015 after he and his family, for safety reasons, had fled Port-au-Prince for Montreal. In Canada, Patrice was happy he was able to raise his growing family in safety but also despondent to be so far removed from his calling as a lawyer and defender of the oppressed. Patrice has found work in a factory in Montreal in order to help support his wife and children. For the second interview, lacking a Kreyol or French translator, we spoke in Spanish, a language Patrice speaks fluently.

I have a peasant background. I was born in a village called La Réserve on March 17, 1978. The village is close to the town of Jean-Rabel.[1] My mother used to buy and sell things. She was also a farmer with my father. I was the third child in a family of seven. We would go with our parents to work the farm, where we'd plant corn and rice.

When I was born, there was a school in our village, but it only offered a few grades. I spent two years in primary school in La Réserve, and then I went to Jean-Rabel to finish primary school. During the summer, I returned to the village, and that's when the massacre occurred. It was July 23, 1987. You can read about it. People were killed all over the area. On that day, the bourgeoisie, the elite, and the peasants that worked for them killed many peasants and children of peasants.

My uncle lived on one side of the village, and my grandmother and father lived on the other side. As the massacre began, children whose parents were part of the peasant movement tried to find a place to hide. I was leaving my uncle's house to go to my father's house when I saw the mob coming. I ran, but they caught me. They said I was the son of my uncle, who was the local chief of the peasant movement. They tied me up because they thought that I was my cousin—Frederic Joseph. That's when they lined us up. There were eleven of us children. They cut the heads off of ten of us. I was the only one they didn't cut. My father's friend was among the people that were cutting off heads. Yes, my father's friend was a criminal. A group of peasants were hired to kill another group of peasants, and he was one of them. But he didn't kill me. I was spared. I was a child. We were all children.

After that, my family went into hiding. We stayed in a big cave in the mountains for about seven days, because we feared that

---

[1] Jean-Rabel is a town of more than 100,000 in the Nord-Ouest Department, about 150 miles north of Port-au-Prince.

the murderers might come back to the village. My uncle and my cousin dressed like women and ran away to Port-au-Prince. After the seven days, my family and I snuck down the mountain. Even then, there was still blood in the river. Nicol Poitevien, one of the men who claimed responsibility, said that they killed 1,042 communists during the Jean-Rabel massacre.[2]

To this day no one is in prison as a result of what happened. I've grown up with these memories. Why did they want to kill the children of the peasants? Why wasn't there any system of justice to protect the people?

WAS IT WORTH IT TO COME HERE EVERY YEAR AND CRY?

We didn't leave Jean-Rabel only because of the massacre. We left because there weren't good schools in the area. My mother was illiterate. She didn't know how to read or write. But even after the massacre, even though she was illiterate, she still wanted her children to make it to school. So we moved to the Artibonite Valley, to Gonaïves.[3]

When I was fourteen, I remember going to a death celebration party.[4] When I got to the graveyard, I came across some priests who had come to the graveyard to remember the children who were murdered during the dictatorship. I started to speak, saying that we were

---

[2] Outside of Jean-Rabel, paramilitary groups acting upon orders from a local land oligarch, Rémy Lucas, killed at least 139 peasants (300 according to various human rights groups and the OAS, and 1,042 according to Nicol Poitevien, one of the self-proclaimed killers).

[3] Gonaïves is a city of more than 300,000 about 45 miles southeast of Jean-Rabel and 90 miles north of Port-au-Prince. It is the capital of Artibonite, the largest of Haiti's ten departmental divisions.

[4] The Day of the Dead in Haiti is observed through Vodou ceremonies as well as part of Christian holidays (All Souls' Day) on November 1 and November 2. Rituals tend to focus on, and honor, the spirits of the dead and those spirits (or *loas* in Vodou) that function as gatekeepers to the afterlife.

here to remember our friends and family, but we haven't had any justice yet. Was it worth it to come here every year to cry? Or should we stand up and fight for justice? People started to yell, "Justice! Justice!" That's when we began marching in the streets and calling for a strike.

After that, I realized that there were other young people in Gonaïves that cared about the same issues. We were young but engaged, and we got together to try and solve problems in the neighborhoods. If there was no electricity, we looked for ways to pressure the government to get it back. We would go out to the countryside and work in the grassroots movements. I'd show the peasants how to read and write. We decided that the peasants needed to know how to read and write in order to better understand their reality and then to act to transform that reality. We held classes for children who didn't get the chance to finish school.

We also decided to build a community radio station to spread our movement. We called it Radio Salt, because salt is a key ingredient in cooking. In order to prepare the good food of transformation and liberation, there needs to be salt.

For a couple of years during high school, I worked with a pastor doing social work. He'd noticed me studying in the streets. I had to be outside to study, because we didn't have electricity in the house and had to go out in search of a lighted place to read at night. At eighteen, I finished high school. I was wondering, *Should I go to the law school in Gonaïves or go to Port-au-Prince?* While I was trying to decide, this pastor invited me to work in a hospital in Port-au-Prince.

I remember driving into Port au Prince from the north and it was night, and from a distance it was, wow, all these lights, with the lights of the rich people. But as we drove into the city, I could see how people had to sleep on the ground in their huts and saw that it was like other places in Haiti.

So without any background in administration, I was given a job as a hospital administrator. I didn't last very long at the hospital, because I understood that wasn't where I was supposed to be. They were just making money off the people who they were supposed to be providing care to. Too many people were dying. There weren't enough qualified staff working there.

I decided to go into teaching, and received a post at a primary school in Cité Soleil.[5] They paid 12.5 gouds an hour.[6] I taught at a recently opened public high school too, though I wasn't getting paid there. And finally, I became the director of youth in a Seventh-day Adventist Church, which also wasn't a paying job.

I had many housing problems in Cité Soleil. I moved to four different houses in one year. In all these houses, when they realized that I didn't have money to pay, they kicked me out. But then I had a friend in Cité Soleil who allowed me to stay at his mother's place in the housing projects. While I was living in that place, I continued to go to the university and study, and I eventually became a lawyer. My mother died the same year I graduated. Just a few months before, I received my law diploma.

TODAY, THAT GIRL IS MY WIFE

Now this is the part of my history that is very important, because in that house in Cité Soleil, there was an old lady who didn't even have a cooking pot. She used a small can to boil the food for us to eat. She had grandchildren who lived with her as well. When I didn't have money to go to school, they would give me some money, some small amount of money. A little girl, someone else's child, used to live in the house too. The girl used to wash clothes and iron for me. I began to understand that she loved me, but she was too little. I decided that

---

[5] Cité Soleil is a large, densely populated unplanned neighborhood of more than 400,000 in northwest Port-au-Prince.

[6] At roughly the time Patrice was teaching, 12.5 gouds equals approximately US 75 cents.

I didn't want to lose the trust that the family had put in me, so I left the house. I went to Delmas, to a group of friends from Jean-Rabel who had a house.[7]

Today, that girl is my wife, Guilaine Augustin. We married in 2006. She was nineteen, and I was twenty-seven. When we got married, she became pregnant and couldn't go to school. After she had the baby, I encouraged her to go back to school. She studied communication and administration and graduated university with a degree in administration.

GIVING THEM A FAIR PLACE TO TEACH

I studied and taught. Even as a lawyer, I still wanted to teach. So I studied in the Human Sciences and Social Services programs at the State University of Haiti and began working in a center for research in social economic development. During this time I took a position as the director of the Department of Environment for the Ministry of Environment in the Artibonite Valley. As part of my job I attempted to organize local committees on the environment and health like I had done in Gonaïves earlier. But there was corruption I couldn't change. And so I left that post after only six months.

After this bad experience in government, I began working for a private organization that promotes the right to education. I thought that there was a place for me in that area, fighting for the right to education—not only in Haiti but also throughout the world. Eighteen countries were a part of the network. Because of the work I was doing in that network, I went to Bamako, in Mali, for three months, to study education. When I came back from Africa, I was so inspired I started thinking of founding a school for human rights in Haiti.

---

[7] Delmas is a large residential and commercial suburb in the northeast of Port-au-Prince, adjacent to the city's airport. Individual neighborhoods in Delmas are referred to by number, since the suburb is organized around numbered streets that radiate out from a central road (for instance, Delmas 45, Delmas 18, et cetera).

And that's when January 12 happened, and everything changed, including the direction my life would take. I became an advocate for the displaced. I began working with Mario Joseph and the B.A.I.[8] I asked if I could work with the people in the tent cities because most of the lawyers didn't want to work in the tent cities. I was helping the displaced in partnership with other organizations. I started a committee against expulsions. You see, when the initial shock of the earthquake was over, many entities—the government, private landowners, et cetera—began trying to push poor people out of the tent cities created in the aftermath. For instance, on the square at the Airport Road, the mayor of Delmas came with police and took people's tents and then threw them away.[9]

After my wife finished school, the two of us decided to follow my dream and create our own human rights organization. We founded the Defense of the Oppressed[10] with the mission of providing lawyers to defend the poor and illiterate in the tent cities suffering displacement as a result of January 12. We looked all over Haiti to find other lawyers to embrace this cause. The fact is that we didn't find many. There's Mario Joseph, of course, and the B.A.I. But where are all the other lawyers?

Here's the situation: Lawyers are on the side of those with money. If you don't have money, you don't find justice. The people who have money can buy the judges. They can buy the public attorneys. They can buy the police. We work with a team of activists and lawyers who believe that they should be on the side of those that are suffering, not the people with money.

---

[8] Mario Joseph is a human rights attorney and director of the B.A.I. (*Bureau des Avocats Internationaux*), a public interest legal and human rights organization in downtown Port-au-Prince. For more on the B.A.I., see Mina's narrative, page 115.

[9] For more on tent cities after the 2010 earthquake, see *Bidonvilles* in the Glossary, page 309.

[10] D.O.P.; in French: *Defenseurs des Oprimées/Oprimés*.

So we made do without enough lawyers. Our program began training people living in the tent cities directly. We taught them about the rights of the land, the right to adequate housing. We call these people "popular jurists." Popular jurists walk directly into these tent cities. When the lawyers are not there, they will start working. These jurists gather all the evidence and pass it on to attorneys who use the information to file cases. In this way we work together to prevent the authorities from kicking people out before giving them a fair place to live.

Our network is pressing the government to provide a decent program of housing for the people. We try to be there for them when the justice system is not fair, when the owner of the lands come to push them away, when they don't have anywhere else to go.

I WANT TO TAKE YOU BACK IN TIME, BACK TO THE MASSACRE

So I want to take you back in time, back to the massacre at Jean-Rabel. They arrested some of the murderers in the first Aristide administration, but when the coup came, they all got released.[11]

A few years back, I went to one of the massacre planners' store. No one recognized me because I had left the area when I was a child. I wanted to see how he was living. I bought something just so I could see him face to face. He was living free and comfortable. I felt so frustrated. This was a government that came from the working class, but unfortunately Aristide didn't bring justice to the victims of Jean-Rabel. When I visited, everything that happened on June 23, 1987—all the murders—came back into my head. The reality I found is they continue to dominate.

---

[11] Here Patrice is likely referring to the coup which overthrew leftist president Jean-Bertrand Aristide in 1991. For more on Aristide and the coup, see Appendix I, page 293.

Back then it was all about the communists.[12] The elite said that the peasants wanted to kill people and take their property. Today the language is still about class. Even if the bourgeois no longer specifically use the word communist, peasants are still frequently accused of wanting to take everything for themselves.

Other people in Jean-Rabel, however, haven't forgotten what happened there. I found that a number of people were still seeking education and a better life for peasants. So with D.O.P., we opened a free workshop and encouraged the students to sign up so they might help peasants who were victims of the massacre at Jean-Rabel. As you might imagine, memories of my own experience have been recovered as a result of this work. Our intent is to raise the level of awareness. People need to understand that they have a right to justice.

There are signs of hope. Frederic Joseph, the boy I was mistaken for in the massacre, is alive and well and currently a justice of the peace. He is a judge and I'm a lawyer! One day we hope to judge the criminals responsible for the massacre in our home place.

THERE WAS A CRIMINAL CASE

Not too long ago, a man that I was representing died in the hands of police officers. He was killed for defending his right to live on land, which was close to the police station in Delmas 33. I filed a case against the police. At that time I happened to be friends with the Delmas chief of police. He asked me to enter into negotiations with him. But this was a criminal case. I told him, we must continue the legal process. So I took the case before the judge, who was also my friend. In Port-au-Prince, everybody in the law knows everybody else in the law. The judge didn't understand my reply.

---

[12] Expression of communist sympathy or possession of communist literature was a crime in Haiti punishable by death under the Duvalier regime, beginning with the passage of explicit legal restrictions in 1969. For more on the Duvalier regime, see Appendix I, page 293.

He wanted me to continue trying to negotiate a settlement with the police.

So I sued the judge. I took the case before a special commission which addresses judges' discipline in the country. Then a friend of his called me and asked, "Why did you do that?" He said, "You know the judge and the judge knows you." I said, "Because he knows me, he should not have requested negotiation. He should have known that I wouldn't accept it." I was starting to feel the pressure from the authorities to back off, to not fight so hard on behalf of my clients. I was gaining a reputation, becoming known as an attorney who wouldn't back down.

Then a customer at my wife's restaurant[13] was murdered one step out of the entrance. The man looked like me, almost the same height. I used to go to my wife's restaurant every night after I left the office and have some beers. The murder happened at the same time as I normally came in. I had to ask myself, was that a message to me or not? Soon after that, I decided to move to another neighborhood. And so we moved houses and sold the restaurant. That was hard. The restaurant was in Santo near a busy street. We had many customers. It was a big part of our family income. My wife wanted to find another place to start up a new business. Without a business it would be very difficult to live because I didn't make a lot of money at my job. We moved to Delmas, but we didn't have any money to rent a house. An American association supportive of our work, the American Jewish World Service, helped us find another home.[14] A.J.W.S. wanted me and my family to be as safe as possible. They provided us with protection. My son could never go to school on his own, so we had someone with us all the time.

---

[13] To make ends meet, Patrice's wife, Guilaine, started a restaurant in the suburb of Santo, northeast of Port-au-Prince.

[14] American Jewish World Service provides humanitarian relief in countries across the globe.

Then one day I was in the office and I saw a lot of cars, around ten of them, out front. That was shocking. They were from the MINUS-TAH.[15] My guard went to ask why they were there. They didn't want to explain. When I called someone from MINUSTAH, he told me not to worry. He told me that they heard on the news that I was at risk so they wanted to support the police in protecting me. I thanked him for his support but said he must move the men.

My wife was the most afraid. She never wanted me to go with a bodyguard because she thought that would decrease my safety. She said, if somebody is always accompanied by a bodyguard in Haiti, it means he has a lot of money. And everybody knows that even accompanied by a guard, they can still easily kill you if they wish. This was not a way to live, to have someone with you at all times, when you go to court, go home, or wherever. To be honest, I felt like I was in jail. I'm not a president, like Obama! When I went to court, there was always somebody standing at the door, for security.

To make matters worse, my wife was pregnant, and her pregnancy was very complicated during the last months. Her doctor was concerned about her level of stress. Then I received threats from the police. A police car started following me when I left the office or my house. It was like being hunted all the time. The last thing I wanted to do was leave my work, but for the sake of my family I arranged for us to take temporary refuge in Canada.

---

[15] The United Nations Stabilization Mission in Haiti (MINUSTAH) was initially authorized following the 2004 coup d'état as peacekeeping forces brought in to stabilize the political situation and protect human rights and the rule of law after Aristide's ouster. They were given greater mandate following the 2010 earthquake to support reconstruction and stability efforts. For more on MINUSTAH, see the Glossary, page 309.

HOW COULD I STAND THERE
AND JUST KEEP TALKING?

When we arrived in Montreal I planned to return to Haiti in three months, but we had a new baby eleven days after our arrival. Leaving my wife alone with the child would have been irresponsible. We had nobody around like family; no mother, no father, no brother, no sister. So I decided to stay in Canada longer. I also started to study international law at the Université de Montréal.

We had to find a house fast, because we were living in a friend's house and we didn't have enough space. In addition to my schooling, I knew I had to find any work whatsoever to support the family. I found a job thanks to a friend's advice. I got the minimum wage, which is like $10 an hour. Taking that was so hard because I wasn't going to be working as a lawyer. But I had no choice. Within two months, we had already accumulated a very large debt. Our first electricity bill that winter in Canada was enormous! The landlord didn't put insulation in the house, and we didn't know better because it was the first time we were in a country with such a harsh winter.

I currently work in a factory that builds machines. I have an extra workload every day, but I earn a lower wage than other workers. I believe I have the lowest wage in the factory. The others make $20 an hour or even $18. I make $14. I'm also the only black man there. I think it's a matter of discrimination. I work at the management level now, but I still don't get a fair wage. I often miss Haiti because this experience is so denigrating.

To take part in the labor market here, my wife studied to be a hairstylist. When we first arrived, she had to choose between college and technical school. She looked for a job for a long time, and then she finally found one in a large hairstyling company where she's working now. She's also working for the minimum wage because, at the moment, she's a hairdresser's assistant.

From here, my wife and I try to keep D.O.P. going, but it's not the same. I speak with colleagues regularly about our caseload and we meet on the phone to discuss strategy. But, as time has moved on the contact has become more distant. It's difficult to be part of the organization when I'm so far away and working a factory job.

In May 2014, I went back to Haiti. As part of that trip, I returned to Cité Soleil for the celebration of a D.O.P. project there. Cité Soleil is where I had lived and worked, and of course it's where I got to know my wife. Going back there was one of the most emotional moments in my life. On the other hand, I felt very frustrated because things are so bad there now people only want food to eat. Food. The most basic human right. There I was talking about other human rights, when in reality there are many children who just need money to buy some food. People needed to eat. How could I stand there and just keep talking?

And then I had to go back to my family in Canada. It's hard. It's hard because many people in Haiti don't understand. They say, "Why don't you come back? Yes, there are threats, danger, but this is your work, this is *Haiti*." You know, in leftist activist circles in Haiti, responsibility toward family hasn't always been a top priority. Many great people, great fighters, haven't been there for their kids. And this is so difficult for me. It feels like I have to choose between my wife and family and my work. But with two young children in a new country, I knew that my wife and I needed to be together. At first, with a newborn, she couldn't work. Now she works. So in the morning I have to rush to drop the kids off at day care and pick them up at the end of my shift. I'm also studying to get an international law degree. I've had to start everything from scratch here.

I listen to the radio or TV and keep up with what's going on in Haiti. I also hear about the many problems at the D.O.P. office—many problems that I cannot fix because I'm not there. Funders know that I'm not in the country. They don't say that they won't support us; they say, you're in Canada and it is not the same. For example, some international organizations were in charge of paying rent for our office. Now they say they can't pay, and the deadline is right around the corner. As for myself, I don't have a single penny. The strange thing is that if I were in Haiti it would be easier to get the money together. Sometimes, here, I feel like I'm already dead.

Every year, so many intellectuals leave Haiti—but they could be so useful to our country. If I had no family, I'd be in Haiti at this moment. I am involved with other victims of Jean Rabel and groups allied with D.O.P. We are trying to get the prosecutor to again bring cases against the killers of Jean Rabel. When I finish my education, our plan is that I'll go to Haiti for some months, stay there, and travel back here to be with my family. But we need a lot of money to achieve that. And I'll have a foot in Haiti and another foot here. My wife doesn't want to go back so quickly. She doesn't trust any of the changes in politics. When I got to Montreal I wanted to establish a new D.O.P. office here so that I could keep working on human rights. But it's not been possible, at least not yet. Being out of Haiti, I sometimes feel like someone who is just watching.

TAYLOR MERCITA

26, mother

Taylor Mercita, the mother of a three-year-old, recently lost her job. Taylor lives with her mother and depends on her support. She wants to learn how to drive heavy trucks and bulldozers in order to save money to go back to school.

Four months ago, I was with my boyfriend. We went to the beach and spent about three hours. We made good love, we swam. That's my best moment of the year so far. He told me he loved me but I haven't been so lucky with relationships.

Sometimes people tell you they love you but they really don't. I'm talking about the father of my child. He was an accountant. One day he lost his job and he couldn't find another one. I didn't want to commit myself to a person who couldn't guarantee me a better life. I saw that our life wasn't going to be all right. It's both our fault that we're not together anymore. We're still friends. He always takes care of our child and we talk on the phone. Our son, he's three years old. His name is Bercame Falaise.

I regret that I had a child before finishing school. I've only reached junior year of high school. If I'd finished high school, I would have been a civil engineer. I don't think it's too late to continue school to make my dream come true. I used to get seven out of ten on every test. I was very smart.

For now, I can't say anything about if I'll get married again or if I'll be back together with my son's father. You never know in life the people you will meet.

If I can settle now, I will. That's something that I am looking for right now. I would date someone just because he helps me. If a man is willing to help me, I'll open my heart to him because that means the person loves me. I don't like to date people just for their money. Men don't have to support me, because I always find jobs to take care of myself. I know there are some bad people out there and I've already told you I'm not lucky in love. How do I know when a man loves a woman? I don't know. One day I'd like to know.

NADEGE PIERRE

38, mother

Driving north on Route Nationale #1 out of Port-au-Prince, the land is dry, covered in dust and thorn bushes with mountains rising quickly to the east and Port-au-Prince bay lying to the west. The once-barren hillsides are now dotted with tens of thousands of tents, mostly fading shades of gray and blue, and an increasing number of cement-block buildings. This desolate stretch— which has been the city's trash dump for decades—is called Titanyen. During the Duvalier dictatorship, many of the regime's victims were buried here. After the earthquake, Titanyen became the site of the nation's largest concentration of mass graves. The number of dead laid to rest here reaches into the tens of thousands.

In January 2013, a few hundred yards up the road from the graves, we spoke with some of the displaced families who now call Titanyen home, including Nadege Pierre and some of her family. We sat on their single shared mattress on the plastic tarp floor of their tarpaulin tent to talk.

I have nothing. This is what made me choose this place. If I had something, I would not have chosen this place. We had this little tent and bought some wood and put the tent on it. No one helped with the house. No organizations. Some *blan*—foreigners—came last month and they offered medical checkups but they didn't really offer anything.

The house we were in was destroyed. We lived in Cité Soleil.[1] The house fell down on January 12, 2010 in the disaster. After that we lived near the post office on the Plaza.[2] At the refugee camp on the Plaza, there were some organizations that took our names but they didn't do anything. Where we were was very crowded. Everyone was in the same situation. Their houses were all broken. We all built tents to live in. Then the burning started.[3] It was always at night. Only God knows who was burning our homes. Jesus knows.

Everything of ours was burnt down, so we came here. This was in January 2012, almost two years after the earthquake. No one helped me find this place in Titanyen. I looked and looked. I don't know anyone here. I only recognize a few people who stay in this area.

Someone gave us this little ground to stay on but I don't really know who owns this land. Even if I had money, I wouldn't build a home here. I can't really do anything here. We've been displaced for three years, since the earthquake. There have been homes burned in this camp too already.

Here there are really no services. Even this little bit of water we had to buy, bucket by bucket, for 5 gouds. When I have a little money to get food, I have to take a bus to buy anything. The only thing we can buy here is a little food for the children. We're here for one year now. We have nothing.

I have eight children. One of my daughters has her own child. They are all here. Right here. I have a lot of family. I am thirty-eight years old. I had children frequently. We are all here. I still have a lot

---

[1] Cité Soleil is a large, densely populated unplanned neighborhood of more than 400,000 in northwest Port-au-Prince.

[2] Large tent cities, or bidonvilles, were constructed on the plaza outside the former site of the National Palace after the 2010 earthquake. For more on bidonvilles, see the Glossary, page 309.

[3] Large-scale looting and burning of bidonville tent camps began around two years after the earthquake.

of family in Bainet where I was born.[4] I don't want to go back there. My mother has died. My father has died. I'm not going back.

I am pregnant with my ninth child. I don't know when it is due. There are no doctors here. Only God knows if I can deliver in a hospital, if there will be enough time.

My husband is out, in the street. *L'ap chache lavi li.*[5] He doesn't have any work. He's looking for a little food.

I was in Port-au-Prince for a long time before the earthquake. I came to the city when I was about twelve years old. I didn't finish school. My mother died when I was young and my father didn't have much. I had to work from thirteen to fourteen years old. I was always paid for work but never very much. I washed, ironed, things like that. I always stayed with my family but I always worked.

I was in Cité Soleil since 1988. We had a little house of our own. It wasn't in very good shape, and then it was destroyed. We didn't have the means to rebuild it so we made a tent on the Plaza. And then this was burned down. There are still a lot of people in Cité Soleil, a lot like it was before. I wouldn't go back even if I could. People are suffering there and we are suffering here. I think there is worse. I feel pain for everyone who is still in Cité Soleil. Things are too "hot," too many people, too much crime.

On the anniversary last week there were a lot of people. They didn't stay. They appeared and then they left. They didn't really do anything for a memorial. It was for nothing. They stayed for an hour, no more. They didn't bring anything. Lots of foreigners came. The president was here; he didn't stay.

I am grateful to be alive. God is taking care of my children. It's God who knows what time, what place he will send me. God will put someone else in my path to take me to another place. I have confidence in God. I have confidence.

---

[4] Bainet is a small coastal town in the south of Haiti, between Jacmel and Les Cayes. It is about 70 miles from Port-au-Prince.

[5] Literally translated: "he is looking for his life," or trying to make a living.

Carrefour is the south coast of Port-au-Prince. To get to Okai, to Jérémie, to Léogâne, all those places, you have to go through Carrefour. It is hilly and rocky. The epicenter of the earthquake was south of the city. This part of town was completely destroyed. The place where they took all the bodies, where they have the memorial, is in the north. It's a wasteland, a burial place. They've been burying people there forever.

—*Jean Pierre Marseille*

PIERRE YVES JOVIN

64, morgue director, Port-au-Prince General Hospital

Pierre Yves Jovin has been the director of the morgue at the General Hospital in Port-au-Prince since 2009. In January 2013, we met in his office at the morgue, which is tucked in the back of the main hospital campus. The campus was still recovering from the earthquake three years earlier and was as much construction site as working hospital. During the earthquake, the morgue building did not fall, but without electricity—like the rest of the hospital— it could only function as a space to collect the dead. Bodies surrounded the building, stacked two and three deep. At night, front loaders and dump trucks had to be used to move the dead to mass graves.

I took my first job at the General Hospital in 1979. In 1981, I was promoted to supervisor. Then I was responsible for the oxygen section from 1991 to 2009. At the General Hospital, we've never been really stable since 1986, at the end of the Duvalier era. We may see some semblance of stability for three months or even a year, but before you know it, there's a strike, they fire the director and bring another one. Each director comes with their own system; they have their own way of leading. As soon as there's a strike, all projects are abandoned and we have to start over. That's how it's been.

I've been the head of the morgue for three years now. When I took office, I couldn't find any files left from my predecessor. I'm trying to put together a system. However, if I were promoted or fired, my successor would not follow my footsteps, and start over doing their own thing without keeping what I've done that was good. That's our mentality as Haitians—most of us.

The administration doesn't really care about the staff. Imagine that in this difficult life, a staff member is getting paid 5,000 gouds a month.[1] What can this do for someone? There are some people who've been working here for months without pay. The worst part is that no one tells them when they are going to get paid. Whoever you talk to, they say they don't know anything. So we end up hoping God's goodness will take care of us. It can't be like this. People have to eat and dress. Those staff members will become frustrated at the government, the administration, or another staff member who gets paid. See here, I get paid every month. Those people who haven't been paid in a while—can I ask them to do something for me like I do the others? No. No! Even though they may do it because of their good will, they may not do it well.

I HAD A JOB TO DO

When the tragedy happened, I had already left work and was on the staff bus on my way home. I live in Mariani.[2] On our way we saw a lot of people running. The driver didn't really know how to maneuver the bus to avoid them. We didn't know that the earthquake had just passed. The driver stopped and we got off. We saw dead people and electrical wires on the ground. I saw schools collapsed, walls with children stuck under them. When I got home, my neighborhood was okay. I thank God every day for His blessings. That night, everyone slept outside under the stars. We all were praying.

---

[1] At the time of the interview, 5,000 gouds equals approximately US$125.

[2] Mariani is a suburb west of Port-au-Prince.

The next day, I had to come to work because I had a job to do. I left home at 4 a.m. and walked to the hospital. I arrived at 10 a.m. I had to walk around people and rubble in the streets. It wasn't until I came here that I saw the amount of work that was waiting for me! We didn't have space for the cadavers. We had to put them outside on cardboard. Imagine! From what I remember, we had 8,032 bodies laid out on the cardboard on the first day. Those were only the ones people brought that day to the General Hospital. I didn't include the ones I found here.

I stayed at the morgue from January 13 until January 22. I had to stay to pile up the bodies. I did that all day, after the truck brought them, so that they could be picked up for burial later that night. They were dropped at Titanyen for mass burials. The cemetery, too.

We just inaugurated a mausoleum at Carrefour-Feuille. Congressman Lochard had a memorial for victims there. This became a mass grave after the earthquake. It holds more than 5,000 people. After that day, there was no time for fancy things. People were buried in sheets or cardboard or nothing. You'd be a prince to have a coffin.

On January 12, there was much solidarity among my people. If we see cadavers on the streets, we don't need to know who they are to take them off the street. Either the government disposes of them, or, if they're taking too long, the population does.

ONE MORGUE FOR THE WHOLE NATION

The morgue had a lot of issues. We received cadavers from January 12 until January 24. The morgue building couldn't hold any more people—only this office we're sitting in now didn't have corpses in it. We also had no electricity. The cold rooms stopped working. Not until early February were we able to freeze corpses again. We had firefighters come to clean out, and the U.S. Marines sent technicians to come to fix the drawers and cold rooms for us. The morgue couldn't hold any more people.

Several months later, the cold rooms stopped working again. The administration checked with Operation Blessing and Partners In Health to see if they could help. With the help from these two organizations and another one I can't remember right now, they were able to find a freezer truck like people use to ship frozen food. We disinfected the truck. We moved the cadavers into the truck. The cadavers stayed in the truck, I can't really remember, but not too long. Not even a month. Not many; about 500 to 600 of them. What happened was that some parents of the dead were here, and when they saw that the cadavers were decomposing, they hurried and took them. When the morgue was repaired, the cadavers were brought back inside.

We just cleaned out and buried 207 people. We have some people that no one has claimed. The cadavers come from the Justice Department. We have about fifty now that were brought from the police, waiting for autopsies, pathology, et cetera, since the first of January.

Our morgue will never reach the standards of other countries as long as we don't have county morgues. You see what I mean? Each county should have its own morgue. The hospital morgue should only be for patients who died at the hospital. Then the cold rooms would not be overcrowded. We only have this one morgue for the whole nation.

We had a physician who was the medical examiner for the morgue. He passed away two years ago. Now we don't have one. That's why if there's a corpse that needs an autopsy, it may take months before it receives one. Sometimes, if the family members are pressuring us, they just tell us to give them the body without finishing the investigation.

You see, we shouldn't have those types of problems, especially in regard to staff. It's so important to the proper functioning of the morgue. The government is investing money in carnivals and other silly things instead. The physicians are asking for everything they will need to perform. They don't want to work without the tools and help they will need. You may find one who doesn't care, but the good ones won't accept poor working conditions. That's why the medico-legal department at the hospital is not really functioning. It's handicapped.

And I can't remember how long I've been asking for a digital camera. I should have a way to keep archives.

When I first got to Port-au-Prince, sometimes I ate, sometimes I didn't. Sometimes I just stayed *pye a te*—feet on the ground—and resigned myself. When I found that the suffering was too much in Port-au-Prince, I went back *andeyo*—outside. Outside the capital people live even worse than here. For people in rural areas who grow their food, there are times when you grow a lot. Too often you lose everything. You get to a point where you can't stay in a place or you will die. I sold two chickens and returned with my children to Port-au-Prince.

Compare the life we are living now to the life we lived years ago. You go and buy bread that used to be one dollar and three gouds. Now it's ten gouds more. Now a gallon of water is selling for how much, 6 or 7 gouds? Now if you don't have 25 gouds you can't eat. Sometimes I lie down and sleep, but I never don't wake up. I wake up and I sit and think and calculate and calculate.

—Annette Guy, maid, Delmas

SNAKE

24, graffiti artist and teacher

Alexandre Sonel, a.k.a. Snake, is a painter and graffiti artist from Cité Soleil. Not long before our interview, his mother passed away after being sick for quite some time, and his father was shot while riding in a tap tap—he was caught in the crossfire between two rival gangs.[1] Snake teaches art at Konbit Soley Leve (Rising Sun Collective), a social movement that was founded in June 2011 by residents of Cité Soleil.

I'll never forget the first time I tried graffiti. It was a Friday and I was going to another neighborhood not too far from mine to buy some food. As I was eating my food, I was observing some children who were playing on the side of the street. I enjoyed the sight, so I grabbed a piece of charcoal and started to draw on the wall, then I sprayed it. It was depicting the scene: the children playing with kites or with hoops, the street vendor selling food next to the pile of trash, and the destroyed houses in the background. I wrote: HAVE A CONSCIENCE FOR HAITI.

I was born and raised in Cité Soleil. The neighborhood is very vulnerable. Most of my friends either left or joined gangs. I too became a difficult child when I was nine years old. I started following

---

[1] A *tap tap* is a kind of taxi.

my friends around and participating in their pranks. My only blessing was that my parents took the time to give me instruction. My father died recently from the upheavals in the community. I still live here because I have a goal: I am fighting for the children in this neighborhood.

At Konbit Soley Leve, we educate the community. We teach them to use the resources we have. We appoint unlikely individuals as role models. A woman who sells her goods on the street to make ends meet is a great example. We started Konbit Soley Leve with cleaning up the community first. We used what we had. We attached a piece of wood to a side of an old fan and used it as a rake. We took sides of an old TV box and attached a rope to it. We used it as a wheelbarrow. We started in one neighborhood, and other people saw our initiative and followed.

I work with six or seven children in the afternoons for one month or two. By the end of that time, my students know many techniques of painting. My friend Alashkar is good with floral art; she teaches kids how to do it as well. Konbit Soley Leve is all of us. We all can bring the positive and meaningful change we want.

I have five brothers and four sisters. My brothers live with me; my two older sisters have their own place, and my two little sisters are with an aunt. After my dad died, I thought it wise to send them to my aunt. I send them some money when I can. My oldest brother is twenty-five years old, and my youngest sister is nine.

From what I remember, my parents suffered a lot here in Cité Soleil. I used to ask myself why they did all they did. I realized later that it was for us, their children. My father was a roof contractor. He used to leave the house, sometimes, at 2 or 3 o'clock in the morning to walk to work. Before he died, he used to make 1,000 gouds a day.[2] My dad didn't know how to read or write. His parents didn't think that it was necessary to send him to school because gaining

---

[2] At the time of the interview, 1,000 gouds equals approximately US$25.

knowledge would only benefit his future children and wife, not them. I am glad he didn't follow his parents' example, and saw to it that we were in school.

My mother, she didn't see any sacrifice as too big. Her name was Andrelise Raphael. She used to sell anything she could to provide for us. She became sick and died November 7, 2014.

Then, a few weeks after, on December 16, as my dad was coming back from work, there was a fight between two neighborhoods. The tap tap that he was in had one person who was probably involved in the conflict. When people from one camp stopped the car and asked that man to get off, he didn't want to. Those people just shot at him while my father was still inside.

I went to many hospitals and couldn't find my father. The next day, my friend called me and confirmed that my father died. He said he was at the General Hospital morgue and gave me his bracelet number. I went and found him. I was told later that he died in an ambulance on his way to the hospital. Some siblings and friends were very mad and wanted revenge. I understood that they were grieving. I took my brothers to the side and told them that it won't change anything to seek revenge. We may not even get to the person who did that, but end up killing an innocent man in the process like what happened to our father. They listened to me and let it go.

I know the people who did this to my father. As a matter of fact, I worked for them after my father died. They were sitting with me while I was working, and we were joking and eating together. One of them I consider to be my friend told me that he learned of what happened to my father. He said he wasn't there when it happened. I know that he would have never told me even if he was the one who pulled the trigger. I told him that it's fine. Life goes on. My only revenge would be to resolve that conflict between those two guys who divided the Cité. I would preach peace. That would be my revenge.

My father taught me something that I don't think I could have learned in school. I remember in 2004, when Aristide left, people from the Cité were looting. My dad said we will not participate in the looting. Even if we die hungry, we will not steal someone else's property. I remember something else that happened in 2003-2004. Usually, when my father leaves in the morning, my mother used to start getting a meal ready. She would boil the beans and wait for my dad's return. If he found a job, then we would eat. That day, he didn't find a job, he had just gone out to look. When he came back, he said that he didn't have any money. He didn't even have money to pay for the bus. My mom suggested that we buy from neighbors on credit. Since he wasn't sure if he would get a job the next day, or anytime soon, he said no. Then, my mother put some salt in the beans and we all ate. These things really marked me.

My mother used to tell me to never follow people unless their actions are good. She taught me not to envy others. I remember the times when she used to play with me during bath time or take me to school. When she became sick and asked to be sent *andeyo*, we used to go visit her.[3] My dad, however, was still here with us. She died five days after she came back to Port-au-Prince. My father was with us throughout everything. After my mother died, we were with him to encourage and support him. Those few days before his death, we became really close to each other. I guess since his wife died, he felt that he had to spend all his free time with us. We laughed, cried, and ate together. He used to watch me and my brother paint. He was probably using us to forget my mother's death. He used to tell us how proud he was of us because we were on the right path and stayed with him.

When my mom was alive, we used to be very close. But I often think about my dad—not because I loved him more but his death troubled me a lot. I have a picture of my parents and my godparents. I usually want to cry when I am looking at that picture, but I try not

---

[3] *Andeyo* means "outside" in Kreyol. Haitians use the term to refer to everywhere outside of Port-au-Prince.

to because I see it as a weakness. Also, if I cry, I may want to make the perpetrators pay for what they did to my father. Therefore, I don't cry. Instead, I focus on my goals.

I want to create a nonprofit. The idea is to have one or two artists from ghettos to help create the organization together. We would teach children and young people our craft. Maybe later we could have a professional school where youth can learn a trade. I would like to have peace at Cité Soleil. As our proverb says, "Clean your house before cleaning someone else's." I want the people who were causing the trouble to be the ones preaching peace. My parents died proud. I think their dream for us was to follow them in the example of courage.

I'm very happy to say that my wife's first daughter—she's also my daughter—was given a free pass to a great college in Santo Domingo for getting the highest point in a spelling contest in her high school! When I met my wife twenty-one years ago she had a one-year-old kid, Esperanza Jose Metellus. Her father passed away. And from the first day I saw her, I became her permanent father. I love her like my blood children. I paid for her school the best way I could, and now some of her dreams are coming true.

—*From an e-mail by Jean Pierre Marseille, March 2016*

JEAN PIERRE MARSEILLE

44, journalist/fixer/translator/salesman

Jean Pierre is a father who lives in Port-au-Prince.

My name is Jean Pierre, but my original name is Jean Marseille. My father's name is Waldeck Marseille. My mother's name is Jocelyn Pierre. After I was deported from the United States back to Haiti in 1994, I took the name Jean Pierre to change my identity. Some people call me JP. My Facebook name is Johnny Pierre. Money G is another name. That's a street name a friend of mine, Teddy, gave me because I'll always be hustling. That's it for names.

I had to give myself a birthday, too. My parents say I was born in 1971 in the spring, but they're not sure what month or day. They say around March, so I picked March 24. Twenty-four is my lucky number.

My wife's name is Guerda. Her first kid's name is Esperanta, age twenty-one. She's going to school and lives in Santa Domingo.[1] Together my wife and I have David Jean, our oldest. He's in twelfth grade, his last year at classic school. Only two more classes and he's

---

[1] Santo Domingo is the capital of the Dominican Republic.

finished with high school! I'm going to try to send him to the university in Santo Domingo with Esperanta. Then there's Medjine. She's fourteen and going to seventh grade this year. After her is Donald. He's ten and in sixth grade. Annesamma is eight. She's also going to the sixth grade this year. Geyonce, we call her Gigi, is seven. She's going to the fifth grade this year. She's my wife's sister's daughter. Her mother died of cholera in Cap-Haïtien after the earthquake.[2] Our families were close, so I adopted her. I had no choice. Out of her whole family, we are the only ones that have a house and have it together enough to take care of her. She's my daughter now. I gave her a birth certificate. I consider her one of my own. And finally there's little Diego. He's four. He's what we call our mistake kid! My wife and I didn't plan on having any more kids, but after the earthquake, the two of us got together, and you know, it just happened again. When we we found out, it was so shocking that I cried. One more responsibility. I was so worried. How was I going to make it with all these kids?

ONE DAY A WOMAN CAME UP TO HER HOUSE WITH A BABY IN A CARDBOARD BOX

I grew up in Cap-Haïtien, raised by my grandmother, but the truth is I wasn't even born here. I remember when I was six, seven years old, and I asked my grandmother why does everybody in this house call me *etranjè*?[3] And they didn't say it behind my back. They said it like it was a good thing. It meant that I was from somewhere else.

My grandmother told me that one day a woman came up to her house with a baby in a cardboard box. About a year before that my father and mother had left on a boat looking for a better life. Both

---

[2] Cap-Haïtien is a city of 200,000 in the Nord Department on Haiti's northern coast.

[3] *Etranjè* means "stranger," "foreigner," or "alien."

my parents were born in Cap-Haïtien. They'd been neighbors. They hooked up, got married, and made my older brother, Jaco. But things were rough then. This was 1970. The Tonton Makout would kill you for anything. So my parents sold what they had and put some money together and were able to buy passage. They left Jaco in Haiti. Their final destination was the United States, but to get to the United States at that time, you had to first go through the Bahamas.

Turns out I was in her belly when she took the boat, what people in the U.S. call a banana boat. Haitians used to take them to flee to the United States. These boats were always overfilled. Sometimes the boat would hold eighty people. Sometimes as many as a hundred. Sometimes they would throw people out in the middle of the sea. I guess at that time my parents were taking a chance. But they did make it to the Bahamas. They were only supposed to stay there for a month. But because my mother was pregnant, they ended up staying longer. They couldn't leave. She couldn't go on a boat to the U.S. pregnant like that.

So I was born. My mother had me in a hospital in the Bahamas. My mother once told me that my birth certificate had my little footprints on it. That's what they do in the Bahamas. They place the footprint of the baby on the birth certificate. Technically, I'm a citizen of the Bahamas. They changed the law in 1970 and said anybody born in the Bahamas was a citizen. If I could prove this—I don't have a birth certificate anymore—I would be in the Bahamas right now. But I never saw this birth certificate.

After I'm born, I'm a problem. They can't go to the States so they decide that they are going to work and rent their own place in the Bahamas. My father worked in the cane fields, and they saved a little money.

After six or seven months, my mother still wanted to go to the States. Her only dream was to get to the United States. I slowed her down. They decided they'd both go, but my mother went first.

There was never a plan to bring me because I was too young.

The boat was too much of a risk. So they decided to send me back to Haiti to stay with my grandmother until they could get themselves situated in the U.S. But they couldn't just ship me back to Haiti. My father paid a woman to take me. I don't know who she was. After my mother left, my father was lonely. He wanted to go chasing after her. So he fixed a little bed in a cardboard box—put my papers and me inside—and handed the box to that woman. She took me on a boat and smuggled me back to Haiti. I was eighteen months old. That was my first deportation.

When that lady brought me to my grandmother, there was no birth certificate in the box. That woman probably stole it and resold it because that was a big business. Everybody wanted to leave Haiti at that time. But everybody knew where I was from and being an etranjè was good for me. To be from another country other than Haiti was always better. The Bahamas were good. To have an actual Bahamian inside the house was like a gift. So I got special treatment.

I grew up on a farm in real countryside with little houses made out of bamboo. The place was part of the commune of Limonade and within walking distance to the larger city of Cap-Haïtien.[4] There was a lot of dirt and dust and no roads. I used to ride a donkey to school. I lived with my mother's mother, my brother Jaco, my uncle, aunties, and all my cousins. I didn't have needs for anything. I ran around there on the land, and I played with the cows and goats and all the animals. I drank natural milk straight from the cow. I was a spoiled kid! My grandmother super-loved me, and my grandfather always brought me fruit. It was the best time in my life. Even if I didn't have the United States glories—the fancy cars and the big money—when I was a kid, I had all the family love that I needed. My grandmother made me feel special, and she treated me really good.

---

[4] Limonade is a commune in the arrondissement of Cap-Haïtien, which is a part of the Nord Department, a large tract of land in Haiti's north. For more on Haiti's administrative divisions, see the Glossary, page 309.

She raised me up. My grandmother was the head of that household. She used to get on the donkey to go downtown to sell the crops her husband had harvested from the farm. She was a highly respected person in that community in Limonade because she had a lot of land and was my mother's mother. My mother was a hero because she was one of the first persons to leave Limonade to go to the United States.

And so the days went on. But my grandmother had always assured me that one day I would leave to join my original family. At that time my parents were living in Belle Glade, Florida. And they had another boy, my brother William. My mother used to send cassette tapes. That's how I first heard my mother's voice.

Finally, my mother sent for Jaco and me. I was around ten or eleven. When it was time for me to go to the United States, I went and hid because I didn't want to leave my grandmother. I didn't want to go. I loved my mother, but I didn't know her as a person. I was in school. I had some friends in Limonade that were really close to me. I knew my wife even. When we were kids we used to walk together to school. I didn't know I was going to marry her! But we'd rendezvous every morning.

My grandmother found me. She knew my hiding spot in the big forest near our farm, near the mango tree. When I stole something from the house or did something bad, I'd go there and hide for a couple of hours. My grandmother always knew that place, but I didn't know she knew until then.

She said, "Come and sit down on my lap." And she sat me down, and she spoke to me. She said, "You know, out of everybody in the world, I love you most. I think I love you even more than your mother, but I'm getting old, and this country's not getting any better. It would be better for you if you go to the United States. Maybe you can get a better life. And one day you can come back and see me and bring me nice gifts because I know you love me."

I loved my grandmother dearly. That's what made me go. My grandmother, she was the only one. I remember it so well. A couple, a man and a woman, came and took me off the farm and brought me to the city. Port-au-Prince was so beautiful back then. I remember walking on Champ de Mars with this couple.[5] They were selling fried meat and bananas. The streets were crowded. There were all these fun things for kids to do. They had clowns in the streets, and people were riding bikes. The streets were clean. That was my first time I ever saw concrete. I saw the White House.[6] It was my first time seeing something that big in my life. It was so beautiful. Then, the man said, "Tomorrow, we'll be leaving for Florida." You know how it is when you're a kid. They never explain anything to you. And I'm like, "Leaving where? I'm not here? This is not the United States?"

And the next day I got on a plane for the first time in my life. This couple were pretending to be my parents. I remember that the lady, the stewardess, was really nice. She said "If you want to throw up, just grab this bag, and do like this." Now, I'm really excited to see the big America. I'm thinking, Where am I going? What will my mother look like? What are my brothers like? What's the United States going to be like? Is it going to be like heaven?

Well, it turned out that mother owed the couple a lot of money, $5,000. They held me in Miami under house arrest until my mother paid up. But that special day, months later, two women and one man came to the door. I gave the man a handshake, and I kissed both the women. I knew one of them must be my mother because of the happiness in their faces. One of them said, "*Ki moun nan nou se manman ou a?*—Which one of us is your mother?" I really didn't know. In my mind, I'm like, *Eeny, meeny, miney, moe.* I picked the one that looked most like my grandmother. Lucky me.

---

[5] Champ de Mars is a park near the former site of the National Palace.

[6] Haiti's national palace. Destroyed during the earthquake and later bulldozed. See Jean's earlier comment about Sean Penn, page 110.

My mom said, "You remember me!" She started to cry. I started crying, too. I was relieved, and very, very happy. I hugged my mother. I thought it was going to be the best time in my life, but I was on a long road. Because nothing's ever perfect. How many times do I have to learn this? When I got to Belle Glade, things weren't great. My parents had split up. My father was violent. My mom was always busy trying to help us survive, working two jobs. She didn't know when I went to school and when I didn't. She never said, "Let me see your report card," or "How did you do in school today?"

I remember being so lonely. Kids beat me up all the time because I was Haitian and couldn't speak English very well. "You stink, Haitian. Take the banana boat back to Haiti." "You're dumb." "You're ugly." Nobody wanted to be my friend. They changed the way I thought about myself. All those people, all those bad names, made me feel less than I was. Eventually I got into the drug life. I was fifteen. I wanted to be cool. I wanted to buy a car. I wanted to have friends and girlfriends. I wanted to correct all the reasons I was picked on. I wanted to take away all the Haitian style.

You could make good money selling. I had other jobs, putting people's groceries in bags and stocking shelves, but that's $3.25 an hour at minimum wage. I was so tired. I had to go to school. I'd get off work at 3 a.m.

The first time I sold I made $400. Sometimes, in a day, I could make $600 or $700. Then, I didn't get beat up as easily.

I watched TV and found out the way to dress and act. I spoke English. I knew slang. When I was eighteen, I bought a Cadillac. I got the new hairstyle. I dropped out of high school and made a name for myself. I became cool and very violent. I got addicted to cocaine. I was depressed. I had thoughts of sucide. I didn't have anybody to give me advice. Only my brother Jaco who worked shit jobs, he tried to set me straight one time, but I didn't listen.

THE GUY SAID HE HAD A
WARRANT FOR MY ARREST

I remember it so well. By then, I was twenty-two. Around four o'clock one day, a U.S. Marshal comes to our house in a four-door gray car and knocks on the door—*boom boom boom boom*. My mom goes to the door. The guy said that he had a warrant for my arrest. My mother said, "What for?" The guys said for "a failure to appear for driving under a suspended license and possession of marijuana." A five-dollar bag of weed. The Marshal said, "Don't worry. Just a simple violation charge." When I went to court that Monday, I was afraid, but deportation was nowhere on my mind. The judge told me that, personally, he'd give me time served, but that I had an immigration hold. I thought, *Man, this must be a mistake. I have my green card.* I called my mom. She found my green card and brought it to court.

Because, you see, you couldn't be deported under Reagan if you had a green card. He was president when I arrived in the United States in 1982. I was twelve when I first came to Florida. I always tell whites from the U.S. that I meet, "You know who my favorite president is? Ronald Reagan." And they can't believe it. "Why do you like Ronald Reagan, man? He was a terrible president." Not for us! Haitians in the United States love Ronald Reagan. Ronald Reagan made it clear—if you had been in the U.S. for over five years, you could have a green card; they would not deport you. I got my green card with the help of Ronald Reagan, but Bill Clinton became president in 1994. And Clinton's new deportation law hit me like a rock. It turned out you *could* be deported if you had a green card. If your crime was bad enough.

And my crime was bad enough. I should say crimes. Because my deportation was not based on a single crime. It was an accumulation of crimes. But the fact is you only need one minor felony to get deported. When I appeared in court on the possession, the judge and an immigration official told me they'd been looking for me since my first major charge—a felony for throwing a deadly missile, a brick, into an occupied vehicle. But the reason I got deported was because of a conspiracy charge. It's called "conspiracy to deliver or purchase cocaine within a thousand feet of a school zone."[7] They charged me with that, but they didn't find any drugs. I *was* selling drugs, but I never got arrested for selling drugs. First it was the possession charge and then I got roped into the whole conspiracy thing. So they had an immigration hearing and I lost. They put me in the county jail. But they said if Immigration didn't come to get me within a month, they had no choice but to release me. I asked the guard, "Does Immigration not come sometimes?" He said, "Sometimes they don't." So I was counting every day. Twenty-nine days later, a guard called out: "Jean Marseille." They came at the very last minute. Immigration shackled my feet and wrapped a chain around my waist. For the first time, I really felt like a prisoner. They transferred me to three other county jails until I finally got to Oakdale, Louisiana, a federal detention center where there's a federal administration department and immigration court where they keep people that are about to get deported. I saw these big barbed-wire fences. It was also the first time in my life I saw snow.

I THOUGHT I WAS AMERICAN

I didn't think about Haiti very much after my grandmother died when I was in the eighth grade. I didn't go back for the funeral. I couldn't. And I'd never gone back to visit. Never. Not once after I came to the U.S. I thought I was American. I pretended to be anyway. But once I was in Oakdale, I got interested because I knew I had no chance of fighting the deportation. I started studying up on events in Haiti. From what I heard on the news, Aristide had gotten pushed out of the country and he wasn't being allowed to

---

[7] Or "possession with intent to distribute within a thousand feet of a school zone."

come back.[8] His supporters were getting killed in the streets. I also read that the Makouts were back and out there raping and shooting people.[9] I tried to understand the situation there, what kind of environment it was. How could I live in a place with so much violence? Was there even any electricity? What about the roads? And I also heard from someone at Oakdale that deportees sent there were getting shot when they arrived at the airport.

While I was waiting for my deportation hearing, my mom sent me a letter and told me something amazing. She said she went to Haiti with all this pèpè and made a killing.[10] And do you know what she did with the money? She bought me a house in Port-au-Prince. Seriously. The house I live in now. She knew I was going to get deported and did her best to set me up here. She sent me the address of her cousin, and told me to contact her when I got to Port-au-Prince.

After a couple months, I had my deportation hearing. My public defender spoke well but didn't know much about me because I had only met him the day of the hearing. And I had a criminal record, so what could he do? The judge sentenced me to deportation.

In the middle of the night, U.S. Marshals came and got me and another Haitian guy, a friend of mine named Geral. Once again, I was shackled. I felt so stupid. I wasn't a dangerous person. Why should I be shackled? They put us on a small, private plane like a Learjet, a U.S. Marshal's plane. It was not a commercial flight. There were three Jamaicans—dreads[11]—on the plane. They dropped the Jamaicans off

---

[8] Jean-Bertrand Aristide was elected president of Haiti in 1990 and removed by coup in 1991. He returned to the presidency in 1994–95 and then was again elected in 2000. For more on Aristide, see Appendix I, page 293.

[9] The *Makout* were a feared paramilitary group under the Duvalier regimes during the second half of the twentieth century. For more on the Makout, see the Glossary, page 309.

[10] *Pèpè* refers to used clothes collected from international donations.

[11] A person with dreadlocks.

first. But only two were taken off. And I'm like, "Yo, man, why you here? I thought you was a Jamaican?" Then, for the first time this guy spoke Kreyol, he says, "I'm Haitian, too." And I said, "All this time we're together on the plane, you're hiding that you're Haitian?" He said, "I have nowhere to go." He was terrified. So was I. I was thinking, "These Haitians are going to kill us." They weren't supposed to deport anybody to Haiti at that time because Haiti was considered unstable. It was so bad that they had already stopped commercial flights to Haiti. But they brought us on a U.S. Marshal plane. These Americans were ditching us.

When the plane touched down, the U.S. Marshals grabbed me and the other guy, and took us with our cuffs on down the ramp. It was kind of like when Obama gets off the plane with the Secret Service, walking down the stairs, waving. Except when I got off the plane in Haiti, I saw dead bodies on the tarmac. You think I'm joking? The marshals took us into the Haitian police station in the airport and said, "These two guys were deported." The marshals didn't speak Kreyol, and there was no translator. The Haitian cops didn't understand English. So I translated. My Kreyol was at least understandable. It wasn't as great as it is now, but I left Haiti speaking Kreyol and I had always spoken Kreyol with my mother. The marshals took the handcuffs off and were like, "Here you are." They handed the three of us to the Haitian cops and took their handcuffs back with them. They went back to their plane. I was getting very scared now. And these Haitian cops started asking us for money.

Before I had signed my name agreeing to deportation, the U.S. Marshals gave me ten bucks. That's the money they give to everybody that is getting deported. I also had a little extra money that my parents sent me from my account stashed under my balls. It was like a hundred bucks total. I said, "Hey, listen, I've got family in the government. I'm of the family of Madame and Mr. Charles Cherenfant. Charles Cherenfant was my mom's cousin's husband, a guy that used to work at the White House with Duvalier, an old Makout. He had been shot once and was famous for having only one hand. Because Aristide was gone, the Makouts were in power again. "Oh!" One cop heard the name. "Let me see the address." He looked at the paper I had carried, and said, "You. You move to the side. I know the family." He sat me down. I pointed to Geral, "He's with me." And so me and Geral waited there until that officer was off work. He was so nice to me. The other guy, the dread—I don't know what the hell happened to him.

Outside of the airport, the day was cloudy. There was smoke in the streets and soldiers. We didn't take a car. We walked from the police station. We walked for about an hour through fields and past shanty houses. Again, I saw dead bodies. It turned night. Dark. And I'm nervous. I offer the cop ten dollars, but he doesn't take it. I'm thinking that this cop is going to shoot me in the bushes. And if we do make it to the house I'm wondering—will this woman, my mom's cousin, remember me? Is this cop really a good guy? Will these people accept me? It's been eleven years since I left. All these things were on my mind.

We reached a house and the cop called out, "Madame Cherenfant. Madame Cherenfant!" My auntie—she's not really my auntie, but I call her that—comes out. She looks at me. "You Jocelyn's kid?" I felt like somebody who was choking that finally gets fresh air. I said, "Yeah." Ahh, it felt really good. I looked behind me. The cop had disappeared. I never saw him again. To this day, I haven't seen that cop again.

My auntie took us in. That first night she cooked us fish. Couple days later Geral went on his way, somewhere. Soon things became pretty tough for me. I mean I didn't know anybody. No one at all. And Haitians were suspicious of American deportees. They thought all American deportees were killers and murderers and thieves. I had a bald head then and had a lot of gold teeth. Also, I was really fat. 195 pounds. Huge belly. Now I weigh 155, 160. People were scared as hell of me. I was the first deportee in my neighborhood.

Then my auntie began stealing the food that my mom was sending me. She'd hide it in her room. Also, she tried to give me a curfew. I just got out of prison and I have to be back at the house by eight o-clock? Remember I'm twenty-two years old. I wanted to find a girl. I was lonely. I dressed up and walked around the neighborhood, talking to people with my messed-up Kreyol, trying to get my groove on. But nobody would give me a chance.

Not long after, I met this guy named Fenix. He took me to his house and let me meet his wife and daughter, and we had a real big dinner. He made believe that I was his friend. In Haitian slang he says, "I know you done been through war 'cause you were deported, you know how to shoot a gun, you know how to do all that stuff, right?" I said, "Yeah, I can do that. I'm tough." I didn't want the guy to think I was a wussie. He explained the plan. It had to do with stealing gas. Back in those days, there were a lot of people selling gas because Haiti had an embargo on it.[12] There was no gas coming in, and so gas was very expensive. We were going to go to a big open field by the airport and rob some gas merchants. And you know, I was tired of sitting at home in my auntie's house. So I said, "Okay, I'll do it." I figure I have to do something. How can I make it in this place? Can I make it as a robber? Maybe I can buy some fresh clothes and look good. Maybe I can get some money and get back to the States somehow.

The next day we park the getaway car and walked into the big open field by the airport. There was a goat track you would follow through the wild grass. Fenix stopped walking and pulled out a .38. He said, "Here's the gun. You pull the gun out on them, and I'll collect the money." I had an uneasy feeling. I mean we're talking about gasoline. If I shoot that gun, shit could blow up. I said, "Yeah, give me the gun."

---

[12] For more on the embargo following the Aristide coup, see Appendix I, page 293.

He gave it to me, and I took about five or ten steps back and pulled the gun on him. I said, "You're going to take me home. What are you bringing me on a suicide mission for?" Fenix was scared. Remember, he thinks I'm a high-class criminal from the United States. He says, "Yo, yo, yo, calm down! I'll take you home. Come on, man. Put down the gun." I was shaking. I put the gun in my pants. Back in the car, I told him, "Look, I didn't come here to die ugly." When we got to my aunt's house, I took out the .38, took out the bullets, and gave Fenix back the gun. I said, "Come get your bullets in the morning." I was happy to be alive. I realized that that was not the way out.

I ASKED FOR A GIRL I'D REMEMBERED AS A KID

Three months later, I was so embarrassed about my deportation and myself that I removed all the gold from my teeth. Then I went to Cap-Haïtien for a visit to see if I could find my old friends. When I was walking around the neighborhood, I asked for a girl I'd remembered as a kid. Her parents and my grandmother used to walk us together to school. I was two years older, and we would have a rendez-vous together. We would go take a peepee, and she would show me hers and I would show her mine. I didn't have any intention in marrying her at the time. I just wanted to see an old friend. And when I first saw her after all those years, I saw that she already had a kid. I wasn't too into that. And I was too busy trying to figure out what I was going to do with my life in Port-au-Prince.

I still didn't have any friends. I needed some kind of support that was family, so I went back to Cap-Haïtien. My wife—she wasn't my wife yet—agreed to come live with me in Port-au-Prince. But I had to start making a living. I had enrolled in a program they had to help deportees reintegrate into society. I learned Haitian history and some French. I knew that I needed to know where the heck I was, how to get myself out of certain situations, get information, have a conversation. I found out later that program was just a hustle, but that was okay. The little bit of French helped me get jobs. I could understand French-speaking communities.

Then came the American invasion that brought Aristide back.[13] That saved my life. All those Americans spoke English, and I could relate. The soldiers knew I was a deportee. I didn't have to tell them. The way I talked, the way I looked, my goatee, everything. They knew I wasn't from here. And they didn't know what *they* were doing here. People were getting rowdy in the streets and people were killing Makouts—but those soldiers were helpless. I was able to get work, and sell them boots and hustle. I helped them get their freak on, got them weed, packs of cigarettes. They'd give me twenty bucks for a pack of cigarettes. "Keep the change, man. I got you, man. Keep the change."

Around the same time, I got my first real translating job. I went to the airport, and I saw this heavyset white guy with dark hair and some shorts on coming off the plane, and I said, "Hey, you speak English?"

He did, and he worked for NPR News.

I said, "You need somebody to translate for you?"

That's how Money G started getting his hustle on.

IF I HAD STAYED IN FLORIDA, I WOULD HAVE DIED IN FLORIDA

If given the choice I would rather come back here a thousand times over going to prison in the U.S. In some ways now I figure it was God's plan for me to get arrested and deported. I was either going to shoot somebody, or I was going to get caught up in some crossfire. No question in my mind, if I had stayed in Florida, I would have

---

[13] For more on the U.S. intervention in Haiti, see Appendix I, page 293.

died in Florida. I wouldn't have my wife and my kids, the people that inspire me, that keep me alive.

Listen, I'm shit in the United States. I'm nothing but a drug dealer, a convicted felon. So getting deported to Haiti was the best thing that happened to me. I've never been in trouble in Haiti. I have a clean record and a good driver's license. I don't steal shit from the people I work with. I don't have no bad reputation. I'm a respected journalist who has worked with the *L.A. Times* and the *Miami Herald*. I'm working real hard so my kids won't have to hustle. I work as a translator, but I do other types of trades in order to make it. I sell Coca-Cola drinks. I have a charcoal business—I sell charcoal made from wood for boiling water and cooking. I sell bags of water, those see-through plastic bags, you see that are sold all over the neighborhoods. Yeah, I sell water, too. Because everything costs something in Port-au-Prince. You gotta buy water. Lucky for me, I have a refrigerator and a freezer at home, so I buy gallon bags for three or four dollars and freeze them. They sell faster.

Our house is open for business. My wife sells the charcoal. She also sells pèpè[14] and rice and beans out of the house. People come to her. I'm a positive type of guy. I always think I'll be able to pull off a business. No matter what type of business I'll try it and see if I can make it work. Every job's a hustle. There's a word for hustle in Kreyol. *Brase*.[15] That word's used all the time.

THE GROUND WAS RUSHING AND SHAKING

The day of the earthquake, I was having lunch with a writer and filmmaker. I worked with her, and she often helped me get jobs. But that day she told me that she was leaving for France, and I realized that I was going to be without work. I didn't expect any journalists

---

[14] *Pèpè* refers to used clothes from the U.S.

[15] *Brase* means to stir or to brew.

to be coming to Haiti anytime soon, and I was really depressed. I was feeling real low and hungry. And I was having problems feeding my kids. My mission that day was to get some money from Chantal to buy some food, go back home, and cook.

Chantal gave me some money and I left.

When I got home, I gave my wife what Chantal had given me, and I went into the backyard. My wife was in the kitchen cooking, and I was talking to her through the window. I was telling her that things really had to change because the situation was really hard. Then, all of a sudden, I heard something like *godou-godou-godou*. The ground was rushing and shaking. Everybody was home for our family dinner, but the kids—Dave, Medjine, McDonald, Annesamma—were spread all over the house.

I hit my head against the wall and knocked a tooth loose. I fell on my knees and was trying to ask for forgiveness. I felt that Jesus must really exist and this must be the last days. I'm not kidding, I thought it was the end of the world. I said my last words, "Jesus, save me. I don't want to have suffered all this time on earth and then go to hell." How could I spend all my time suffering on earth to then die and go to hell?

After I calmed myself down, I went looking for my wife and kids. My wife was on the floor waving her hands in the air, saying, "Jesus Christ," I got her up and we got all the kids assembled. Everybody was fine!

We all went out of the house. We couldn't stay in the house anymore. I checked out the house—no cracks or anything. My house is built properly. And I was like, "Wow, must have been an earthquake." There was dust everywhere and people were yelling out "Jesus! Jesus! Jesus!" And people were screaming, coming out of buildings with dirt on their faces, running back and forth. Some people came out with broken legs. We had the second earthquake. *Du-du-du-du*. More aftershocks. More screaming. Houses were falling. People tried to save people.

A little while later I called Chantal. I had a Voila cell, but most people had Digicel phones, which didn't work. Voila was still working. Chantal told me she was okay but she was really paranoid because she was worried she wouldn't be able to get a flight out. Then I got a call from another journalist in the States. The word was spreading. He asked if I was all right, and my first thought was "He's on the way to Haiti." Immediately, I knew I had to go to the airport. I put my shoes on. I would go help some journalists and make a little money also. I told my neighbors that I would come back with a fresh car to help people, even though I didn't have a job yet.

So I headed toward the airport. That's when I saw the worst things. Delmas wasn't that bad.[16] There weren't many houses really destroyed. But as I'm walking, I start seeing people with cut legs, people trapped under roofs. I stopped to help this guy grab his wife from beneath the rubble. It took a long time. I realized that I had forgotten about myself. I'm like, "What am I doing?" I have to go to the airport.

By the time I did get there, it was almost dark. The first newspeople here were from China. They didn't need me because I guess they didn't speak English. I stood by the door waiting and then the jobs started coming. There weren't enough interpreters. But the fact is, the situation was pretty easy to understand at first. People needed help. Everybody can relate to that. You don't need language. It was simple. The streets were messy. We walked where we could. I was doing the translator job, but I was trying to help, too. I took the injured to the hospital. At the General Hospital I saw all these dead bodies on the ground. All over the hospital. Everywhere! There were no doctors. But there were bodies everywhere.

By the time I made it home, it must have been two days later, I was so tired. Even though we weren't supposed to go into the houses,

---

[16] Delmas is a large residential and commercial suburb in the northeast of Port-au-Prince, adjacent to the city's airport.

I went into mine to sleep. And who cares? At that time I was starving and happy to be alive.

There were so many sad people, but there were people showing each other love. The poor and the rich became one. You would see a big bourgeois guy, afraid to sleep in his mansion, and he was sleeping on the street with everyone else. We became closer to our neighbors during this time.

All the news channels were talking about violence in the streets and looting, people acting crazy. It wasn't true. It took a month for the dirty hearts to come back. But that first week, even if you were the biggest monster, you'd have a heart. Greediness comes about because of food. You can't really blame people.

Some bodies they only found later. I lost a lot of friends. Some friends, I don't know where they are to this day. They never found their bodies. They just disappeared. They could be anywhere. Like my friend Teddy. He was a deportee. Two days before the earthquake, we were together. After the earthquake, I went to his house, and it was flat. I am still hoping that he comes by. "Jean! Yo, Money G!"

I'm not saying that the earthquake should have happened, but it helped me in my situation at that time. I had six or seven months without work before it happened. After it, I got a lot of work. I felt professional, working as a translator. I felt like a journalist myself. I felt like I was educated, like I'd been to college, and was helping all these people. I felt like I was living in some dream.

I get more respect here because I'm from the United States and ended up with an education. When people in my community have problems, they come to me. They say, "I need to borrow $200. My kid is sick." I do the best I can to help them out. When people want advice, they come to me. The other day, a friend offered me $250 to fill out a letter for him from the U.S. Embassy. I said, "No, man." I gave him a hug and did it for free. In other times, I would have taken the money, but I'm not looking to be rich. Respect is more important. I just want to be able to feed my family and pay for my kids' education. It's not hard to satisfy me. I have my bad days, don't misunderstand, but I also have my good days here, many of them.

APPENDICES

INTRODUCTION TO THE APPENDICES

In Port-au-Prince, in the days following the January 12, 2010, earthquake, a Haitian friend lamented out loud—as we sat together, but speaking to no one in particular—that "Haiti needs to stop changing history." The scope of the disaster was just settling in, but she was referring to the country's legacy of setting historical precedents.

Haiti is a small nation, occupying the western third of the Caribbean island of Hispaniola. It is smaller in size than the U.S. state of Maryland. But the history of the "New World" cannot be understood without considering Haiti. Haiti has also been central to a number of events of global significance—from first contact with western Europe, through slavery, colonialism, and revolution, to creation and maintenance of external debt, and, most recently, the global response to the 2010 earthquake.

It is likely that Christopher Columbus made first contact in the New World in northern Haiti in 1492. Less than half a century later, the indigenous population was decimated—more than 90 percent of the island's original inhabitants having died from disease, enslavement, or other brutalities. By the end of the eighteenth century, the colony of Saint-Domingue was producing more than two-thirds of France's overseas wealth, with sugar the dominant cash crop.

A deadly industry was created to transform sugar cane into granulated sugar and liquid molasses. Sugar cane grows year-round, and the colony's industrial sugar mills ran around the calendar and around the clock. The industry depended on relatively cheap and expendable slave labor. It was less expensive to import a new African slave than to slow the agricultural or industrial production. Life expectancy for a slave in colonial Haiti was twenty-one years.

The importance of the 1791–1804 Haitian revolution cannot be overstated. It has been an inspiration for the world's oppressed and a source of great fear for the powerful for more than 200 years. While the United States continued to profit from chattel slavery for a full sixty years after the Haitian revolution and lived with such convoluted inhumanities as the "three-fifths compromise," Haiti made its politics plain. For example, the 1806 Haitian Constitution states: "Every African, Indian and those issued from their blood, born of colonies or foreign countries, who might come to reside in the Republic, will be recognized as Haitians ..." Citizenship could be obtained after one year of residence. Haiti's mere existence, let alone its open shores, was an affront to colonial world order. In the words of anthropologist Ira Lowenthal, "Haiti was the first *free* nation of *free* men to arise within, and in resistance to, the emerging constellation of Western European empire." It would be another 150 years before much of the colonized gained independence. The roots of what became the modern human rights movement are contained in the Revolution and Haiti's early governance.

Soon after independence, Haiti encountered a number of all-too-modern consequences typical of the post-colonial world. This includes the first example of foreign debt creation. In 1825, under threat of invasion, Haiti agreed to pay "reparations" to France for property seized during the revolution, namely themselves and the land of the former colony. With no cash reserves or sanctioned foreign trade Haiti had no money to pay this "debt." It had to borrow from France (and others) to meet the payment. This initial debt, equivalent to $21 billion in today's money, was paid well into the twentieth century, to say nothing of further indebtedness accrued over the intervening decades. Traces of this initial debt were paid until 1947.

In a direct analogy to what is called "structural adjustment" in the post-WWII global economic era, Haiti's internal development and foreign trade was heavily influenced by its creditors. Non-economically productive sectors such as public health, education, and environmental and food sustainability were neglected in favor of agricultural and natural resource exportation.

Though politically independent, throughout the nineteenth century Haiti developed according to the priorities and the constraints of creditors in Europe and the United States and fell ever further into debt. The twentieth century saw the increasing influence of the United States—including a military invasion between 1915–1934, continuing with a number of U.S.-backed governments until the 1957 election of François Duvalier, whose rise to power was part of a backlash against the elite, light-skinned governments that followed U.S. occupation. This brutal Duvalier family dictatorship lasted until 1986.

Most recently, Haiti suffered a "natural" disaster of unprecedented concentration. Only a small number of natural disasters have caused greater casualties: flooding in China in 1931, the Bhola cyclone in present-day Bangladesh in 1970, and the Tangshan earthquake in 1976. The earthquake on January 12, 2010, is estimated to have killed 220,000–316,000 people in its immediate aftermath. As a recent comparison, the Indian Ocean tsunami in December 2004 carried a similar death toll but this was spread over many hundreds of miles of coastline and more than eight nations.

The devestation of the earthquake in Haiti was concentrated in Port-au-Prince, the city's southern suburbs, the small urban center of Léogâne (closest to the epicenter), and as far south as Jacmel on Haiti's south coast. The intensity of images and stories that followed the disaster may well have given most people in the world their framework for understanding (and misunderstanding) Haiti.

It is impossible to understand the devastation of the earthquake without understanding the city of Port-au-Prince. But this does not work in reverse; Haiti and its capital city are, of course, much more than a single disaster or any single narrative. The recent loss of lives, homes, crops, and vital public infrastructure brought by Hurricane Matthew in October 2016 reminds us that Haiti and Haitians continue to struggle and deserve the world's attention, understanding, and generosity.

We recognize that the following appendices are wholly inadequate in providing an understanding of the country's history and society. We offer them instead to help readers grasp the ways the narratives in this book are part of that larger history of a city and nation.

—*Evan Lyon*

APPENDIX I: HAITIAN TIMELINE

Our focus in this collection has been Port-au-Prince, and we've consciously chosen to avoid any attempts to provide a full account of Haitian history or politics. Still, some context is important. Because Haiti's history of colonization, revolution, governments, invasions, and heads of state—from Toussaint Louverture to the U.S. occupation to Papa and Baby Doc Duvalier—are a part of the stories some of our narrators have chosen to tell about themselves, we offer this timeline as a reference. We also have a few recommendations for further reading on the subject (see page 343).

5000 BC: Humans first reach the island that, in modern times, would be divided into present-day Haiti and the Dominican Republic.

300 BC: Farming villages are established on the island around this time by a division of the Arawak culture which is prevalent throughout the Caribbean and coastal South and Central America.

Pre-1492: Before contact with Europeans, the island is inhabited by a Taíno-speaking people who refer to the island as *Hayti*, or "land of mountains."

1492: Christopher Columbus establishes the first European settlement in the Americas near present-day Cap-Haïtien. He names the island *La Isla Española*—"the Spanish Island," later anglicized to *Hispaniola*.

1490s: The Spaniards enslave much of the indigenous Taíno population. The indigenous population rapidly declines from disease introduced from Europe. Abuse and mass killings by the Spaniards cause the remaining population of Taíno speakers to nearly disappear.

1517: The first African slaves are brought to Haiti to replace the dwindling population of indigenous slaves. Up to a million Africans will be brought to Haiti as slaves over the coming centuries.

1550: The indigenous population of the island has been reduced to an estimated few hundred people from an estimated hundreds of thousands at the time of Columbus's arrival.

1659: King Louis XIV of France establishes a permanent settlement on Tortuga Island near Hispaniola's northern coast. The island has long served as a base for French pirates. Some of the island's French inhabitants soon migrate to Hispaniola and establish plantations. A French colony is established in Turgeau heights (just southwest of modern Port-au-Prince) and a hospital is built there.

1664: The French West India Company is established to direct expected commerce between growing French Caribbean colonies and France.

1670: The first major French settlement on Hispaniola is established and is named Cap-Français (now Cap-Haïtien).

Late 1600s: Hispaniola is a hub of the "triangle trade" in which manufactured goods pass from Europe to Africa, slaves from Africa to the Americas, and slave-produced crops from the Americas to Europe.

1697: Spain sends troops to drive away French colonists from Hispaniola, including from the region that had come to be called Hôpital (present-day Port-au-Prince) after the hospital built there. French settlers drive off the invading Spanish troops. Spain soon cedes the western part of Hispaniola to France as part of the Treaty of Ryswick. The French-controlled portion of the island is then renamed Saint-Domingue.

1706: French colonial authorities fear English invasion of Saint-Domingue and also seek to impose authority over pirate communities living in Hôpital. Authorities dispatch a ship named *Le Prince* to the bay near Hôpital in order to assert control of the area. It is this ship that will eventually give the city of Port-au-Prince its name. French nobility begin to claim land grants in the Hôpital region.

1742: The French found Port-au-Prince on the Gulf of Gonâve with the intention of making it the central port of the French-controlled portion of the island. The location is chosen partly because the surrounding heights make it easier to defend from land and sea attacks than other settlements within Saint-Domingue. Port-au-Prince is made capital of the colony by 1749.

Early 1700s: Through the first half of the century, trade from agriculture based on slave labor expands. Cotton, sugar, indigo, coffee, and other agricultural exports make Saint-Domingue a great source of wealth for French landowners. Those landowners bring more slaves to the colony to meet economic demand, and those slaves face brutal and often fatal working conditions in the fields. Many slaves escape to the colony's mountainous countryside and form independent communities. Some communities of former slaves begin raiding

French settlements. Both slaves and former slaves share religious beliefs derived in part from West African *Vodun* but also incorporating elements of Roman Catholicism, Taíno beliefs, and other religious traditions. Though Haitian *Vodou* is commonly practiced by the 1700s, Roman Catholicism remains the only religion slaves are allowed to practice publicly in Saint-Domingue.

1750s: Kreyol is now spoken by the majority of the population in Saint-Domingue. The language is a creole, or relatively stable mixture of other languages. Kreyol is based on eighteenth-century French with elements of Spanish, Taíno, various West African languages, and Portuguese.

1751: Separate earthquakes two months apart destroy much of Port-au-Prince.

1751–1758: A former slave named François Mackandal leads a rebellion against slave owners. Some historians believe Mackandal might have been a Vodou priest, or *houngan*, and likely encouraged slaves to poison colonists and livestock. Mackandal is captured in 1758 and burned at the stake by French authorities. The colonial authority then begins passing laws that severely restrict the rights of nonwhites in Saint-Domingue, including the rights of tens of thousands of free people of color (*gens de couleur libres*, often shortened to *gens de couleur*), including those with white and African ancestry known as *mulattoes*. At this time, whites make up only 10 percent of the population of Saint-Domingue.

1770: A powerful earthquake devastates Port-au-Prince.

1787: By this year, Saint-Domingue produces about 60 percent of the world's coffee and 40 percent of the sugar imported by France and Britain. It accounts for almost 40 percent of France's foreign trade.

This output is maintained through the exploitation of approximately half a million slaves.

1789: The French Revolution weakens French rule abroad and gives colonial subjects new concepts to employ in demanding their own rights. At this time, Saint-Domingue has a population of around 30,000 gens de couleur, some of whom have become wealthy plantation owners and many of whom are slaveholders. Many gens de couleur seek greater civil liberties and suffrage, including the large community of gens de couleur living in the mountains south of Port-au-Prince.

1791: Slaves begin to revolt in the north, and soon over 100,000 slaves and free people of color are involved in the rebellion. On or around August 14, 1791, Dutty Boukman, a Vodou houngan and a leader of the revolution, presided over a great ceremony at Bois Caïman in the north of Haiti. A week later 1,800 plantations had been destroyed and 1,000 slaveholders killed. Within two weeks, the revolutionaries control most of the northern territories of Saint-Domingue.

1792: By early in the year, former slaves control much of Saint-Domingue. The French Legislative Assembly grants full civil rights to all free men of color in all of France's colonies, partly as a way of subverting the rebellion on the island. The Assembly also orders 6,000 French troops to the island to stop the revolt.

1793: France and Great Britain go to war, and Great Britain forms an alliance with Spain to drive French troops out of Saint-Domingue. Spanish troops are joined by former slaves to drive out the French. By the end of the year, French authorities have begun negotiating with revolutionary leaders including Toussaint Louverture to switch alliances and join France if slavery were to be abolished.

1794: Slavery is formally abolished in all French colonies. Toussaint Louverture and some of the forces of former slaves and gens de couleur join France against Spain and Great Britain. Louverture's lieutenants include former slaves Jean-Jacques Dessalines and Henri Christophe. Aside from British and Spanish soldiers, Louverture's troops also battle former slaves still aligned with Spain. Louverture wins a string of military victories.

1795: In the Treaty of Basel, Spain cedes all of Hispaniola to France. Because of weakened French authority, Louverture is able to assert control over all of Hispaniola and makes himself governor of an effectively autonomous state.

1801: Louverture issues a new constitution for Saint-Domingue that calls for an autonomous state with Louverture himself appointed governor for life. He also has the power to choose his successor, and future governors would be appointed for five-year terms. The constitution also bans all religions other than Catholicism and upholds a plantation system called *fermage* in which the government would lease land to managers, and former slaves would be legally obligated to stay on the land and help cultivate it. After the declaration of this constitution, Napoleon Bonaparte sends a French force, an expedition led by his brother-in-law Victor Emmanuel Leclerc, to reassert control over Saint-Domingue.

1802: After losing effective control of the island, Louverture is promised his freedom if he integrates his forces into the French army. He agrees, but is arrested anyway and is imprisoned in France, where he soon dies. After France begins to reassert slavery in Saint-Domingue under Napoleonic rule, another rebellion forms. In October, former French allies such as Dessalines, Christophe, and Pétion join the rebellion.

1803: Britain is again at war with France and blockades Saint-Domingue, making it impossible for Napoleon to supply or reinforce troops there. Rebels defeat remaining French troops throughout Saint-Domingue. By the end of the year, rebels, now led by Dessalines, have completely routed the French. Leclerc and many of his remaining troops fall prey to yellow fever. Dessalines rips the white stripe from a French flag to create what will become the first flag of independent Haiti.

1804: On January 1, Dessalines signs a declaration of independence. The newly independent people of the former Saint-Domingue adopt the indigenous word for Hispaniola, *Hayti*, as the name of the new nation.

1805: Dessalines establishes a new constitution and becomes the emperor of Haiti. Dessalines is determined to find a capital other than Port-au-Prince due to the presence there of powerful gens de couleur families, especially those living south of the city in what will become Pétionville. The new capital is established in Artibonite and named Dessalines. Approximately 3,000 to 5,000 French- and Kreyol-speaking whites remaining in Haiti are massacred on Dessalines's orders, and their former lands are taken by the state. Dessalines makes white ownership of land illegal and reasserts the principle of fermage, so that most Haitian citizens are categorized as either laborers (serfs) or soldiers, with soldiers making up 10 percent of the adult male population.

1806: Pétion and Christophe work to overthrow Dessalines. Dessalines is assassinated in October, after which the country is divided in two. Pétion becomes president of the southern Republic of Haiti while Christophe becomes king of the Kingdom of Haiti in the north.

1806–1820: King Henry Christophe builds the Citadel overlooking Cap-Haïtien. Built to defend against recolonization, the fortress remains a symbol of the hostile world dominated by foreign, mercantilist powers that Haiti was willing to fight for its independence.

1816: Pétion implements a constitution that includes a bicameral legislature made up of a senate and democratically elected chamber of deputies, the influence of which can still be seen in Haiti's system of governance today.

1818: Pétion dies of yellow fever and Jean-Pierre Boyer becomes president of the Republic of Haiti.

1820: After a coup in the Kingdom of Haiti and the suicide of Henri Christophe, Boyer is able to reunite Haiti without bloodshed. He makes Port-au-Prince the capital of the reunified Republic of Haiti.

1822: A fire destroys major parts of Port-au-Prince.

1825: After pressure from a French fleet of warships, Boyer begins negotiations with France over formal acknowledgment of Haitian independence. France demands payment of a large indemnity for the property it lost during the revolution—i.e., the slaves and land—in exchange for acknowledgment of Haitian sovereignty. The original agreement grants a debt to France of 150 million francs (though the final number is negotiated down to 90 million francs). The enormous debt will have devastating consequences for the nation's development. Boyer continues the practice of Haitian serfdom by passing the Code Rural. Though the code breaks up some large plantations and distributes land to smaller farmers, it also requires farmers to meet production quotas to help pay Haiti's debt to France and also forbids farmers from moving into cities or selling their farms, among other restrictions.

1843: Another devastating earthquake hits Haiti. Jean-Pierre Boyer is removed as president and flees to Jamaica. He eventually dies exiled in France.

1844: The eastern two-thirds of Haiti splits from the Republic of Haiti and becomes the Dominican Republic. The Republic of Haiti does not recognize the new state and launches numerous unsuccessful invasions of their new neighbor over the coming decades. Haiti finally recognizes Dominican statehood in 1874.

1847–1858: A year after being chosen as Haiti's new president, Faustin Soulouque declares himself emperor and seeks to elevate a new black nobility by massacring mulattoes who hold power throughout Port-au-Prince. Emperor Faustin organizes a secret police and a paramilitary known as the *Zinglins* who terrorize his political enemies. Faustin is overthrown in a coup in 1858.

1862: The United States recognizes Haiti as a sovereign nation. Decades later, Frederick Douglass becomes the first U.S. Consul-General to the Republic of Haiti.

1898: The burden of Haiti's debt to France reaches half of the national budget.

1910: Fearful of foreign influence in the Caribbean, U.S. President William Howard Taft loans Haiti a large sum of money to help it pay off its debt to France. The plan ultimately has little impact.

1911–1915: Seven Haitian presidents are killed or overthrown.

1914: U.S. President Woodrow Wilson orders the Marines to invade Haiti. Although he claims to be motivated by the desire to protect Haitian citizens from anarchy, his aim is to protect American interests and prevent a possible German invasion. By transferring $500,000 from the Haitian National Bank to New York, the United States effectively gains control of the country's finances. Port-au-Prince is placed under martial law by the U.S.

1915: The Haitian-American Treaty of 1915 creates a mixed Haitian and American military force controlled by the U.S. Marines. It officially gives the American government control of Haitian finances and the legal right to intervene in the country's politics. The U.S. installs a pro-American president, Philippe Sudré Dartiguenave.

1917: The U.S. tries to force Haiti to adopt a new constitution allowing ownership of land by foreigners, which had been forbidden after the Haitian Revolution. When the Haitian legislature rejects the new document, the U.S. forces the president to dissolve the legislature.

1918: The burden of Haiti's debt to France reaches 80 percent of the national budget.

1919–1929: Government policies such as forced labor, press censorship, and racial segregation lead to popular unrest. Groups of armed resistance become popularly known as the *Cacos*. U.S. Marines clash with the Cacos and assassinate their leader, Charlemagne Péralte.

1929: The Haitian legislature meets for the first time since 1917. In December, U.S. Marines fire into a crowd of protesters in Aux Cayes killing twelve and wounding twenty-three. The "Cayes Massacre" becomes a rallying cry to end U.S. occupation.

1934: The U.S. officially withdraws, but maintains direct financial control of Haiti until 1941. Between 1915 and 1934, an estimated 15,000 Haitians have been killed by U.S. troops or the police under U.S. control.

1946: Léon Dumarsais Estimé is elected president of Haiti. He is the first black president of Haiti since the end of the U.S. occupation. He appoints a physician and political ally named François Duvalier as the director of the National Public Health Service. Duvalier has been active in programs to eradicate diseases in Haiti such as typhus and malaria. Many of his patients have called him "Papa Doc," a nickname he takes into political service.

1947: Haiti fully repays the indemnity France demanded in return for recognition of independence in 1825, nearly 125 years after the original deal was struck.

1950: Estimé is removed in a coup and Duvalier returns to practicing medicine. He soon goes into hiding in fear of reprisals for his former support of Estimé.

1956: After declaration of an amnesty, Duvalier emerges from hiding and runs in the election for president of Haiti. During his campaign, Duvalier stokes popular resentment against the powerful mulatto elite. He paints his opponent for office as part of this elite and gains popular support in rural Haiti as well as support in the military. He wins the election with over two-thirds of the vote, though there are reports of voter fraud and intimidation at the polls.

1957: After inauguration, Duvalier exiles many political opponents.

1958: Following a failed coup by exiled military officers, François Duvalier replaces top generals in the army with his appointees. He also begins organizing a paramilitary group that he calls the National Security Volunteers but will become popularly known as the *Tonton Makout*. The Makout will terrorize Haiti for the next several decades.

1962: The United States suspends most economic aid to Haiti

partly due to allegations that Duvalier is appropriating the funds for himself. In turn, Duvalier renounces U.S. aid.

1964: François Duvalier is elected president for life, ruling over a police state marked by corruption and human rights abuses. By this time his Tonton Makout paramilitary is over twice the size of the official army.

1965: Duvalier begins persecuting suspected communists after Fidel Castro aligns Cuba's revolution with communism. Strict laws against promotion or possession of communist literature are passed. Duvalier and the Makouts kill an estimated tens of thousands on the pretext they are keeping suspected communist dissidents out of Haiti. Many educated Haitians, including doctors and lawyers, flee the country fearing political persecution by Duvalier's regime. However, Duvalier's anti-communist rhetoric earns him the tolerance, if not greater support, from the United States.

1971: François Duvalier dies. His nineteen-year-old son, Jean-Claude "Baby Doc" Duvalier, succeeds him as president for life, though reluctantly. Duvalier cedes direct rule to councilors so he can focus on his social life. After some minor reforms, including a slight relaxation of press censorship, the Nixon administration re-establishes economic aid to Haiti. The Makout continue to terrorize Haiti and human rights abuses are rampant.

1978: After the outbreak of swine fever virus among Haiti's domestic pig population, the U.S. pegs further agricultural aid to the condition that Haiti exterminate its native domestic pigs and replace them with breeds from the U.S. However, the new livestock are not adapted to Haitian climate or food sources and fare poorly. Much of the new pig population is soon lost, causing massive economic hardship and starvation in rural Haiti.

1980s: Haiti's tourism industry (important to its economy) is decimated following reports of AIDS and instability.

1985: After years of economic hardship and political repression, a string of popular uprisings, strikes, and riots begin throughout Haiti. A parish priest and vocal exponent of Liberation Theology named Jean-Bertrand Aristide returns from exile and begins giving popular political sermons out of Saint-Jean Bosco Church in Port-au-Prince.

1986: Jean-Claude Duvalier flees in the wake of popular unrest. The Reagan administration encourages Duvalier to leave but refuses to grant him asylum in the United States. However, Duvalier is flown out of Haiti on a U.S. Air Force plane.

1986–1990: A series of governments fail, creating a vacuum of authority as the Duvalier period comes to a close.

1987: Haitian Kreyol is made the official second language of the country, ushering in an era where the majority of the population can, for the first time, read official laws and policies. Approximately 10 percent of Haitians—the upper class and better educated—are fluent in French.

1988: More than 100 armed Tonton Makout break into Aristide's Saint-Jean Bosco Church during service and attack parishioners with guns and machetes. At least thirteen are killed and seventy injured, though Aristide escapes and goes into hiding. The attack is one of many failed attempts on Aristide's life during the 1980s. He becomes an increasingly popular figure throughout Haiti.

1990: Jean-Bertrand Aristide is elected by popular vote in what is considered the country's first truly democratic election.

1991: Aristide attempts numerous political reforms, including bringing the military under civilian control and investigating human rights abuses. His policies anger the nation's elites, and in September, just a few months after his inauguration, he is overthrown in a coup. Aristide states that he believes the C.I.A. has backed the coup that removed him from office. The United Nations establishes a trade embargo to force Haiti's new rulers to step down. However, the Bush and Clinton administrations grant a number of exemptions to U.S. businesses operating in Haiti.

1991–1994: Thousands of small boats filled with Haitian refugees try to reach Florida.

1993: Numerous Aristide supporters still in Haiti are targeted for killing by paramilitary organizations. The United Nations authorizes a peacekeeping force to enter Haiti as part of an effort to reform Haitian civil society.

1994: U.S. President Bill Clinton sends an intervention force to Haiti. The troops restore President Aristide to power. Aristide disbands the Haitian military.

1995: René Préval is elected in Haiti's first peaceful transfer of power between elected presidents.

1996: U.S. and UN peacekeeping forces leave the country. Aristide breaks with a political party he helped form to start a new party called *Fanmi Lavas* ("the Family of the Flood").

2000: Aristide is re-elected with over 90 percent of the vote. The U.S. and other nations issue sanctions following the lopsided election and claims of electoral fraud.

2004: After an uprising against President Aristide, U.S. forces airlift him out of the country, allowing him and his family to escape into exile. Aristide spends the majority of this exile in South Africa.

2004: The international community establishes the United Nations Stabilization Mission in Haiti (MINUSTAH), tasking it with maintaining security, stabilizing the political process, and monitoring and promoting human rights.

2006: René Préval is re-elected to the presidency.

2008: Several people are killed throughout Haiti during riots protesting the high cost of living. Hurricanes kill almost 800 people and force hundreds of thousands from their homes.

January 12, 2010: A 7.0-magnitude earthquake strikes ten miles southwest of Port-au-Prince. Two strong aftershocks follow shortly thereafter. Millions are displaced, approximately 250,000 people are killed, and most of the government and medical infrastructure of Port-au-Prince is destroyed.

January 14, 2010: The search for survivors continues. In the absence of heavy-lifting equipment, people sort through rubble using their bare hands. Lost infrastructure—including the shutdown of the international airport—make it difficult to reach victims and relief workers with supplies.

January 15, 2010: Destruction at airports continues to prevent international volunteers and supplies from getting into the city.

January 20, 2010: A 6.1-magnitude aftershock hits west of Port-au-Prince. The U.S. announces that it will send another 4,000 troops to assist with the relief effort.

October 16, 2010: Thirty-eight-year-old Jean Salgadeau Pelette becomes the first Haitian to die of cholera in more than a century. He contracted the disease through exposure to contaminated river water in Mirebalais, a town in central Haiti. The cholera bacteria was introduced by UN troops through negligent sanitation practices at the MINUSTAH base in Mirebalais.

October 27, 2010: The number of cholera deaths reaches 303. Most victims have been infected in the area surrounding Mirebalais.

December 3, 2010: The nationwide death toll from cholera reaches 2,071. As many as 91,770 cases have been reported, with 43,243 people hospitalized. By August 2015 those figures would balloon to 700,000 cholera cases, with more than 9,000 Haitians dying from the disease.

2011: Popular musician Michel Martelly is elected president.

2012: A study by the Inter-American Development Bank puts the earthquake's cost between $7.2 billion and $13.2 billion, based on a death toll of 200,000 to 250,000, and estimates that the country's economic growth is likely to be significantly set back by the disaster for years.

2012: Hurricane Sandy kills dozens of Haitians and destroys crops and property.

2012: The *New York Times* reports that 357,785 Haitians are still living in 496 tent camps, and that only $215 million of the $7.5 billion disbursed after the earthquake has been spent on permanent housing. By 2014, the International Organization for Migration (I.O.M.) would report this number was cut in half to 170,000.

APPENDIX II: GLOSSARY

2010 Haiti earthquake: The earthquake that hit Haiti on January 12, 2010 was unprecedented in its scale and magnitude of impact. In total it is estimated to have caused as many as 250,000 fatalities, cost up to $13.2 billion, destroyed 280,000 residences and commercial buildings, and displaced more than 3 million people. With the epicenter located close to Port-au-Prince, the earthquake devastated the greater Port-au-Prince commercial area, leveling hospitals and destroying communication systems and electrical networks.

arrondissement: Each of Haiti's ten *départements* is further divided into *arrondissements*, totaling forty-two in all. These arrondissements are the second-largest political subdivision within Haiti.

bidonvilles: The 2010 earthquake leveled in excess of 200,000 structures throughout the Port-au-Prince area, leaving more than 1.5 million people to form makeshift dwellings clustered into what would become 1,555 *bidonvilles*, or tent cities. Five years after the earthquake, that number was down to 79,397 people in 105 sites. While the effort to close camps has been relatively successful, the International Organization for Migration has focused on rental subsidies, funded by donors and pushed by the government but largely unpopular with displaced

Haitians wary of long-term dependency. The I.O.M. has recently shifted its approach toward building two-story houses for quake victims able to show proof of home ownership, with the provision that they house another victim rent free for two years.

Citadelle Laferrière: A UNESCO World Heritage Site and one of the largest fortresses in the Americas, the Citadelle Laferrière was built by Henri Christophe in 1820 in Haiti's Nord-Est Department.

citizenship issues in Dominican/Haitian relations: The Dominican Republic (DR) and Haiti have had a difficult political relationship since the Dominican Republic won independence from Haiti in 1844. In 2013, that tension was expressed in the passage of a decree that reviewed all national birth records from 1929 to 2007, retroactively restricting citizenship of tens of thousands of Dominicans. These former citizens were left facing deportation. In response to an outpouring of international criticism, the Dominican congress passed a bill in 2014 that extended citizenship to those who could provide proof of registering their birth. To date, fewer than 9,000 people have registered under this program, despite over 110,000 potentially qualifying, leading many to doubt the sincerity of the Dominican Republic's efforts to appease conflict between the two countries.

commune: The third tier of political divisions in Haiti after *département* and *arrondissement*. Forty-two arrondissements are divided into 140 communes and 570 communal sections.

corvée labor: Unpaid labor imposed by the state. At various points throughout the initial stages of Haitian independence, the state used corvée labor to force civilians to work under brutal conditions without remuneration in order to complete a variety of public works projects, notably King Henri Christophe's palaces and fortifications and the expansion of Haiti's road networks. During American military occupation from 1915-34, troops took advantage of corvée labor laws, long unused but never repealed.

deforestation: Haiti is more than 98 percent deforested. This process began under colonization and intensified with coffee production in the early eighteenth century. Currently deforestation and resulting soil erosion is driven by charcoal production. Charcoal is produced by the poor to pay for food, shelter, and other necessities.

département: The highest-level administrative division in Haiti. There are ten départements in Haiti, each with its own regional capital. The départements are divided up in arrondissements and further into communes.

external debt: Money owed to foreign creditors (governments, banks, individuals) has hampered Haiti's economic growth since independence. In 1825, newly independent Haiti struggled against the threat of French invasion and a return to slavery, and agreed to pay an indemnity and reduce its import and export taxes by 50 percent. Ultimately totaling 90 million francs, this indemnity was largely financed through loans from French financial institutions. The indemnity wasn't repaid in full until 1947, with loan payments accounting for 50 percent government expenditure in 1898 and 80 percent by 1914. Debt further skyrocketed under the Duvalier dictatorship, growing from US$302 million to over US$1 billion between 1980 and 2004.

Fanmi Lavalas: A Haitian political party formed in 1996 after a leading leftist political party Lavalas (Kreyol for flood) split to become the Struggling People's Organization and the Aristide-led Fanmi Lavalas. Fanmi Lavalas strongly opposed neoliberal policies and austerity measures supported by the Struggling People's Organization.

Front Révolutionnaire Armé pour le Progrès d'Haïti (FRAPH): A right-wing paramilitary group that emerged in 1993, aimed at repressing support for Jean-Bertrand Aristide in the aftermath of the coup that ousted Aristide from the presidency in 1991. Led by Emmanuel "Toto" Constant, the group worked in tandem with the military regime using violence to maintain political repression and authoritarian control.

gens de couleur: French for "people of color." Originally short for *gens de couleur libres*, or free people of color, the phrase was a common way of referring to free blacks or people of mixed race in France's West Indian colonies prior to the abolition of slavery. Pre-Haitian Saint-Domingue was legally divided into distinct classes based on race and land ownership, with the white plantation and working class set apart from the freedmen (*affranchis*) and slaves. Post-independence, Haiti inherited the division between mixed-race, French-speaking gens de couleur, and black, Kreyol-speaking Haitians, laying the foundation for race-based discrimination that continues today.

Hispaniola: the area of land comprising both Haiti and the Dominican Republic.

Kreyol: Spoken by all Haitians, the language is a creole, a stable native language combining other languages, in this instance predominantly eighteenth-century French with elements of Spanish, Taíno, various West African languages, and Portuguese.

loa: Loa, also spelled *lwa*, are the sprits of Haitian Vodou and serve as intermediaries between God (Bon Dye) and humanity. Vodou ceremonies are centered on invitation of a priestess (*mambo*) or priest (*houngan*) calling the loa to take part in the service. Loa arrive by possessing a worshiper and acting or speaking through them. Most loa are linked by syncretism to Catholic saints based on iconography or other characteristics.

restavek: A child domestic worker taken into a more affluent household ostensibly in exchange for receiving education and board. In reality, the majority of restaveks are trafficked or forced into slavery, vulnerable to abuse, and often escape to a life on the streets. Before the earthquake, about 250,000 restaveks lived in Haiti and an additional 2,500 had been trafficked into the Dominican Republic. Approximately two-thirds of all restaveks are girls.

Saint-Domingue: The French colony on the island of Hispaniola that would become the Independent Republic of Haiti in 1804.

Saint-Soleil School: a popular movement in Haitian art, drawing on symbolism from Vodou rituals and relying heavily on abstract forms.

Taíno: The indigenous people who populated the island of Hispaniola when Columbus arrived in 1492. Estimates put the pre-contact population at roughly hundreds of thousands to several million. While historians emphasize the disappearance of Taíno culture along with its population, its legacy continues in current Haitian and Dominican traditions, with many making efforts to claim direct Taíno lineage.

Temporary Protected Status (T.P.S.): A temporary legal residency status within the United States granted to citizens of specified countries. T.P.S. was established as a legal, nonpermanent form of residency by an act of Congress in 1990 in response to armed conflict in El Salvador. The T.P.S. visa is typically granted during a specific window of time to citizens of specified countries that are under a state of emergency due to warfare, natural disaster, or other humanitarian crisis. T.P.S. status is not intended to be a pathway to such permanent status documentation as green cards, but it does allow for work authorization in some cases. Currently, T.P.S. visas are administered by the Department of Homeland Security. T.P.S. status can be terminated for individuals at any time.

Tonton Makout: The paramilitary force formed by dictator François Duvalier ("Papa Doc") to suppress political opposition. Literally translated, Tonton Makout means "Uncle Gunnysack," a Haitian bogeyman who stuffs children into a bag at night. By regularly employing state-sanctioned rape and murder, they perpetuated a culture of terror that maintained their absolute command. Human Rights Watch estimates that the Duvalier regimes are collectively responsible for the death of 20,000 to 30,000, with the Tonton Makout responsible for the majority of violence.

United Nations Stabilization Mission in Haiti (MINUSTAH): The United Nations Stabilization Mission in Haiti was initially authorized following the 2004 coup d'état that ousted President Jean-Bertrand Aristide. After the 2010 earthquake, the UN peacekeeping forces were given a greater mandate to support reconstruction and stability efforts. MINUSTAH came under scrutiny when reckless sewage disposal at the UN base located on the Artibonite River near Mirebalais was directly traced to the outbreak of cholera, infecting hundreds of thousands of Haitians. The case triggered a re-examination of how peacekeeping personnel are used in disaster recovery.

United States Agency for International Development (U.S.A.I.D.): The division of the U.S. government responsible for foreign aid, U.S.A.I.D. has had a presence in Haiti for over fifty years.

Vodou: Practiced throughout Haiti, Vodou dates back to the eighteenth century or earlier and combines various elements of West African religious practices with Roman Catholicism and other belief systems. The same religious practices that developed in Haiti into Vodou have also found expression in other global religions, such as

Louisiana Voodoo, Vodun (practiced in Ghana, Togo, Benin, and Nigeria), Santaria in Cuba, Candomble in Brazil, and Dominican Vudú. The spirit of humans, saints, and the semidivine *loas* are central to the Vodou belief system, and much of Vodou ritual centers around honoring, summoning, or driving away loas and other spirits. Many core Vodou beliefs—especially around sickness and other forms of suffering—are shared by a majority of Haitians, regardless of personal religious beliefs.

APPENDIX III: HEALTH AND JUSTICE AFTER THE EARTHQUAKE

CHOLERA

A few short months after the earthquake, in the midst of the resulting rubble and chaos, Haiti was struck by an unexpected epidemic: cholera. The cholera outbreak highlighted the structural failings of the country's health, water, and sanitation infrastructure that needed both emergency and long-term responses in order to eradicate cholera from the country.

The disease had not existed in Haiti for over a century and entered the country through the UN's peacekeeping mission to Haiti (MINUSTAH). At the time of the disease's appearance, however, its origins were unknown. It was clear, however, that the disease was deadly and would continue to spread rapidly and kill if not properly addressed.

One of the first people to contract cholera in Haiti after the earthquake was named Jean Pelette. He was thirty-eight years old, from Mirebalais in the Centre Department, and had a history of severe mental illness. Like others in Mirebalais, Jean Pelette used the Latem River that flowed through his town for washing—his body, his teeth, and his clothes. Despite having access to potable water at home, Pelette also regularly drank from the river. Pelette died on October 16, 2010 after developing acute diarrhea. His was not an isolated case. At the time, sixty-one cases of watery diarrhea were reported in the area.

But the epidemic did not stay isolated in Mirebalais for long. On November 9, the *New York Times* issued reports suggesting that the disease had made it to Port-au-Prince. The case in question, a young boy living in a post-earthquake tent camp, served as proof that the bacteria was moving quickly through the country's departments.

By January 2013, just over one year after cholera's appearance in Haiti, 642,832 cases would be recorded with a fatality rate of 1.2 percent. Despite these grave statistics, studies have shown that these numbers likely vastly underestimate the true incidence, as many died at home or just before making it to hospitals or clinics where their illnesses could be recorded.

While there were undeniable victories during the response to the crisis, the scale of the epidemic raises questions about why the disease afflicted the nation as intensely as it did. For one, the strain of cholera found in Haiti is a bacterium that can exist outside of a human host for almost two weeks in warm conditions. The disease spreads through the consumption of water that has been infected with contaminated feces. About a quarter of those infected show symptoms, but asymptomatic carriers can still spread the disease. So cholera is a particularly deadly disease in warm places with ailing water and sanitation infrastructures, such as Haiti.

Clean water and sanitation coverage in Haiti is among the lowest in the world. Before the earthquake, 69 percent of Haitians had access to an improved water source and 17 percent had access to improved sanitation facilities. Among urban Haitians, 85 percent had access to an improved water source and only 24 percent had access to an improved sanitation source. The destruction wrought by the earthquake reduced these numbers further.

The cholera epidemic was further exacerbated by the post-quake healthcare shortage. In the quake, 60 percent of Haiti's already struggling health care system was destroyed. The treatment of incoming patients depended heavily on quickly constructed health centers. In his book *Haiti After the Earthquake* physician/anthropologist Paul Farmer describes the public response to the network of care centers, "These sites were soon deluged with people standing, or trying to stand, in line for intake into these centers. Such rapid treatment responses saved lives, probably thousands of them."

The Haitian government has made marginal advances in addressing the underlying, structural failings that led to the outbreak. In 2012, public health agencies outlined the ten-year National Plan for the Eradication of Cholera. The plan focuses on increasing access to potable water and improved excreta-disposal systems, increasing national capacity for solid-waste management, increasing access to primary health care, and strengthening the national capacity for epidemiological surveillance. While the emphasis on structural rebuilding is promising, the agency estimated the cost for the implementation of this plan at US$2.2 billion. By 2015, according to a statement made by outgoing UN coordinator in the Response to Cholera in Haiti Pedro Medrano Rojas, only 20 percent of that budget had been procured. It may be a long time before these problems are addressed in a truly comprehensive way and the risk of cholera, to which the country's most vulnerable are still exposed, is truly eradicated.

When news of cholera's emergence first broke, the mystery of how the strain entered the country and the Artibonite River was of great concern. As public health authorities struggled to understand and contain the outbreak, authorities and journalists began tracing the origin of the epidemic to a UN camp located upstream of Mirebalais. In December 2010, a leaked French report suggested that sewage from the UN site had escaped into Mirebalais citizens' water source. The UN initially refused to comment on these and other reports. By 2011, with rumors rising of UN involvement, an independent report was commissioned to explore the cause of the cholera epidemic.[1] The report emphasized structural factors necessary for the spread of cholera (the use of river water by Haitians for drinking, the farming of paddy fields, lack of immunity, poor sanitation, fleeing by residents from cholera-infected areas). The report seemed to do little other than blame Haitians for the conditions in which they live. One of the lead authors of the UN report, in light of new genomic evidence, changed her opinion to blame the UN camp for contaminating the water source with the disease.

These realizations raised questions of human rights and justice. A document entitled *Violations of Rights Related to the Ongoing Cholera Epidemic*, by the Institute for Justice and Democracy in Haiti (I.J.D.H.), clearly lays out the rights-based violations by both the UN and Haitian state against cholera victims. Endorsed by forty-seven related rights organizations, this document makes the clear case that both bodies have failed to protect the rights of cholera victims. The I.J.D.H. emphasizes that while the Haitian state must be held accountable for its own failures, the actions of the UN restricted the state's ability to ensure certain rights. Ultimately, the Haitian state is called upon to make reparative actions in the realm of water and health, but also to defend the rights of its citizens by exerting pressure on the UN to take responsibility for its part in the crisis.

Litigation has also exerted pressure on the UN. Lawyers at I.J.D.H. and the Bureau des Avocats Internationaux (B.A.I.) filed claims against the UN on behalf of 5,000 cholera victims seeking an investment in the water and sanitation system in Haiti, individual compensation for victims, and a public apology. Fifteen months later, these claims would be deemed "not receivable by the UN." Cases are ongoing and remain unresolved. Importantly, however, on August 17, presumably because of outside pressure, Secretary General of

---

[1] A. Carvioto et al., *Final Report of the Independent Panel of Experts on the Cholera Outbreak in Haiti*, United Nations, un.org, May 4, 2011.

the UN Ban Ki-Moon released a statement admitting that the UN should be playing a larger role in the response to the cholera outbreak in Haiti because of the UN's hand in its entrance into the country.

The cholera epidemic has surfaced complex questions of public health, basic services, human rights, and international justice. By late 2016, there had been 780,029 incidences and 9,160 deaths from cholera in Haiti.

SEXUAL VIOLENCE

In stark contrast to the case of cholera, the recorded history of sexual violence in Haiti extends far beyond the earthquake of January 2010 to the voyages of Christopher Columbus, with both natives of the island and the explorer himself documenting abuse. In the twentieth century, rape was used as a weapon of control during the regimes of François Duvalier (1957–1971), his son Jean-Claude Duvalier (1971–1986), and General Raoul Cédras (1991–1994). High levels of sexual violence continue into the twenty-first century, with pervasive gender inequity, systemic misogyny, ineffective policing and criminal justice systems, and a culture of shame for victims. Reporting and prosecution rates are extremely low. Victims of sexual violence include both men and women, but women are most often affected.

An unrelenting contributor to sexual violence in Haiti—rooted in tremendous inequality—is the *restavek* system. In Kreyol *restavek* means "to stay with" and refers to the practice of poor families sending their children to work as unpaid domestic servants to wealthier families in exchange for shelter, food, and, sometimes, the opportunity to attend school. In the chapter of a paper detailing violence against women and girls in Haiti entitled "The Girl's Body as Property: The Practice of Restavek," Benedetta Faedi describes this system as emerging from the time of independence and lasting until the present. Faedi reveals that almost 10 percent of female restavek children are victims of sexual violence. This is a risk 4.5 times higher than for a non-restavek female child.[2]

At its core, the restavek system results from the problem of structural poverty. Poor families send their children away in hopes that they will have better lives. To end the restavek system forcing Haitian children into potentially harmful living arrangements, the problem must be addressed as a result of systemic poverty and financial insecurity.

Increases in sexual violence in the period of trauma and insecurity following the 2010 earthquake are well documented in the setting of massive displacement and tent camps. Formal camps offer displaced people basic necessities, such as shelter and clean water, but continue to be replete with sexual violence. Informal camps fare even worse.

Before the Haitian earthquake, a number of sources had documented rises in sexual violence following natural disasters in other countries, for example following Hurricane Katrina, the December 2004 tsunami in Asia, and the 2005 Kashmir earthquake. In Haiti, reports of rape taking place in Haiti's relief camps emerged less than a month following the earthquake. In February 2010, the *Independent* reported that camp dwellers and outsiders were taking "emergency measures" to curb the incidence of the crime. This included informal groups of camp residents that patrolled the premises during the night with knives and iron bars, girls wearing jeans under their skirts as a protective measure, and the establishment of health centers specifically for women.[3]

A year after the earthquake, Amnesty International published a report entitled, *Aftershocks: Women Speak Out Against Sexual Violence in Haiti's Camps*. This report states that in the 150 days following the earthquake there were 250 reported rape cases throughout the

---

[2] Benedetta Faedi, "The Double Weakness of Girls: Discrimination and Sexual Violence in Haiti," in *Stanford Journal of International Law* (Winter 2008).

[3] Nina Lakhani, "Rape on the Rise in Haiti's Camps," *Independent*, February 6, 2010.

camps. The report's press release states, "There is no security for the women and girls in the camps. They feel abandoned and vulnerable to being attacked. Armed gangs attack at will, safe in the knowledge that there is still little prospect that they will be brought to justice."[4]

But increases in sexual violence after the earthquake were not isolated to displacement camps. Political instability in the country also contributes to the continued violence against women and girls. As previously mentioned, sexual violence has existed as a weapon of political subjugation throughout world and Haitian history. Faedi, in her report on restaveks, also describes the way political gangs use the bodies of women as a means to punish the women's family members.

Despite the prevalence of sexual violence, the disappointing truth is that very few rape cases in Haiti, as with many other countries, are reported or result in a prosecution in the Haitian criminal justice system, much less a conviction. Not only can the process of prosecution be difficult and inefficient, but it can also result in negative consequences for those who choose to take action against rapists. The I.J.D.H. and the Bureau des Avocats Internationaux (B.A.I.) report that, according to a 2012 UN study that observed rape complaints over a three-month period, only one out of sixty-two complaints in the sample made it to a courtroom. Thanks in part to the work done by B.A.I., the numbers of both prosecutions and convictions have increased slightly in recent years. For example, their work in 2012 resulted in seven trials and convictions.

Fear of retribution from the families of accused and convicted rapists, as evidenced in the narrative of Loutchama and her mother Adrienne Phatal included in this book, is one of the reasons these attacks go unreported and under-prosecuted. I.J.D.H. reports Loutchama's mother as having stated, "My feeling is, I lost. The lawyers put in my mind the idea of going to court, but in the end

---

[4] Amnesty International, *Aftershocks: Women Speak Out Against Sexual Violence in Haiti's Camps*, amnesty.org, January 6, 2011.

I lost a beautiful daughter, and what did I gain with this 'justice'? Nothing."[5]

On a positive note, work done by civil society organizations and NGOs appears to be slowly curbing sexual violence and advocating for victims of sexual violence. In 2005, rape was criminalized. In terms of the overall reduction of incidents, the grassroots Haitian NGO KOFAVIV, with support from the Goldin Institute, in a 2015 report documented 575 fewer incidents of attacks against women than they did in 2010. The data of one NGO tells us only so much, but it does demonstrate the potential for improvement on this issue and the existence of an ongoing fight for a more just and violence-free Haiti.

H.I.V./AIDS

The global H.I.V./AIDS pandemic emerged in the early 1980s simultaneously in New York, San Francisco, and Port-au-Prince, spread though sexual transmission. As a consequence of this early introduction of the virus and years of poor access to health care and prevention services, Haiti has the highest prevalence of H.I.V. in the Caribbean and Latin America. In 2015, an estimated 1.7 percent of the adults aged fifteen to forty-nine years had H.I.V. with approximately 8,000 deaths from AIDS-related illness that year.

Initial efforts to respond to the H.I.V. crisis in Haiti grew from a partnership between the Ministry of Health and two NGOs, the Haitian Group for the Study of Kaposi's Sarcoma and Opportunistic Infections (GHESKIO, 1982) and Partners In Health (1987). GHESKIO was the first institution in the world established specifically to fight H.I.V./AIDS and, alongside Partners In Health, has provided preventative and treatment services for decades. In 2002, Haiti became a recipient of aid from the Global Fund to Fight AIDS,

---

[5] Lisa Armstrong, "The Rapist and the Girl Next Door, the Paradox of Prosecuting Rape Cases in Haiti," ijdh.org, May 7, 2014.

Tuberculosis, and Malaria (G.F.A.T.M.). Since then, H.I.V. has remained a leading health concern in Haiti, but substantial progress has been made in preventing and treating H.I.V. infections nationwide.

Understandably, the severe destruction brought by the 2010 earthquake placed provision of H.I.V./AIDS healthcare in jeopardy. The weeks immediately after the catastrophe were characterized by the struggle to cope with the loss of many healthcare professionals, as well as clinical environments, with care moved to tent cities. Amid the confusion, it was impossible to tell how many H.I.V./AIDS patients were unable to attain regular antiretroviral treatment.

Since the earthquake, large-scale studies have reported a return to pre-earthquake levels of treatment and infection rates,[6] while further reports have linked successful programs to a pre-established infrastructure (Partners In Health and GHESKIO) working with significant funds provided in large part by the Global Fund and the US President's Emergency Plan for AIDS Relief (PEPFAR). Many still suffer from the linked problems of H.I.V., loss of healthcare infrastructure, and sexual violence. Still Haiti has reached near universal antiretroviral treatment coverage with 50,078 patients being treated as of June 2013. GHESKIO treats 40 percent of these patients in and around Port-au-Prince.

TUBERCULOSIS

Tuberculosis (TB) has infected and killed humans for millennia; the disease has never gone away. Globally, as of 2015, tuberculosis surpassed H.I.V. to become the leading infectious killer of adults. In Haiti, tuberculosis has always been a leading health concern despite the fact the disease is curable in nearly all cases. Since TB is an

[6] See J. A. Walldorf, et al., "Recovery of HIV Service Provision Post-Earthquake," *AIDS* 26 (2012).

airborne infection, everyone in proximity to the disease is vulnerable. Poverty, poor nutrition, and difficulty accessing healthcare, however, lead to greater illness and death among some communities. On a global scale, over 95 percent of TB deaths occur in low- and middle-income countries. While TB remains a leading health problem in Haiti, with an incidence rate (number of new infections per year) of 200 per 100,000 people, Haiti is not ranked among the nations designated as high-burden countries.

The introduction of H.I.V. in the early 1980s has only worsened the problem. The annual risk of developing tuberculosis for people living with HIV is between twelve and twenty times more likely than it is for those without the virus. The emergence of multidrug-resistant tuberculosis (M.D.R.T.B.) in Haiti has been recognized as a problem since the 1980s, with multidrug-resistance an ever-increasing issue. On a global scale, Haiti has relatively low M.D.R.T.B. rates. Multidrug-resistance is a particular problem in Port-au-Prince—though it must be stated very clearly that most Haitians, either in Port-au-Prince or in the countryside get sick and too-often die of drug-susceptible TB.

As in other instances, the 2010 earthquake produced considerable difficulties for the provision of treatment for those suffering from tuberculosis. Damage to buildings and the death of healthcare professionals led in some cases to hospitals manned by a single staff member. Tuberculosis rates in Port-au-Prince remained above pre-earthquake levels well into 2012.

APPENDIX IV: PORT-AU-PRINCE INFRASTRUCTURE, PLANNING, AND THE EARTHQUAKE

Many of this book's narrators describe the immense physical destruction caused by the earthquake, including the leveling of whole neighborhoods. The following provides background on Port-au-Prince's development, construction, and urban planning that substantially exacerbated the disaster.

Haiti is an exceptionally centralized nation: Port-au-Prince contains 80 percent of its industrial, commercial and banking facilities, as well as more than half of its hospitals and universities. Port-au-Prince grew rapidly during the last half of the twentieth century. In the 1980s and '90s, the population increased by approximately 115,000 each year. This expansion was largely driven by economic hardship *andeyo*, or outside of the city. Economically driven deforestation and soil degradation, as well as the flooding and undermining of the domestic Haitian market with cheap foreign rice and other food staples, have destroyed agricultural livelihoods in many parts of the country, triggering mass migration to Port-au-Prince.

There were very few public resources and little infrastructure to support impoverished newcomers in Port-au-Prince. With afford-able housing options scarce, many build shelters wherever they find a sliver of empty land. As a result, much of the city consists of informal settlements, many located in areas at high risk of natural disasters (steep, unstable slopes and ravine bottoms, for example). This growth pattern, combined with crushing poverty and a lack of urban plan-ning, means that most neighborhoods lack connections to critical services like water, sewers, and roads.

Poor recordkeeping and contested property rights have also hampered efforts to improve urban conditions. "It [is] very difficult to trace the ownership of any piece of land in Port-au-Prince," said Braulio Eduardo Morera, an architect with international design firm Arup, who worked on the earthquake reconstruction effort. "In most places, because the informal settlements had been there for so long, claiming rights over land, even if you had a property register, was very difficult. That creates environments where no one knows who's in charge of what."

One fact not in dispute, however, is the built environment's role in the devastation. As a saying commonly heard among disaster-relief specialists and geologists goes, earthquakes don't kill people, buildings do. After surveying the post-quake damage, seismolo-gist Roger Bilham wrote in *Nature*, "The disaster could have been averted had sound construction practices been adhered to through-out the region."

Due to lack of funds and material resources, Port-au-Prince builders cut corners wherever possible. Haitian design and con-struction practices at all levels are very poor by seismic standards, and the government cannot enforce existing building codes. Struc-tural reinforcement, for instance, is underutilized. Earthquake-safe construction standards require the embedding of steel reinforce-ment bars, or rebar, at strategic locations within concrete structures. Port-au-Prince builders often employ them incompletely or simply leave them out, and the rebar common in Haitian buildings is often substandard and ineffectual, lacking necessary design elements or utilizing recycled material that has been damaged.

The concrete mixes used in Port-au-Prince are also problematic. Concrete is made of cement, water, and materials known as aggregates. The quality and quantity of each component, as well as the process by which they are joined, are critical for creating solid buildings—including an adequate portion of the cement, the most expensive element in concrete. Tragically, too little cement was used in building Port-au-Prince.

Estimates placed the total number of people living in temporary shelters in the first months at 1.3 million. Another half million moved in with family or others who had shelter. Tent camps sprang up around the city. Six months after the quake, the UN reported, "While many have settled in well-organized, managed camps, others survive in spontaneous settlements where services are intermittent at best."

The six largest camps were concentrated on parks, public squares, or empty lots. For a time, the provision of water, food, and other services at these sites drew people from around the city. Conditions were far from ideal, however, with frequent reports of overcrowding, lack of food and water, and lack of personal security—including an epidemic of sexual violence.

In March 2013, the International Organization for Migration (I.O.M.) claimed that 320,000 people were still living in hundreds of camps scattered around the city. By January 2015, the number had shrunk to 80,000—considerably fewer, but still a huge number considering people had been living in tents for five years since the initial disaster.

One promising development to emerge from the reconstruction effort has been formal recognition of the city's vast squatter settlements. Before the earthquake, the government planned to forcibly relocate 1.2 million people who lived in neighborhoods that had existed for decades but were not recognized on any official level.

After working with international design, planning, and policy experts that offered help with reconstruction, the idea of relocation was abandoned, and the government committed to integrating these settlements into the city. According to architect Darren Gill, who spent several years working with Architecture for Humanity in Port-au-Prince, "Getting these informal communities (literally) onto the map was probably one of the greatest achievements of urban planning in post-earthquake Haiti."

APPENDIX V: SUGGESTED READING

While we hope this collection of oral histories has provided a picture of contemporary Port-au-Prince, it is only the beginning of the story of the city. This list of suggested reading is by no means complete or definitive. Also, many of the great books from and about Haiti still remain untranslated from French and Kreyol.

Street of Lost Footsteps by Lyonel Trouillot

Love, Anger, Madness: A Haitian Triptych by Marie Vieux-Chauvet

The Enigma of the Return by Dany Laferrière

The Black Jacobins by C.L.R. James

Masters of the Dew by Jacques Roumain, translation by Langston Hughes

Haiti After the Earthquake by Paul Farmer

Silencing the Past by Michel-Rolph Trouillot

The Dew Breaker by Edwidge Danticat

Haiti: The Aftershocks of History by Laurent Dubois

The Comedians by Graham Greene

The Uses of Haiti by Paul Farmer

Avengers of the New World by Laurent Dubois

Life in Haitian Valley by Melville Herskovits

The Infamous Rosalie by Evelyn Trouillot

ACKNOWLEDGMENTS

Special thank you to David Krause and Dominican University, the Abundance Foundation, and the Lannan Foundation for generous grants that helped get this project off the ground. Big thanks as well to Ann Schukat and Don Menn who assisted us at a pivotal time. Also thanks for generous support from San Francisco State University, the Pozen Family Center for Human Rights and the Bucksbaum Institute for Clinical Excellence at the University of Chicago, the MacDowell Colony, where portions of this book were edited, and the great staff at Voice of Witness, especially Director Mimi Lok, Managing Editor Luke Gerwe, and Resource Development Associate Natalie Catasús, and Education Program Director Cliff Mayotte. Thanks to Haiti Communitere, Steph Price and the English in Mind Institute, Megan Coffae and her patients and colleagues at Ti Kay Haiti, Zanmi Lasante, Partners In Health, Deia (Andrea) de Brito, Pastor John Pierremont, Adam Bessie, Jean-Robert Lafortune of Haitian-American Grassroots Coalition, Marleine Bastien of FANM or Fanm Ayisyen nan Miyami, Sandy Dorsainvil and the Little Haiti Cultural Center, Régine M. Roumain and the Haiti Cultural Exchange, Michèle Voltaire Marcelin, Elsie Saint Louis at HAUP (Haitian Americans United for Progress), Haitian American Museum of Chicago (HAMOC), the Haitian American Community Association of Chicago, Joe Sciarillo and Jean Xavier at AAN (African Advocacy Network of San Francisco). And thanks to the narrators whose stories do not appear in the book but who offered their time and shared part of their lives with us: Wilson Jean, John Pierremont, Obnes Compere, Regi (Reginald) Lysias, Jean Xavier, Daniel Tillias, Rene Gueldy, Rejine Albin, Yanick Etienne, Eddy Laguere, Harry Nicolas, the Commission of Women Victims for Victims (KOFAVIV) of Port-au-Prince, Mona Augustin, and others who for safety reasons we can't name. And finally, an enormous thank you to the family of Jean Pierre Marseille.

EDITOR BIOGRAPHIES

Peter Orner is the editor of two previous oral histories, *Underground America* (2008) and *Hope Deferred: Narratives of Zimbabwean Lives* (coeditor Annie Holmes, 2010), both published by Voice of Witness. Orner is the author of two novels, two story collections, and most recently, a memoir, *Am I Alone Here?* His fiction and nonfiction has appeared in *The Atlantic*, *New York Times*, *Granta*, *The Paris Review*, and *Best American Stories*. His work has been awarded the Rome Prize from the American Academy of Arts and Letters, a Guggenheim Fellowship, and a Fulbright to Namibia. Orner has taught at the University of Iowa Writers' Workshop, The MFA Program for Writers at Warren Wilson College, the University of Montana, Northwestern, and Charles University in Prague. Orner is a longtime professor at San Francisco State University and recently accepted a faculty appointment at Dartmouth College.

Evan Lyon is a physician, advocate, researcher, and author on health and human rights. He is on the board of the Pozen Family Center for Human Rights at the University of Chicago and is a contributing editor at the academic journal *Health and Human Rights*. He has collaborated with Partners In Health (www.pih.org) in Haiti and at other sites for more than eighteen years. He has served on the faculties of Harvard and the University of Chicago medical schools. Lyon teaches health and human rights at the University of Chicago. Closer to home, Dr. Lyon is the Chief Integrated Health Officer for the Heartland Health Outreach, a nonprofit organization dedicated to providing primary health care, behavioral health and addiction services, H.I.V. care, dental services, and housing for people experiencing homelessness in Chicago.

Laura Lampton Scott's fiction and nonfiction have appeared in *Michigan Quarterly Review*, *Tin House* online, the *Guardian* online, *Okey-Panky*, *Literary Hub*, and other publications. She previously served as associate editor on *Hope Deferred: Narratives of Zimbabwean Lives* (coeditors Peter Orner and Annie Holmes, Voice of Witness 2010). Scott has taught fiction at the University of Montana and currently teaches at Literary Arts in Portland, Oregon. She is a MacDowell Colony fellow.